Celebrity Weddings
&
Honeymoon Getaways

Elizabeth Arrighi Borsting

OPEN ROAD PUBLISHING

OPEN ROAD PUBLISHING

We offer travel guides to American and foreign locales. Our books tell it like it is, often with an opinionated edge, and our experienced authors always give you all the information you need to have the trip of a lifetime. Write for your free catalog of all our titles, including our golf and restaurant guides.

Catalog Department, Open Road Publishing
P.O. Box 284, Cold Spring Harbor, NY 11724

E-mail:
Jopenroad@aol.com

1st Edition

The author has made every effort to be as accurate as possible, but neither she nor the publisher assumes responsibility for the services provided by any business listed in this guide; for any errors or omissions; or any loss, damage, or disruptions in your travels for any reason.

TABLE OF CONTENTS

CONTENTS

CONTENTS

CONTENTS

SIDEBARS

CONTENTS

SIDEBARS

1. Introduction

Imagine exchanging vows at the posh Beverly Hills hotel where singer Paula Abdul and her husband said "I Do," or celebrating at the historic Georgia B&B where John F. Kennedy Jr. and wife Carolyn Bessett gathered after their nuptials. Better yet, why not follow in the footsteps of actress Heather Locklear and musician Richie Sambora by escaping to the same secluded beachfront hotel on the island of Maui?

With this guide, I'll put you on the guest list to some of the most famous weddings and celebrations in history, from contemporary heartthrobs such as Luke Perry and Chris O'Donnell to Hollywood legends like Elizabeth Taylor and Clark Gable. You'll also visit some of the most romantic honeymoon locations imaginable and discover who checked in as Mr. and Mrs. Although this book focuses primarily on Hollywood icons, I've also included luminaries from the fields of music, politics, literature, and sports.

Potential brides and grooms will find this guide invaluable when selecting a wedding, reception, or honeymoon site. I'll take you on a tour of each hotel where you'll visit wedding backdrops, peek into ballrooms and salons, sample various restaurants and, of course, open the doors to the many guest rooms and honeymoon suites.

Even if you're not about to take a trek down the aisle, this guide will prove beneficial for planning romantic getaways or sleuthing for celebrity haunts. During your literary sojourn, you'll discover some of the most famous and exclusive hotels, ranches, inns, and bed and breakfasts scattered throughout North America and be privy to the lists of celebrities who have checked in before you. In addition, each destination includes a history of the hotel and, whenever possible, a bit of celebrity-related trivia.

With this unique guide as your wedding planner and travel companion, you'll enjoy star status as you visit the hotels and inns where the rich and famous, past and present, have tied the knot or relaxed in post-nuptial bliss. I am confident you'll have a famously wonderful time!

2. Planning A Great Wedding & Honeymoon!

During the 1960s and 1970s, traditional weddings took a back seat to simple celebrations. The church was replaced by beaches and parks, white wedding dresses and veils were tossed aside for blue jeans and flower wreaths, and tuxedos and wing tips gave way to bell bottoms and sandals.

Thankfully, the Age of Aquarius has passed, and big weddings along with age-old traditions are back in vogue. While this book highlights some of the most celebrated weddings and honeymoons in recent years, keep in mind that many of these newlyweds had limitless budgets.

For couples who must stick to a budget but still desire a celebration with star-studded qualities, here are some tips.

Budget Tips for Weddings

• Saturdays tend to be the most popular for weddings, so consider choosing another day of the week for your nuptials. You'll have better negotiating power with wedding and reception sites, photographers, florists and other related services.

• If you've always dreamt of being married at a posh location, but don't have the means to turn your dream into a reality, consider limiting the guest list to close friends and family only. It's easier to host an elegant sit-down meal for 50 than for 500.

• By limiting your guest list, you'll have more money to spend on elegant touches and things that may be more important to you, such as a cappuccino bar, additional flowers, photography, entertainment and, of course, the honeymoon!

• When selecting flowers for your wedding and reception, you'll save money by choosing blooms that are in season. Be sure to ask your florist what is in season during your wedding month.

Budget Tips for Honeymoons

- When you are on your honeymoon, LET EVERYONE KNOW! You'll be amazed at the upgrades, complimentary bottles of champagne, and extra service you receive when casually mentioning your new marital status. Even the most astute hoteliers are in love with those in love, so be sure to inform your travel agent or hotel when making reservations, and ask if there are any special packages or amenities available for honeymooners. If you're not honeymooning but still celebrating a special occasion, such as an anniversary, don't be shy; mention that too.
- The same rule applies to airline travel. If traveling by plane, you may get upgraded at ticketing if you mention you're on your honeymoon and are dressed appropriately. However, there are no guarantees, especially if a flight is full.
- When planning your honeymoon, try to avoid peak seasons when prices tend to soar. The summer months are the most popular time of year for traveling, as are certain holidays such as Memorial Day and Labor Day weekends.
- If you're visiting a big city with hotels that cater to a business clientele, such as New York or San Francisco, arrange it so you're there on a weekend when hotel occupancy tends to be low. If a quaint country inn is more your style, avoid the weekends when prices and occupancy are higher.
- If there is a hotel you've always wanted to stay at, but you just can't afford it for the duration of your honeymoon, compromise and stay only a night or two. Then find more affordable accommodations somewhere else for the remainder of your stay.

How This Book Is Organized

At the beginning of each hotel entry is a **Celebrity Guest Register**. Those names in italics and listed first indicate the featured couple or couples. When only one spouse is of celebrity status, then only their name appears under this section. Those names that are not in italics have at one time or another been a guest of the hotel.

Included in each entry are **prices** for accommodations, ranging from the least expensive room to the most elaborate suite. Keep in mind when making overnight arrangements that prices are determined by the size of the room, location of room (waterfront view, city view, or *no view!*), season (beach properties are more expensive during the summer, while mountain resorts can be pricey during the winter months) as well as other factors such as recent renovations, current occupancy rate, and so on.

If a hotel or inn provides complementary breakfast, afternoon tea or other amenities, I've listed it. I've also highlighted special hotel packages and amenities geared towards couples, but many offer an array of packages.

Most of the hotels listed in this guide have endured more trials and tribulations than many of the Hollywood couples they have hosted and, in some cases, have aged better, too! Each property, whether built before the Civil War or just recently erected, has a story to tell. Architectural enthusiasts and history buffs will especially enjoy each **history section** which details everything from a hotel's past owner and architectural style to its demise and restoration.

The properties chosen for this book cater to couples planning a wedding and reception, with the majority capable of coordinating all details, so I've listed a section called **Getting Married**. Included are descriptions of the areas available for ceremonies and receptions as well as ideas for hosting pre-nuptial gatherings. In some cases, when an establishment has an array of ballrooms and salons, I've selected those best suited for wedding celebrations and have omitted those facilities geared toward business meetings and conventions.

Unless specified, each property offers the services of a wedding or event coordinator that will assist you in the planning process. Most of the properties featured in this book offer on-site catering as well as an available list of reputable services, from photographers and florists to musicians and clergy.

There's also a section on **Famous Nuptials & Celebrated Honeymoons**. This section details at least one famous wedding and/or honeymoon that took place at the featured property. Whenever possible, I have tried to provide as much insight as possible without being overly intrusive to the celebrity couple. Details vary and may include famous guests who attended, wedding attire, menu selection, which room or rooms the celebrities occupied and so on. Featured couples are highlighted and appear first under each entry's "Celebrity Guest Register."

Another section is called **Celebrated Occasions**. From time to time, a hotel will have hosted a wedding-related gathering for a celebrity such as a rehearsal dinner, engagement party, or bridal shower. I felt it meaningful to include a few of these celebrations as well.

In order to be included in this guide, each property had to provide overnight accommodations, so travelers could feel as if they were "sleeping with the stars." The **honeymoon section** that accompanies each entry gives you a basic floor plan for the type of accommodations offered as well as amenities and recreational activities offered. If a celebrity has stayed in a certain room or suite, you can be sure it's mentioned.

3. Alabama

THE TUTWILER HOTEL
2021 Park Place N.
Birmingham, AL 35203
800/845-1787
205/322-2100

Accommodations
$89-$172

Celebrity Guest Register
- *Tallulah Bankhead*
- Robert Wagner
- Stevie Wonder
- Charlton Heston
- Michael Bolton
- Charles Lindbergh
- Billy Joel
- Janet Jackson
- Stephanie Powers
- George Foreman
- Neil Diamond
- Patti LaBelle
- Henry Kissinger
- Tommy Lee Jones

A History
The Tutwiler Hotel has been a Southern tradition since its opening in 1914. Financed by Major Edward Magruder Tutwiler, the original hotel occupied a 13-story red brick building at the corner of Fifth Avenue and 20th Street in the heart of Birmingham.

The gala opening on June 15, 1914, was the talk of the town and featured an afternoon reception and a formal eight-course Buffet Muscovite - or Russian Service - dinner for an astronomical $3 per person. Shortly after its opening, The Tutwiler attracted Alabama politicos and society mavens who enjoyed the generous Southern hospitality they had grown accustomed to.

During the '20s, '30s, and '40s, The Tutwiler hosted a number of Hollywood celebrities and heroes passing through town to promote their latest project. For more than a half-century, The Tutwiler was the hub of social activity until its decline in the 1960s. In 1974, The Tutwiler was in the news again when it became the first major structure in the nation to be razed by implosion. The end of an era had come to pass, and all that remained were remnants of a once grand establishment.

Eleven years later, a group of investors, led by Major Tutwiler's grandson, Temple Tutwiler III, decided to bring the Tutwiler back to life. The hotel's new home was in the Ridgely Apartment Building at Park Avenue and 21st Street, a building financed by Major Tutwiler in 1913, and a sister property of the original Tutwiler.

Today, the historic Tutwiler Hotel has recaptured the hearts of Birmingham with its grand edifice and elegant decor.

Celebrated Honeymoons

Alabama native and 1930s screen siren and stage actress, **Tallulah "Dahling" Bankhead**, and her fiancé, actor **John Emery**, who co-starred with Ingrid Bergman and Gregory Peck in Alfred Hitchcock's 1945 thriller *Spellbound*, stayed at The Tutwiler Hotel the evening prior to their August 1937 wedding. The next morning, the two drove to nearby Jasper for a simple ceremony attended by the bride's family, including her father, Senator Will Bankhead. After the reception, the couple had planned to fly back to Tallulah's New York estate, but heavy rains prevented their departure; instead, the new Mr. and Mrs. John Emery returned to The Tutwiler Hotel for their wedding night.

Getting Married at The Tutwiler Hotel

Combining old world charm with gracious hospitality, the South seems to rise again within the confines of the elegant Tutwiler Hotel.

Weddings are held outdoors - weather permitting - on the hotel's **Patio**, a downtown garden oasis surrounded on three sides by the eight-story brick structure. Vows are exchanged among seasonal flowers, and wrought-iron lamps create old-fashioned ambiance for evening ceremonies. There are three salons also available for indoor ceremonies and receptions. The **Ridgely Room**, with its high ceilings and crystal chandeliers, can accommodate up to 144 guests and features an elegant pre-function area for hosting cocktails prior to a formal sit-down dinner. With a cozy setting for receptions of up to 72, the **Woodward Room** offers Southern charm with picturesque windows overlooking downtown Birmingham. The **Lindbergh Room** is ideal for intimate gatherings of 24 and actually features a stylish anteroom complete with fireplace that opens up to the dining area.

Located adjacent to the lobby is the award-winning **Christians' Restaurant**, offering southern comfort for breakfast, lunch, or dinner.

This Birmingham institution is a popular gathering spot for celebrating special occasions. **The Pub** is ideal for post-rehearsal gatherings, and offers an array of light meals and cocktails.

The Tutwiler Romantic Honeymoon

Newlyweds may wish to take advantage of the Romantic Honeymoon package ($179 per couple), which includes a luxury suite, a bottle of champagne with keepsake glasses, a single red rose, an engraved brass room key to remember their stay, turndown service with chocolates and continental breakfast for two.

Honeymooning at The Tutwiler Hotel

The Tutwiler Hotel is an imposing Italianate red brick building topped with terra-cotta cornices that give it a distinctive silhouette. With a coffered ceiling coated in Italian marble and hand-crafted tapestries, the elegant lobby recalls the grandeur of the South's past.

Two wings feature 147 elegantly appointed guest rooms and suites with turn-of-the-century antiques and marble bathrooms; some offer fireplaces and wrought-iron balconies. Two exclusive floors - the sixth and seventh - feature their own lounge with continental breakfast items in the morning and cocktails and hors d'oeuvres in the evening.

The Tutwiler Hotel also features an elaborate art collection that includes paintings donated by the Birmingham Museum of Art.

Heston At The Tutwiler

Actor Charlton Heston used a two-day visit to The Tutwiler in May 1995, to put the finishing touches on a self-penned book. While most writers rely on their laptop computers for creating copy, Heston did it the old-fashioned way...with a hotel typewriter!

---

4. Arizona

ARIZONA BILTMORE RESORT & SPA
24h Street and Missouri Avenue
Phoenix, AZ 85016
800/950-0086
602/955-6600

Accommodations
$130-$1,330

Celebrity Guest Register
- *President and Mrs. Ronald Reagan*
- *Rosalind Russell*
- Tim Allen
- Alec Baldwin & Kim Basinger
- Christie Brinkley
- Nicolas Cage
- George Clooney
- Melanie Griffith
- Magic Johnson
- Jay Leno
- Jerry Seinfeld
- Sharon Stone
- Robin Williams
- James Woods
- Joan Crawford
- *Harpo Marx*
- Bryan Adams
- Patricia Arquette
- Clint Black
- George Burns
- Eric Clapton
- Tom Cruise & Nicole Kidman
- Whitney Houston
- Michael Jordan
- David Letterman
- Wesley Snipes
- Jean Claude Van Damme
- Noah Wyle
- Roseanne

A History
In the early 1920s, the McArthur family envisioned a dream resort for the vast Arizona desert. Plans were drawn up, reworked, and then put into action. The McArthurs ushered in a new era of luxury with the opening of the Arizona Biltmore on February 23, 1929. It became known as the Jewel of the Desert and was a popular destination for Hollywood

heavyweights. Beginning with Herbert Hoover in 1930, the Arizona Biltmore has had the honor of hosting every American president. Not long after its opening, Chicago chewing gum magnate William Wrigley Jr., purchased the resort, making it the centerpiece of the Wrigley empire for the next 40 years.

Renowned architectect Frank Lloyd Wright can be credited with the architectural integrity bestowed on the Arizona Biltmore. While Albert Chase, a former apprentice under Wright, is the architect of record, Wright's influence and style are evident throughout. The entire design process - from the harmony with the terrain and the use of indigenous materials to the interior decor and the lighting - are pure Wright. The full extent of Wright's involvement remains a mystery, adding to the Biltmore's mystique, but many speculate that Wright collaborated with his former student to create this architectural masterpiece.

Architectural history was made with the building of the Arizona Biltmore as pre-cast concrete blocks were molded on-site and used in the total construction of the resort. Emry Kopta, a prominent Southwestern sculptor, designed the distinctive trademark *Biltmore Block* out of the materials to form a geometric pattern inspired by the trunk of a palm tree.

Throughout its history, the Arizona Biltrmore has been loyal to its Southwestern heritage; any expansions or additions have been enhancements and not compromises. Nearing 70 years since its opening, the Arizona Biltmore remains a classic resort, a Jewel of the Desert, that few contemporary hotels can rival.

Famous Honeymooners

Phoenix is not only a destination, it is also a gateway from the western United States to other regions of the country. The Arizona Biltmore has hosted a number of celebrity honeymooners in its history, including **Ronald and Nancy Reagan**, who divided their honeymoon between the Biltmore and the Mission Inn (see Riverside, California); actress **Rosalind Russell** stopped here during her honeymoon in the 1940s; and the comically silent Marx brother, **Harpo**, was such a happy groom while at the Biltmore that he and his bride held hands while skipping through the formal dining room!

Getting Married at the Arizona Biltmore

Drenched in a nature's beauty, desert-style weddings are held throughout the Biltmore's grounds, offering such lovely backdrops as cascading waterfalls, towering palm trees, and flower-filled gardens. The **Aztec Patio**, which can accommodate up to 150 guests, is a favorite spot for exchanging nuptials as the faint sound of trickling water is heard from a nearby fountain.

After the ceremony, guests are ushered to one of three historic ballrooms. The octogonal **Grand Ballroom** is an opulent setting with its unique configuration. A pre-reception area is ideal for cocktails and conversation; French doors open onto a covered loggia with views of Squaw Peak Mountain in the distance. The **Gold Room** offers majestic surroundings for groups of 300. Sandstone walls create a wonderful contrast to the rich, gold hue draped throughout, and elegant chandeliers hung from high ceilings make the Gold Room an exceptional venue for celebrations. A parasol-shaped ceiling and dramatic lighting are hallmarks of the **Atzec Room**. Encased in sandstone blocks, the salon can best be described as 1930s Southwestern with sandstone walls and Art Deco accents. The Aztec Room, which is connected to the Atzec Patio, can accommodate up to 120 guests.

There are a collection of casual-to-elegant restaurants for pre-wedding gatherings scattered throughout the property. **Wrights**, the Biltmore's premiere restaurant, offers a private dining room for rehearsal dinners and features striking Southwestern architecture as well as indoor and outdoor seating. The **Biltmore Grill & Patio** offers an eclectic menu for each meal of the day, and the al fresco setting is best enjoyed in the early mornings. The **Cabana Club Restaurant and Bar** offers casual poolside dining, a swim-up bar and sunset cocktails. The **Squaw Peak Bar**, located in the hotel lobby, offers indoor and outdoor seating for enjoying dry desert afternoons and balmy evenings.

Honeymooning at the Arizona Biltmore

From the lobby's gold-leaf ceiling to the faint smell of burgundy that lingers in the Wine Cellar, the Arizona Biltmore is an oasis of elegance. Covered promenades draped in flora and open walkways lined with fragrant flowers meander through the grounds leading the way to guest quarters.

There are 500 rooms and suites paying homage to Frank Lloyd Wright with Mission-style furnishings and color schemes native to the arrid desert. Private patios and balconies entice guests to gaze at Squaw Peak Mountain, the Paradise Pool, the towering fountains, or the blooming gardens.

The Arizona Biltmore is a recreational oasis boasting two PGA golf courses, a swimming pool skirted with brightly-colored cabanas plus four smaller pools dotted throughout, eight tennis courts, a 92-foot-long water slide and a spa. A selection of lawn games, which harken back to the era of the hotel's beginning, include croquet and shuffleboard.

Joan Crawford At The Biltmore

When Joan Crawford visited the Arizona Biltmore with a former husband, a Pepsi Cola executive, she laughingly refused an assortment of refreshments sent to her room. Displayed on the tray - among other things – was an ice cold Coca Cola!

RAMADA VALLEY HO RESORT

6850 Main Street
Scottsdale, AZ 85251
800/321-4952
602/945-6321

Accommodations
$125-$350

Celebrity Guest Register
- *Robert Wagner & Natalie Wood*
- Janet Leigh
- Jimmy Durante
- Tony Curtis
- Marilyn Monroe
- Bing Crosby

A History

Touted as the first year-round European Plan Hotel in the Scottsdale area, the Ramada Valley Ho Resort, originally named the Hotel Valley Ho, opened on December 20, 1956.

Developer and original owner Robert Lawrence Foehl designed the resort using elements favored by his mentor Frank Lloyd Wright. Sandstone, a material often used in Wright's designs, create the blocks which run the length of the hotel balcony. In order to preserve the hotel's aesthetics, Foehl ordered tunnels to be dug underneath the building in order to conceal obtrusive electrical lines.

During its heyday, the hotel catered to wealthy snowbirds, who flocked west to escape the cold climates of the Midwest and East Coast, as well as to a score of celebrities. Today, the Ramada Valley Ho Resort is considered to be a Scottsdale institution and an oasis for those in need of rest and relaxation.

Famous Nuptials

When actor **Robert Wagner**, star of the television series *Hart to Hart*, married actress **Natalie Wood** (*West Side Story, Miracle on 34th Street*), for the first time (they would eventually divorce and remarry each other for a second time, a union which would last until Wood's untimely death in 1981) they did so without any Hollywood fanfare.

The two exchanged nuptials at the Scottsdale Methodist Church in Scottsdale, Arizona, on December 28, 1957. The 19-year-old bride wore a simple, ankle-length gown embellished with tiny pearls, a sight only about a dozen family and friends were invited to witness. Following the 20 minute ceremony, a small reception was held at the Ramada Valley Ho Resort. The newlyweds enjoyed a honeymoon across the United States aboard the train Super Chief along the California coast.

Getting Married at the Ramada Valley Ho Resort

Located on 14 sprawling acres, weddings at the Ramada Valley Ho Resort are conducted with a Southwestern flair. Couples can exchange vows amid the many flower gardens located throughout the property or, should weather prove uncooperative, in one of two ballrooms.

Both the **Palo Verde** and the **Pow Wow** ballrooms feature tasteful decor with muted hues, soft lighting, and high ceilings. The Palo Verde, the larger of the two salons, can accommodate up to 200 guests and is located in the hotel's conference center. The Pow Wow, located in the hotel's main building, offers a large pre-reception area and can accommodate parties of up to 180.

For family breakfasts, leisurely lunches, or rehearsal dinners, **Summerfield's** provides a casual atmosphere for pre-nuptial gatherings with large picture windows that gaze across the center courtyard. For spontaneous socializing, **Summerfield's Lounge** features a covered patio and offers refreshing cocktails within steps of the swimming pool.

Come Back A Year Later - For Free!

Newlyweds marrying at the Ramada Valley Ho receive a complimentary deluxe suite for their wedding night with a complimentary bottle of chilled champagne. Couples who marry at the hotel also enjoy a complimentary suite on their first-year anniversary!

Honeymooning at the Ramada Valley Ho Resort

Hailed as Scottsdale's best-kept secret, the Ramada Valley Ho is for honeymooners who desire nothing more than to lounge by the pool and stroll down fashionable esplanades in search of boutiques in downtown Scottsdale.

Newlyweds are ushered into a flagstone and mahogany lobby, with nuances of Frank Lloyd Wright's influence. The two-story resort features 292 oversized rooms and suites with Southwestern overtones and decor. Each room, unique in design, offers views of either the swimming pool or colorful gardens.

The resort features three swimming pools, two whirlpool spas, a fitness course, and two lighted tennis courts. Nearby attractions include the exclusive Fifth Avenue shopping district, quaint Main Street, the Phoenix Zoo and an array of championship golf courses.

Where Durante Played For Free!

If anyone could smell a captive audience, it was the legendary entertainer Jimmy Durante. While staying at the resort, he would pass the hours singing and playing the grand piano in the lounge, much to the delight of the hotel guests.

5. California

THE ALISAL GUEST RANCH AND RESORT
1054 Alisal Road
Solvang, CA 93463
800/415-4725
805/688-6411

Accommodations
$325-$400

Celebrity Guest Register
- *Clark Gable & Lady Sylvia Ashley*
- Ava Gardener
- Goldie Hawn & Kurt Russell
- Beau Bridges
- Sally Fields
- Ozzie & Harriet Nelson
- Bob Newhart
- Tom Poston
- Michael York

- Mel Gibson
- Kevin Costner
- Jeff Bridges
- John Ritter
- Ricky Nelson
- Doris Day
- Kris Kristofferson
- Don Knotts

A History
In the late 1700s, conquistador Raimundo Carrillo received the 13,500-acre Rancho Nojoqui as payment for his service to the Mexican government. He chose to raise cattle on his land in the area, now known as Santa Ynez Valley, and established a legacy for future owners of the ranch.

In 1860, when the ranch was owned by Ulpiano Yndart, a terrible drought wreaked havoc on the cattle industry, causing major financial losses to Mexican landowners. For the first time in history, their holdings were made available to migrating Americans, and the land was quickly purchased by the Pierce family. The Pierces renamed the land Rancho

Alisal, a word derived from the native Chumash Indians meaning *grove of Sycamores*, and masterminded a concept for an irrigation system, which brought the water from the Santa Ynez River to a great portion of their land.

By the turn of the century, the cattle were sharing the land with horses at the request of the ranch's new owner Charles Perkins. In addition to raising cattle, Perkins turned his attention to the Sport of Kings and began breeding thoroughbred racehorses. His hobby paid off in 1925, when his horse, *Flying Ebony*, won the Kentucky Derby.

Perkins eventually sold the ranch to Charles Jackson, and under new ownership, the cattlemen's quarters were converted into accommodations. On July 16, 1946, The Alisal Guest Ranch opened for summer seasons. While still a working cattle ranch, The Alisal was immediately hailed as a premiere dude ranch, and received the stamp of approval from Hollywood's city slickers.

More than 50 years since its opening, The Alisal Guest Ranch and Resort still beckons those who have a passion for the great outdoors.

Famous Nuptials

When **Clark Gable** married his fourth wife, **Lady Sylvia Ashley**, it had been nearly seven years since he had lost his wife, actress Carole Lombard, in a tragic airplane crash over Nevada. He was so devastated by her death, many Hollywood insiders predicted he would never find love again. However, on December 20, 1949, at 3:15 pm inside the library at the Alisal Guest Ranch, he married the widow of Douglas Fairbanks, Sr.

The bride wore a conservative navy blue suit with collar and cuffs trimmed in white. The groom, looking dashing as always, chose a blue business suit for the occasion. After he slipped a platinum wedding band on Lady Ashley's finger, the two hosted a reception on the ranch's patio.

Celebrated Honeymoons

For Clark Gable, The Alisal Guest Ranch was the ideal place to hold his wedding. He was an avid outdoors man, a passion that his bride did not always share, but tried to acquire a taste for. After the ceremony and reception, the two spent their wedding night at the ranch, and the next day the newlyweds boarded the Matson Liner Lurline en route to Wakiki for a Hawaiian honeymoon.

Getting Married at The Alisal Guest Ranch and Resort

Being married on a working cattle ranch is certainly a unique backdrop for a wedding ceremony and reception. The ranch offers a trio of au natural settings for exchanging nuptials outdoors, including the **Lakefront Deck**, overlooking a serene body of water; the **Creekside**

Garden complete with a babbling brook and aromatic flora; and the **Poolside Pavilion**, which stands in the shadow of the nearby rolling hills and overlooks the swimming pool.

There are five reception areas that are designed to harken back to the days of the old ranchero. **The Sycamore Room**, which can be divided into three separate rooms for smaller groups of 32-60, can host up to 200 guests, and features high-beamed ceilings, expansive windows, and a stone hearth. The Western-themed **Cottonwood Room** pays homage to Native Americans with a Navajo-style ceiling motif and can host up to 60 guests comfortably. The **Chuckwagon Grill**, overlooking the pool and spa, offers a casual, airy ambiance with its open-beamed ceiling, suspended ceiling fans and wallpaper with a Native American pattern - ideal for intimate gatherings of 56 or less.

A cozy and relaxed setting best describes **The Laurel Room** with its paneled walls, high-beamed ceilings, and plush carpeting, an ideal choice for groups of 40. **The Library** is a choice location for small, informal receptions of 30, and features a fireplace and private bar.

The restaurants at the ranch are for the exclusive use of its guests only and are not available for pre-wedding celebrations. However, any of the reception rooms may be reserved for rehearsal dinners or engagement parties.

How About A Rodeo Theme Wedding?

A specialty of the ranch are the themed-style receptions, including authentic Western barbecues at the rodeo arena.

Honeymooning at The Alisal Guest Ranch and Resort

Few places can claim to be a working cattle ranch *and* a full-service resort, but The Alisal Guest Ranch and Resort offers that and more. Honeymooners who wish to relive the days of the Old West, yet be pampered, won't be disappointed!

There are 73 cottages at the ranch, featuring either a comfortable studio or a spacious two-room suite. Each cottage, configured to ensure maximum privacy, resembles a tiny home with covered porches and garden views; while the interiors are adorned in the classic California ranch design with Spanish accents. Unique touches include wood-burning fireplaces stocked with wood for cold nights, refrigerators with ice makers, and coffee makers with a supply of gourmet coffees and teas. While these amenities offer modern comforts, guests are still expected to "rough it" a bit at the old ranch. The guest rooms offer no television or phones, an actual bonus for honeymooners. Any messages or faxes are immediately delivered to your room, and televisions and phones are located in the public rooms for those who absolutely can't do without.

Each stay includes a hearty breakfast and full dinner served in **The Ranch Room**. The chef prepares each meal with the freshest ingredients to create Western-style grub and other traditional American fare. While breakfast offers a casual setting, dinner is a more dressy occasion: jackets for men and equally appropriate attire for women. After dinner, cocktails and entertainment are available in **The Oak Room Lounge**.

For rugged romantics, there are 10,000 acres and countless trails to explore on horseback; a fleet of boats to sail the waters; a lake filled with bass and bluegill awaiting fishermen; and walking trails for nature lovers. For golf and tennis enthusiasts, there are two 18-hole golf courses and a complete tennis center plus an outdoor, heated swimming pool and spa. There also are a number of lawn games to enjoy: horseshoes, croquet, shuffleboard, and badminton.

Presidential Neighbors

The Rancho del Cielo, the pied-à-terre owned by former President Ronald Reagan and his wife, Nancy, neighbors the ranch's 10,000-acre spread. Other nearby celebrity ranchers include Michael Jackson, who frequently resides at his fantasy homestead Never-Never Land.

HOTEL BEL-AIR
701 Stone Canyon Road
Los Angeles, CA 90077
800/648-4097
310/472-1211

Accommodations
$315–$2,500

Celebrity Guest Register
- *Meg Ryan & Dennis Quaid*
- *George Peppard & Elizabeth Ashley*
- *Casey & Jean Kasem*
- Audrey Hepburn
- Gregory Peck
- Anjelica Huston
- Howard Hughes

- *Charlie Sheen*
- *Leeza Gibbons*
- Princess Grace Kelly
- Marilyn Monroe
- Sophia Loren
- Gary Cooper
- Greta Garbo

A History

During the early 1920s, oil millionaire turned real estate developer, Alfonzo E. Bell, was determined to create the most beautiful and desirable neighborhood on the West Side of Los Angeles. He erected several buildings for his planning and sales efforts and used the main mission-style building as his headquarters. He hired architects and engineers to design the commanding east and west iron gates that still grace the entrance to this exclusive Los Angeles neighborhood. Next he constructed 60 miles of trails throughout Bel Air and erected the Bel Air Stables, so local residents could board their horses after a ride through chaparral-covered trails.

In 1940, hotel proprietor Joseph Drown purchased the former Bel Air land offices and stables. Architect Burton Schutt was hired to convert the buildings into hotel accommodations without compromising the original 1920s style and charm. While the conversion from sales office to luxury hotel was underway, Drown commissioned the design of the hotel gardens, Swan Lake, the Pavilion Room, the swimming pool and the cabanas.

Since its opening day in 1946, the Hotel Bel-Air has been a favorite getaway of the rich and famous. Situated in Los Angeles' exclusive Bel-Air estate district, the hotel is comprised of several Mediterranean-style villas. Alfonzo E. Bell's mission-style headquarters now serves as the hotel's main building and lobby. Its 1920s pink stucco facade is crowned by a bell tower and consists of hand-made, wrought-iron balconies and gates, shaded arcades, intimate courtyards accentuated with fountains and chimneys. The stables have been replaced by a unique oval swimming pool, and the 1940s cabanas have been transformed into additional guest quarters.

Famous Nuptials

Many celebrities have been married at the Hotel Bel-Air, including **Elizabeth Ashley** and **George Peppard** on April 17, 1966; disc jockey **Casey Kasem** and his wife, **Jean**, wed in December 1980; talk show host **Leeza Gibbons** married **Stephen Meadows** in 1991; and **Meg Ryan** and **Dennis Quaid** took an impromtu stroll down the aisle on February 14, 1991.

Celebrated Honeymoons

After a whirlwind five-month romance, actor **Charlie Sheen** and model **Donna Peel** were married at Saddle Rock Ranch near Malibu, California, on his 30th birthday in September 1995. Guests included Kiefer Sutherland, Nicolas Cage, and famous family members Martin Sheen and Emilio Estevez. After a late night reception, which lasted until

2 am, the bride and groom bid guests farewell and headed to a suite at the Hotel Bel-Air.

Getting Married at the Hotel Bel-Air
At the Hotel Bel-Air, couples can expect the star treatment from beginning to end. The tranquil outdoor setting of **Swan Lake** is a natural backdrop for California-style weddings. Named for its graceful inhabitants, Swan Lake is surrounded by pink primrose, miniature yellow daffodils, lavender violas, pink tulips, jasmine and many other fragrant flowers. Swan Lake also is a favorite location for outdoor receptions.

Hotel Bel-Air offers two venues for post-nuptial receptions: **The Garden Room** and **The Pavilion Room**. The Garden Room offers an elegant setting coupled with views of the grounds and can accommodate up to 160 guests, while The Pavilion Room, offering an equally lavish setting, has a capacity of 50 guests. The rooms can open up to create one large salon, accommodating parties of 210.

The Restaurant, simply named, offers French-Californian cuisine. Located at the end of one of the many graceful arcades off the hotel's main building, The Restaurant is an ideal location for rehearsal dinners. The bougainvillea-draped terrace is heated year-round and overlooks the gardens and Swan Lake, making it one of the most desirable locations in Los Angeles. The Restaurant offers breakfast, lunch, dinner, and Sunday Brunch. An elegant afternoon tea also is available for hosting the traditional bridesmaids' luncheon.

The Bar, adjacent to The Restaurant, is reminiscent of old Hollywood with its dark wood paneling, wood-burning fireplace, and baby grand piano. In the evenings, live entertainment makes this watering hole a magnet for hotel guests and nearby residents.

Fresh Herbs Only At The Bel-Air
The Chef's working herb garden - complete with basil, bay leaf, sage, rosemary, tarragon and cilantro - provides couples with an aromatic sanctuary for enjoying one another.

Honeymooning at the Hotel Bel-Air
Situated on 11 sprawling acres, honeymooners enjoy seclusion from the rest of the world. Several stucco structures house the 92 guest chambers, including 33 suites, each varying in size, floor plans, and views. Paths leading from the hotel gardens, landscaped fountain courtyards, and signature swimming pool, segue into the villas' individual entrances.

Five renowned interior designers were commissioned to create the distinctive and unique surroundings found in each room. Special touches include wood-burning fireplaces, terra-cotta tile floors, needlepoint rugs, private patios and terraces.

Guest amenities include 24-hour access to the Fitness Center; complimentary tea service upon check-in; a selection of automobiles for use upon request; 24-hour room service; and much more.

Marilyn Monroe's Guest Cottage

The hotel's Fitness Center, where stars pump iron while in residence, was once the guest cottage of Marilyn Monroe. It also is rumored that early on in her career, this particular cottage provided the backdrop for her most famous photos - where she wore nothing more than a splash of Chanel No. 5!

BENBOW INN
445 Lake Benbow Drive
Garberville, CA 95542
800/355-3301
707/923-2124

Accommodations
$115-$295

Celebrity Guest Register
- *Joan Fontaine and Brian Ahern*
- Alan Ladd
- Clark Gable
- Spencer Tracy
- Basil Rathbone

- Eleanor Roosevelt
- Nelson Eddy
- Jeannette MacDonald
- John Barrymore
- Janet Gaynor

A History
The historic Benbow Inn was named for its original owners, the Benbow family. The Benbows commissioned architect Albert Farr to create a cornerstone for the resort community they envisioned for their 1,290-acre valley located in the heart of Northern California's Redwood Forest.

In July 1926, the Hotel Benbow opened, and its distinctive Tudor-style architecture resembled a graceful English manor. The hotel quickly became a destination for motoring tourists traveling along the newly-completed Redwood Highway. The allure of seclusion and the inn's warm hospitality appealed to film stars of the era. Avid outdoorsman Clark Gable enjoyed riding horses and fishing in the nearby Eel River; many of his contemporaries flocked to the Benbow Inn in search of some much needed rest and relaxation after a grueling schedule of filming.

In 1962, the Benbow family sold the hotel, and each of the four subsequent owners brought with them their own personal touches without compromising the hotel's original charm. In 1983, the Benbow Inn was placed on the National Register of Historic Places, and today it remains one of Northern California's best-kept secrets.

Celebrated Honeymoons

Actress **Joan Fontaine**, star of such classic films as *Dunga Din* and *Rebecca*, married actor **Brian Ahern** on August 20, 1939, at St. John's Episcopal Chapel in Monterey, California. The bride, who wore a period-style gown of white satin complete with a hooped skirt and long train, was attended by her famous sister and rival, actress Olivia de Havilland, best known for her portrayal of Melanie Wilkes in the epic film *Gone With The Wind*. The reception was held at the nearby Del Monte Hotel in Carmel. After the congratulations, the newlyweds sped up Highway One to enjoy a leisurely honeymoon at the Benbow Inn.

Getting Married at the Benbow Inn

Small, intimate wedding ceremonies are the inn's forte. There are two outdoor settings offering splendid views of the gardens and nearby Eel River. The **Rose Garden Circle**, located just below the inn, offers a picturesque setting for exchanging vows. A manicured lawn extends out to touch the English garden filled with roses, marigolds, and other flora. The **Terrace Gardens**, located on an open-air deck, overlooks the river below. An historic bridge gracefully arches in the background to connect the two lands separated by water. Leafy trees, various flowers, and other natural elements make this an ideal setting for both weddings and receptions. The **Dining Room**, which opens onto a scenic terrace, is available for afternoon receptions and features a bevy of antiques, a beamed ceiling, and dark oak Windsor Chairs – making it equally ideal for rehearsal dinners.

For unwinding or reviewing last minute details, a complimentary afternoon **English tea** with scones is served in the inn's charming lobby. In the evening, the **Lounge** is an ideal place to retreat with guests to enjoy a refreshing cocktail or steaming cup of java while enjoying the talents of a pianist.

> ## Design Your Own Wedding Menu
> *While the menu selection is mouthwatering, the inn's award-winning chef also will create a custom wedding menu upon request.*

Honeymooning at the Benbow Inn

Upon opening the door to the Benbow Inn, you feel as if you're on the banks of the Thames River rather than enmeshed in the Redwood Forest. The aroma of fresh-baked scones and brewing tea is most inviting, as guests lounge on overstuffed sofas, converse about the area's history, and read by the wood-burning fireplace.

There are 55 bedrooms and suites located inside the main hotel and in the lower terrace; each room, with its abundance of antiques and chintz fabrics, reflects the English theme. Most rooms offer a view of either the terrace, gardens, nearby mountains, or river. The Honeymoon Cottage, the inn's most expensive chamber, features a vaulted ceiling, king-size four-poster bed with canopy, wood-burning fireplace, stocked refrigerator, spa, and a private patio overlooking the gardens and rivers.

For couples wanting to take advantage of the wooded trails that lead to **Benbow Lake**, the inn will prepare a picnic basket filled with gourmet goodies to enjoy once you arrive at your destination.

> ## Same Honeymoon Spot, Different Hubby
> *Joan Fontaine enjoyed the Benbow Inn so much during her honeymoon with first-husband Brian Ahern that she returned for another honeymoon with, of course, a different husband!*

THE BEVERLY HILLS HOTEL

9641 Sunset Boulevard
Beverly Hills, CA 90210
310/276-2251
800/283-8885

Accommodations
$275-$3,050

Celebrity Guest Register
• Elizabeth Taylor
• Faye Dunaway
• Karen Carpenter
• Henry Fonda

- Spencer Tracy
- Rudolph Valentino
- Greta Garbo
- Charlie Chaplin
- Howard Hughes
- Richard Burton
- Duke & Duchess of Windsor
- John Wayne
- Robert Stack

- Lauren Bacall
- Marilyn Monroe
- Gloria Swanson
- George C. Scott
- Carole Lombard
- Eddie Fisher
- Prince Philip
- Natalie Wood
- Clark Gable

A History

When The Beverly Hills Hotel was built in 1912, the famed Sunset Strip was nothing more than a bridal path. Burton Green, president of the Rodeo Land and Water Company, built the palatial pink palace for what was then considered an astronomical sum, $500,000. The opening invitation listed the hotel's address as "halfway between Los Angeles and the sea," and it would be quite some time before the postal code "90210" would be attached to any celebrity's address.

Green built Beverly Hills' first major structure in the hopes that it would entice the affluent bluebloods from the east to invest in this rustic alcove west of Los Angeles. He lured Margaret Anderson, then manager of the posh Hollywood Hotel, to oversee his premiere property. Not only did she manage it, she purchased the place in 1920. That same year Hollywood's royal couple, Douglas Fairbanks and Mary Pickford, established residence up the hill at Pickfair. Soon the couple's movie star friends began clearing out the bean fields to make room for their own grand estates, and from then on The Beverly Hills Hotel has been legendary.

Today, The Beverly Hills Hotel is often referred to as the "Pink Palace" and is situated at the top of one of the most well known and wealthy avenues in America, Rodeo Drive.

Famous Nuptials

In September 1980, **Karen Carpenter**, the late singer for the brother-sister '70s duo, The Carpenters, walked down the hotel's garden path wearing a white gown fashioned after an 18th-century riding ensemble. Her wedding to a Southern California real estate tycoon was officiated by the well-known Reverend Robert Shuler. After the "I Do's," 450 guests enjoyed a sit-down luncheon reception in the hotel's elegant Crystal Room.

Famous guests included Dorothy Hamill, Herb Alpert, Dean Martin, and Olivia Newton-John , who was lucky enough to catch the bouquet!

Celebrated Honeymoons

Few women can compete with the legendary **Elizabeth Taylor**, both in terms of her successful career and her number of husbands. After each of her weddings, with the exception of first husband Nicky Hilton, the heir to the Hilton Hotel empire, and her most recent union to Larry Fortensky, the bride would escape to one of the many pink bungalows at The Beverly Hills Hotel with her new husband in tow.

She came as Mrs. Michael Wilding, Mrs. Mike Todd, Mrs. Eddie Fisher, twice as Mrs. Richard Burton and finally as Mrs. John Warner, the Senator from Virginia. Usually Elizabeth and her other half would continue the honeymoon at another romantic or exotic location before returning home.

Getting Married at The Beverly Hills Hotel

The Beverly Hills Hotel offers a fairy tale setting for brides and grooms. There are two gardens suited for outdoor weddings: the **Crystal Garden** and the **Polo Garden**. The Crystal Garden is conveniently adjacent to the Crystal Ballroom, and blossoms with hues of white and cream-colored flowers including roses, azaleas, camellias, and flowering magnolias. **The Polo Garden's** manicured lawn and blossoming flora also is a popular setting for outdoor weddings.

The hotel features three tastefully appointed reception salons, which are also used for indoor wedding ceremonies. A sweeping staircase, leading from the lobby to the **Crystal Ballroom**, allows newlyweds to make their grand entrance as Mr. & Mrs. Once inside, a flowing ribbon motif in the ceiling's design draws attention to the dramatic balconies, and three large doors lead to a gazebo in the Crystal Garden. The ballroom can accommodate up to 1,000 guests; a pre-event reception area can comfortably house 650 for cocktails and includes a private bridal room complete with waiting area and full bath. An elegant foyer gives way to the **Sunset Room**, which boasts a floor-to-ceiling bay window stretching the entire length of the parlor to capture the most breathtaking views. The ballroom, which accommodates up to 300 guests, has a daytime ceiling mural complete with blue skies and clouds.

The **Rodeo Room** can be divided into three very private rooms or can remain as one large area for parties of 800. The salon features gold and purple hues, plush upholstered walls, dramatic drapery throughout, and mirrored accents. A cocktail area accommodates up to 400 guests for pre-reception celebrations and features a permanent bar and balcony with steps leading to the Crystal Garden.

For pre-wedding gatherings, the **Polo Lounge** is perhaps the most famous eatery in Los Angeles – if not the country. For decades, Hollywood deals have been made over power breakfasts and two martini lunches, and nothing escapes the watchful eyes of seasoned maitre d's. Other dining choices include the **Polo Grill** for elegant family dinners, **The Fountain Coffee Shop** for informal dining, **The Cabana Club Café** for poolside dining under umbrella-shaded tables, and the **Sunset Lounge** for finalizing last minute wedding details over high tea or a glass of wine.

A Kosher Wedding, Gourmet-Style!
The chef can create and prepare a kosher menu upon request utilizing the hotel's exclusive gourmet kosher kitchen.

Honeymooning at The Beverly Hills Hotel

The hotel offers 203 secluded guest rooms, suites, and individual bungalows in the heart of Beverly Hills. Lush gardens surround the 12 sprawling acres, and distinctive fragrances reveal a mixture of hibiscus, bougainvillea, coconut palms, and orange blossoms. Each room is uniquely appointed and pampers guests with such amenities as marble bathrooms, roaring fireplaces, individual terraces, and private entrances.

For couples who really want to spoil themselves, the Crescent Wing houses the 2,500 square foot **Presidential Suite** featuring a private entrance, commercially-equipped kitchen, resident chef and butler, two individual shower stalls and a state-of-the-art treadmill. Only the four-bedroom **Presidential Bungalow #5** can compare, boasting its own private lap pool! The Presidential Suite is offered at $3,000 per night, the Presidential Bungalow is slightly higher at $3,050.

Guest amenities include **The Pool & Cabana Club** complete with 21 private cabanas, two championship tennis courts, a fitness center, jogging trails throughout the 12 acres, chauffeured limousine service and much more.

Marilyn Monroe, 90210
During the filming of the 1959 movie, "Let's Make Love," Marilyn Monroe and her French co-star, Yves Montand, would make some of their own love in bungalows 20 & 21.

THE REGAL BILTMORE
506 South Grand
Los Angeles, Ca 90071
800/245-8673
213/624-1011

Accommodations
$195-$2,000

Celebrity Guest Register

- *Delta Burke & Gerald McRaney*
- Will Rogers
- Barbra Streisand
- J. Paul Getty
- Howard Hughes
- President Ronald Reagan
- Duke & Duchess of York
- Bob Hope

- *Natalie Cole*
- Henry Fonda
- Ann Miller
- Walt Disney
- President Harry Truman
- Princess Margaret
- Eleanor Roosevelt

A History

In 1922, ground was broken for what would soon be hailed as the most elaborate hotel west of Chicago. The Regal Biltmore opened on October 1, 1923, and was financed by a consortium of local businessmen who then leased the property to the Los Angeles Biltmore Company. The 1,000 room hotel was built for an inflated sum of $10 million and is believed that its namesake was suggested by Cornelius Vanderbilt, who was a friend of John McEntee Bowman, president of The Regal Biltmore Company. Vanderbilt's family coined the name *Biltmore* for their family's 255-room estate in North Carolina. The name is derived from two words *Bildt*, the Dutch ancestral town of their origin (van der Bildt) and *More*, an Old English word for rolling, grassy countryside which described their native Holland. Bowman went on to develop several hotels across the country, as well as in Cuba, bearing the Biltmore name.

Shultze and Weaver, New York-based architects best known for creating the elegant Waldorf-Astoria, were hired to design the hotel. They borrowed architectural elements to reflect the Castillian heritage of California, and created a Spanish-Italian Renaissance design. Museum quality frescos and bas-relief decor that still adorn the public rooms were hand-painted by Italian artist Giovanni Smeraldi and illustrate the elegant style of the 1920s. Five years after the hotel opened, it underwent a $4 million expansion to include 500 additional guest rooms and the Biltmore Bowl.

A number of modern buildings now dominate the downtown Los Angeles skyline, but few can rival The Regal Biltmore's commanding design and elegant interior, both of which pay homage to Hollywood's golden era.

Famous Nuptials

In 1989, transplanted Southerners **Delta Burke** and **Gerald "Mac" McRaney** were married in The Regal Biltmore's elegant Emerald Room before 400 guests. The bride, best known for her role as Suzanne Sugarbaker on the hit television series *Designing Women*, was attended by 10 bridesmaids, including Matron of Honor and co-star Dixie Carter. Not to be outdone, the groom, an alumnus of such television shows as *Simon & Simon* and *Major Dad*, had a set of groomsmen to match.

After the ceremony, the newlyweds waltzed across the foyer to the Crystal Room to celebrate. The couple's Southern hospitality was evident in their selection of musicians. To ensure everyone would eventually make it out to the dance floor, they hired a nine-piece ensemble, a jazz quartet, a 12-piece dance band, a bagpiper and eight trumpeters who heralded the bride each time she entered the room. Guests included Valerie Harper, Markie Post, Hal Holbrook (husband of Dixie Carter), Tim Curry, Mary Ann Mobley and Gary Collins.

Celebrated Honeymoons

After their Tara-esque wedding, **Delta Burke** and **Gerald McRaney** spent their wedding night in one of The Regal Biltmore's elegant suites before heading on an extended European honeymoon. Singer **Natalie Cole**, who also was married at The Regal Biltmore, is said to have spent her wedding night here as well.

Getting Married at The Regal Biltmore Hotel

The Regal Biltmore houses four exquisite ballrooms created in the Beaux Arts fashion perfectly suited for weddings and receptions. The **Crystal Ballroom** features an intricate hand-painted ceiling, a fleet of crystal chandeliers and curved balconies suspended from the mezzanine, and can accommodate up to 800 guests. Down the corridor is the ornate, bi-level **Gold Room**, named for its gold leaf motif. The salon features such characteristics as hand-carved doorways and an arched ceiling, and welcomes parties of 500. The **Emerald Room**, with its beamed ceiling, is adorned in hues of green with gold accents, and can host up to 400 guests. A wooden esplanade and hand-painted friezes are hallmarks of the **Tiffany Room**, which can accommodate up to 400 guests.

There are a number of venues for hosting pre-wedding functions or enjoying a romantic dinner for two. **Bernard's**, well suited for formal rehearsal dinners, is an elegant setting with ornate pillars, rich woods and 1920s silver; while **Smeraldi's** offers casual bistro-style dining for family introductions or informal gatherings; **Saisai** features authentic Japanese ambiance and cuisine, and features five private rooms for dinners. The opulent **Rendevous Court**, positioned beneath a three-story ceiling, features an ornate fountain as its focal point and serves cocktails and afternoon tea.

Two lounges are an ideal meeting spot before heading to the rehearsal: the **Cognac Room** and the 1920s-style **Gallery Bar**.

Honeymoon Package At The Regal Biltmore

Newlyweds may wish to request the special Honeymoon Package, which includes a junior suite, bottle of champagne upon arrival, and breakfast in Smeraldi's for $195.

Honeymooning at The Regal Biltmore

The Regal Biltmore offers 683 tastefully appointed guest rooms, which resemble elegant boudoirs rather than standard hotel chambers. There are 43 suites ranging in size from one to three bedrooms, and feature such amenities as spiral staircases, private elevators, or grand pianos.

The Presidential Suite is equal to having your own private penthouse complete with full kitchen, dining and living room, a master bedroom and two guest rooms. Famous occupants have included Presidents Truman, Kennedy, Ford, Carter, Reagan and Clinton.

The Oscar Goes To...A Napkin!

When the Academy of Motion Picture Arts and Sciences was established in 1927, an event was held in the Crystal Ballroom to celebrate the founding of the newly formed organization. During the gathering, attended by moguls and movie stars, a rough rendering of a statue was sketched on a napkin. It depicted a small – but imposing – figure with his arms folded across his chest. The statue, fondly referred to as Oscar, would later become an international symbol for the motion picture industry.

THE CLIFT HOTEL
495 Geary Street
San Francisco, CA 94102
800/652-5438
415/775-4700

Accommodations
$195-$825

Celebrity Guest Register
- *Donald O'Connor*
- Joe Cocker
- Prince
- Jessica Tandy
- Patti LaBelle
- Alfred Hitchcock
- Rosemary Clooney
- Billy Joel
- Jimmy Stewart
- Hume Cronyn
- Hedda Hopper
- Kim Novak
- Michael Jackson
- Edward G. Robinson

A History

Frederick C. Clift and his siblings inherited from their father a piece of property at the corner of Taylor and Geary near San Francisco's Union Square in the early 1900s. At age 45, Clift abandoned a fruitful law career in hopes of becoming a world-class hotelier. In a brash move, he bought out the rest of his family's interest and was determined to build a luxury hotel that would embody true style and class.

Clift hired architect George A. Applegarth, a graduate from Paris' prestigious Ecole des Beaux Art, to design his dream hotel. He presented the young architect with an ambitious scenario to build "a hostelry of the highest type in both construction and furnishing, and with the most modern conveniences and luxuries as afforded in the best Eastern and European hotels." And, in the wake of the great San Francisco earthquake, Clift wanted it "quake proof!"

Rising from the rubble of Old San Francisco, The Clift Hotel opened in 1915, during the frenzy of the Panama-Pacific Exposition. The original 12-story, 350-room structure was enhanced nine years later when three additional floors were added. During the 1920s, a parade of Packards and Pierce-Arrows glided to a stop in front of The Clift's doors to deposit well-dressed guests.

Throughout its tenure, The Clift has adapted to the social element of the era. During the war years, the hotel was a favorite residence for families of officers being shipped overseas. During the 1950s and '60s, when corporations offered lavish perks, business trips often included the entire family. In order to attract this new clientele, The Clift staged publicity shots illustrating how the nuclear family enjoyed San Francisco while Dad attended important meetings.

Since its opening more than 80 years ago, The Clift has survived and remains a staple of San Francisco hospitality.

Celebrated Honeymoons

Actor-dancer **Donald O'Connor**, best remembered for his co-starring role in *Singing in the Rain,* wed **Gloria Noble** at the El Presidio Wedding Chapel in Santa Barbara on October 11, 1956. They spent their wedding night at the nearby Santa Barbara Biltmore Hotel, and the remainder of their honeymoon was spent at The Clift Hotel, where the groom was starring in a play next door at the Curran Theatre.

Getting Married at The Clift Hotel

The Clift Hotel houses eight banquet rooms on various levels of the hotel, all boasting Art Deco splendor. The Mezzanine salons, named for California's natural wonders, include the **Shasta**, **Sequoia**, and **Yosemite** rooms. The Shasta can accommodate up to 45 guests. The Sequoia can comfortably house 100 guests. The Yosemite, the hotel's main ballroom, can accommodate up to 200; when combined with the neighboring Muir room, which can host up to 50, the room expands to house 250 guests. The **Spanish Suite**, located on the rooftop, features two terraces with breathtaking views of the city and can house up to 100 guests. The **Penthouse Suites** offers two rooms for intimate gatherings of 15 or 20, and features exquisite panoramic views. The **Coach Suite**, housed in the hotel's lower level, offers accommodations for 40.

The French Room is an elegant venue for hosting rehearsal dinners and features fine dining, early 20th-century crystal chandeliers, and Louis XV decor. **The Redwood Room** features romantic Art Deco decor, and with a mood-enhancing piano bar is reminiscent of the 1930s. The Redwood Room is perfect for hosting a bridal luncheon or afternoon tea, or for post-rehearsal cocktails.

Rose Petals On Your Honeymoon Bed

For $450 per night, a special Romance Package is available for honeymooners and includes overnight accommodations in an elegant suite complete with a scattering of rose petals on the bed; a chilled bottle of champagne; two crystal flutes; a pair of monogrammed, silk pajamas – the top for her, the bottom for him; and breakfast in bed. The cost is $450 per night.

Honeymooning at The Clift

Located just blocks from famed Union Square and positioned in the center of the city's Theater District, The Clift rises 17 stories to offer 329 elegantly-appointed guest rooms and suites. Rooms are spacious in size with high ceilings, crown molding and hand-crafted woodwork, Georgian-style furnishings and marble bathrooms. Special amenities include personal butler service upon request and complimentary limousine service to the downtown area.

Hitchcock's Choice

The York Hotel, located just a few blocks from The Clift, was the backdrop for Kim Novak's apartment in the film Vertigo. However, the cast and crew, including Novak, Jimmy Stewart, and director Alfred Hitchcock, all made The Clift their home during filming.

FOUR SEASONS BILTMORE, SANTA BARBARA

1260 Channel Drive
Santa Barbara, CA 93108
800/332-3442
805/969-2261

Accommodations
$335-$1,800

Celebrity Guest Register
- *Heather Locklear and Tommy Lee*
- *Gabrielle Carteris*
- Greta Garbo
- Bing Crosby
- Rosalind Russell
- John Philip Sousa
- Charles Lindbergh
- Michelle Pfeiffer
- *Donald O'Connor*
- Michael Douglas
- Jack Lemmon
- Errol Flynn
- Joan Crawford
- Somerset Maugham
- Kirk Douglas

A History

At the beginning of the 20th century, the Santa Barbara Country Club, which featured a 9-hole golf course overlooking the Pacific Ocean, was replaced with a cluster of seaside guest cottages. The owner, Walter Douglas, built the mini-resort to accommodate guests planning an extended stay. Eventually – long after Douglas' departure – it became known as Montecito Park.

By 1925, the site was acquired by the Santa Barbara Biltmore Corporation, and plans were begun for a new spectacular oceanfront resort. Designed by Reginald Johnson, most of the small cottages gave way to a beautiful Spanish-style structure complete with stucco walls and a red-tile roof. Opening night took place on a chilly evening in December of 1927, and within weeks guest rooms were occupied by Hollywood moguls and starlets.

With the crash of the stock market in 1929, and the bleak years that followed during the Great Depression, the bank foreclosed on the hotel and its owners in 1932. Three years later, the Pacific States Savings and Loan Company purchased the hotel, and major shareholder Robert Odell became the new operator of the Santa Barbara Biltmore.

Odell had his own unique style of management, devoting his attention to every detail of the operation. Under Odell, major improvements were made to the property, including a new waterfront club, a 167-foot swimming pool and an opulent ballroom. Odell and his wife resided in one of the hotel's original 1904 cottages, which served as a backdrop for lavish gatherings for such luminaries as the Barrymores, Greta Garbo, Bing Crosby, and Errol Flynn. The cottage, named for Odell, is now the hotel's premier suite.

During World War II, the Biltmore provided refuge to American soldiers during R&R leave, and Hollywood entertainers motored up from Los Angeles to present shows to the men. After the war, the hotel continued to flourish under Odell's watchful eye; for many famous guests, the Santa Barbara Biltmore was their home away from home.

Nearly 70 years since its opening, the Four Seasons Biltmore, Santa Barbara, is still a sought-after hideaway by Hollywood legends and rising stars.

Famous Nuptials

Actress **Heather Locklear** married first-husband **Tommy Lee**, drummer for the heavy metal band *Motley Crüe* (now married to Baywatch star Pamela Anderson Lee) on May 10, 1986, outdoors at the Four Seasons Biltmore, Santa Barbara. A skin-tight, mermaid-style wedding gown hugged the bride's slim figure as 500 guests, including the groom's tattooed band members, looked on. After 40 minutes, the two were pronounced husband and wife. The guests were ushered to a nearby ballroom where the party continued for hours.

Other famous Four Season Biltmore brides include actress and former talk show host **Gabrielle Carteris**, who played Andrea on the hit television series *Beverly Hills 90210*.

Famous Honeymooners

On October 11, 1956, the El Presidio Wedding Chapel in Santa Barbara was the backdrop for actor **Donald O'Connor's** marriage to his wife Gloria. The groom, who starred opposite Gene Kelly and Debbie Reynolds in the classic movie *Singing In The Rain*, had not one but seven best men. The two spent their wedding night at the Santa Barbara Biltmore and continued their honeymoon in San Francisco, where the groom was starring in a play (see The Clift Hotel).

Getting Married at the Four Seasons Biltmore, Santa Barbara

Whether it's an intimate group of 50 witnessing the nuptials or a cheering crowd of 300, the most spectacular setting for exchanging vows at the Four Seasons Biltmore are the three outdoor gardens. The courtyard setting of the **North Patio** features blooming flora, tropical trees, and lush foliage surrounded by the hotel's Mediterranean structure. Brides descend down a spiral Spanish staircase to make their entrance. Weddings hosted at **La Pacifica**, which overlooks the ocean and not-too-distant Channel Islands, are enhanced with the sound of crashing waves. The **500 Courtyard** is nestled near a collection of cottages, and brides and grooms exchange vows beneath a trellis with the faint sound of the ocean behind.

Each ballroom is positioned near one of the wedding gardens, so all the transportation required from the ceremony to the reception is a simple stroll through the gardens. **The Loggia Ballroom**, for groups of up to 200, boasts 18-foot ceilings, crystal chandeliers, a magnificent fireplace, and graceful mirrors. Parties spill out onto a bricked-in courtyard, where cool ocean breezes refresh guests. Teetering above the Pacific Ocean is **The La Pacifica Ballroom**, where ocean vistas are seen through floor-to-ceiling windows. The ballroom welcomes groups of up to 300. The smaller yet splendid **El Mar** salon offers high-beamed ceilings, suspended chandeliers, an elegant mantle and fireplace, and shuttered windows throughout. A covered terrace, which gazes out upon the ocean, is an ideal location for enjoying pre-reception cocktails.

There are a number of restaurants and out-of-the-way eateries located throughout the hotel. For splendid rehearsal dinners, both **La Marina** and **The Patio** boast spectacular seascape views and award-winning cuisine. Casual gatherings take place outside on **The Patio**, surrounded by a garden-like setting with ocean vistas. **La Sala Lounge** offers a delightful afternoon tea by day with cocktails and entertainment in the evening. Discover coastal breezes on La Sala's outdoor terrace and, on cooler evenings, a cozy indoor fireplace is ablaze with burning wood.

The Four Seasons Biltmore Suggests ...

A recommended vendor list is available – from photographers to florists – and each one is familiar and knowledgeable with the hotel and its policies.

Honeymooning at the Four Seasons Biltmore, Santa Barbara

When exiting the 101 Freeway at Olive Mill Road, a vintage neon sign emblazoned with the words *Biltmore Hotel* points south, guiding you toward your destination. As you round the two-lane road to the hotel's circular driveway, you know you've discovered something special.

The Four Seasons Biltmore, Santa Barbara, is situated on 22 acres of prime oceanfront property. There are 234 guest rooms located in two-story structures; 12 luxurious suites are housed in charming cottages. Each chamber features white-shuttered windows with views of either the flower-filled gardens, the waterfront and Channel Islands, the Santa Ynez Mountains, or the inviting swimming pool. Large floor plans are an added bonus and many offer either a balcony or private terrace and cozy fireplace.

The narrow seaside street connects the hotel to the **Coral Casino Cabana and Beach Club**, where an oceanside swimming pool and white-sand beach await hotel guests. With two pools, two health clubs, a spa, bicycles, three tennis courts, shuffleboard, croquet and a putting green, there's never any reason to venture elsewhere!

No Wonder the Food is So Good Here!

Julia Child, the first lady of gourmet, resides near the hotel. She and her late husband, Paul, would often take brisk strolls through the flower-filled gardens of the hotel. Once in a while, she can be still be spotted near the kitchen talking shop with the chef.

FOUR SEASONS HOTEL
300 South Doheny Drive
Los Angeles, CA, 90048
800/332-3442
310/273-2222

Accommodations
$295-$4,000

Celebrity Guest Register

- *Paula Abdul*
- Ricki Lake
- Rachel Hunter
- Magic Johnson
- Brandy
- Howard Stern

- *Luke Perry*
- Rod Stewart
- Rosie O'Donnell
- Jason Priestly
- Janet Jackson
- Robin Quivers

A History

Since its opening a decade ago, the Four Seasons Hotel has become a hot property for East Coast celebrities who breeze into town for press junkets, agent meetings, and nightclub openings.

The hotel is located on a palm-lined street in a quiet residential neighborhood near Beverly Hills. The 16-story structure rises above the city offering panoramic views of downtown Los Angeles, Hollywood, Beverly Hills, Bel Air and Century City. Because of its close proximity to the movie and production studios, the hotel is often the backdrop for celebrity interviews, press junkets, power lunches and movie deals. The Four Seasons Hotel also is close to such fashionable addresses as Rodeo Drive, Wilshire Boulevard, Melrose Avenue, and Sunset Boulevard.

The Four Seasons Hotel may not have the history of some of its neighboring inns, but it certainly has become a Los Angeles landmark in an incredibly short amount of time, and is a favorite destination for Generation X's rich and famous.

Famous Nuptials

Teenage girls across the United States were reduced to tears after learning *Beverly Hills 90210* hearthrob **Luke Perry** married **Minnie Sharp** at the Four Seasons Hotel on November 20, 1993. It's rumored that the two met after Luke received a piece of "fanny" mail from Minnie, which included a pair of her panties, and decided to give her a call. After the nuptials, everyone headed to nearby Pinot Bistro in Studio City for the reception, which was attended by many of the groom's *90210* co-stars.

Pop singer and former Los Angeles Laker Girl, **Paula Abdul**, wed entrepreneur **Brad Beckerman** beneath a flower-draped chuppah at the Four Seasons Hotel on October 25, 1996. More than 160 guests witnessed the ceremony, including members of the musical group Boyz 2 Men, Rod Stewart and Rachel Hunter, basketball great Magic Johnson, and Rosie O'Donnell.

Getting Married at the Four Seasons Hotel

From concept to conclusion, the Four Seasons Hotel attends to the smallest of details on behalf of the bride and groom. The hotel offers an array of reception salons suitable for small or large gatherings, plus an outdoor area for al fresco celebrations.

The **Wetherly Gardens** is ideal for outdoor California-style weddings and receptions, and features a beautifully landscaped courtyard of white camellias coupled with draped bougainvillea, accommodating up to 250. The elegant **Grand Ballroom** features soft, muted hues, floor-to-ceiling windows and suspended crystal chandeliers. The ballroom can accommodate 500 guests comfortably for receptions, 250 for sit-down dinners. The **Beachwood** and **Benedict** rooms can both host up to 30 guests, and each features an outdoor terrace. The **Almond** and **Linden Garden Suites** feature French doors that open to reveal terraces and garden vistas and can house up to 60 guests. The **Palm Garden Suite** features a terrace and private garden area suitable for receptions of 70. The **Garden Court** is perfect for intimate gatherings of 22, and features a small alcove for pre-reception cocktails.

There are three restaurants located on the premises, ranging from informal to elegant. **The Cafe** is reminiscent of a European-style brasserie, and is open for breakfast, lunch, and dinner as well as afternoon tea. The casual **Poolside Terrace** overlooks the city skyline and nearby Hollywood Hills, and is a perfect place to enjoy the sunshine while lunching with bridesmaids. The award-winning **Gardens Restaurant** features 18th century Italian art, views of the private gardens, and superb cuisine for impressing soon-to-be in-laws. After the rehearsal dinner, the wedding party may wish to gather at **Windows Lounge** for cigars and a martini toast.

King Of All Freeloaders

When radio personality and self-proclaimed King of All Media Howard Stern came west to promote his debut movie "Private Parts," his radio entourage came along too, enjoying a brief stay at the Four Seasons. In fact, Stuttering John enjoyed his stay so much, he managed to charge thousands of dollars to Howard's promotional account...an act of stupidity his boss won't let him forget!

Honeymooning at the Four Seasons Hotel

The elegant Four Seasons Hotel features 179 guest rooms and 106 suites. Each room is designed to feel as if you are a guest at someone's home rather than a visitor at a hotel. Each room offers contemporary embellishments including Asian, geometric, and floral themes, with terraces overlooking Beverly Hills and greater Los Angeles. Special touches include overnight shoeshine, packing and unpacking upon request, and plush terry robes for him and her.

The hotel also features a swimming pool and Jacuzzi spa, a tented exercise equipment center located poolside, massage therapy, and personal fitness trainers upon request.

HIGHLANDS INN
P.O. Box 1700
(Four miles south of Carmel on Highway One)
Carmel, CA 93921
800/682-4811
408/624-3801

Accommodations
$225-$650

Celebrity Guest Register
- *Madonna & Sean Penn*
- Tracy Chapman
- Clint Eastwood
- Audrey Hepburn
- Bette Midler
- Yoko Ono
- Isabella Rossallini
- Natalie Wood
- Barbra Streisand

- Marlon Brando
- Julia Child
- Jeff Goldblum
- Julian Lennon
- Joe Montana
- Jackie Robinson
- Tom Selleck
- Liza Minnelli
- Elizabeth Taylor

A History
In July 1917, J. Franklin Devendorf opened a luxury cliff-side retreat overlooking the magnificent Pacific Ocean. From the beginning, Highlands Inn was a virtual magnet for attracting the rich, the famous, and the celebrated.

Until telephone lines were installed in 1918, reservations for the inn were taken at the neighboring Pine Inn in Carmel. The only thing more inconvenient than not having direct phone lines was the treacherous, one-lane seaside road that lead to Highlands Inn. In 1922, Devendorf sold the inn to California State Senator and Mrs. Edward Tickle. During the Tickles' 24-year reign, the area underwent a few subtle changes: the hilltops, once blanketed with wild strawberries, were now shaded by the pine trees planted by the first owner; and the one-lane country road that hugged the coastal cliff was transformed into Highway One, linking Highlands Inn to the rest of the world.

Although the inn has had several proprietors in its 80-year history (the Tickles sold the property in 1946) every owner has continuously strived to maintain its charm and beauty. As a result, the resort offers the most unobstructed views along the California coast and is still a sought-after haven for those – rich, famous and otherwise – seeking seclusion.

Celebrated Honeymoons

When **Madonna** married **Sean Penn** on August 16, 1985, it was assumed that their wedding would be *anything* but traditional. But traditional it was! The bride, who was also celebrating her 27th birthday, covered her signature bustier with an elegant white gown complete with 10-foot train; a traditional veil shielded her face. The groom, a poster boy for grunge long before it was fashionable, wore an expensive Versace double-breasted suit. Together the two looked like any other couple on their wedding day.

After the ceremony and reception, which was catered by Wolfgang Puck and included such guests as Diane Keaton, Andy Warhol, Cher, Carrie Fisher, Emilio Estevez, Timothy Hutton and Tom Cruise, the two climbed into their black Mercedes Benz and headed for Carmel. When they finally reached Highlands Inn, they registered under an alias and spent the next two nights in privacy.

Getting Married at Highlands Inn

Weddings are a specialty at Highlands Inn, and couples exchange vows beneath a foliage-covered trellis at the outdoor **Wedding Gazebo**, dramatically perched high above the Pacific Ocean. The gazebo can easily accommodate 50 guests seated or 80 standing.

The inn houses six banquet salons, each boasting ocean views with interiors designed to complement the natural beauty that lies on the other side of the salons' thresholds. The **Surf Room** and **Yankee Point** gaze down at the Wedding Gazebo and are connected by a balcony that overlooks the ocean. The Surf Room can accommodate up to 120 guests, while Yankee Point is ideal for groups of 50 or less. The **Grove Salon**, North and South, can be combined to create a reception area for 70; separately the North Salon can house 45 and the South Salon can accommodate up to 30. For intimate receptions of 18, the **Mt. Devon Room** is a cozy venue.

Highlands Inn also houses two award-winning restaurants ideal for romantic dinners and rehearsal dinners. The **Pacific's Edge**, named for its cliff-side setting, features a glass-walled interior and panoramic vistas of the ocean; the **California Market** offers expansive views, al fresco deck dining, and coastal charm.

Honeymooning at Highlands Inn

Towering above the drama of rocks, surf, and sand stands the historic Highlands Inn. Situated on 12 unspoiled acres that practically teeter above the Pacific Ocean, honeymooners can't help but feel removed from the rest of the world.

There are 142 spa suites offering such amenities as wood-burning fireplaces, full kitchens, outdoor decks or balconies, compact disc players and spa baths. The pampering **Townhouse Suites** house spacious dressing areas and rejuvenating spa-like hydra-massage baths. Couples can frolic in the heated outdoor swimming pool or a trio of outdoor spas; enjoy a workout in the fitness center; or take advantage of the inn's all-terrain bicycles. Mother Nature provides some of her own romantic comforts, including wooded paths for jogging, cycling, or strolling; a footpath that offers sweeping 180-degree vistas of the California coast; a nearby nature reserve that was a favorite subject for photo genius Edward Weston; and an infinite view of the Pacific Ocean and its majestic habitat of passing whales.

Marlon Brando's Secret Culinary Delight

When Marlon Brando occupied the Presidential Suite at Highlands Inn, he could have requested any number of culinary masterpieces prepared by the inn's award-winning chef. Instead, he desired nothing more than liverwurst sandwiches for most of his stay!

HOTEL DEL CORONADO

1500 Orange Avenue
Coronado, CA 92118
800/468-3533
619/435-6611

Accommodations
$179-$1,300

Celebrity Guest Register
• *Joe DiMaggio*
• Madonna
• President Ronald Reagan

• *Hedy Lamarr*
• *Rita Hayworth*
• Chris Everett

- John Wayne
- Marilyn Monroe
- Cesar Romero
- Goldie Hawn
- Tony Curtis
- Charlie Chaplin
- Demi Moore & Bruce Willis

- Robert Wagner
- Jack Lemmon
- Esther Williams
- Frank Sinatra
- Bruce Springsteen
- Johnny Weissmuller

A History

The Hotel del Coronado, simply known as *The Del*, has enjoyed as much fame as its many well-known guests.

What would eventually become a grand example of elegant Victorian architectural design began as a vision in the mid-1880s. Railroad tycoon Elisha Babcock and his partner, H.L. Story, purchased the entire Coronado peninsula for $110,000. With idle time and plenty of money, the two decided to build a resort hotel which would be the "talk of the Western world." Construction began in March 1887, and opening day, February 19, 1888, drew thousands of spectators from across the United States.

At the time of its opening, The Del was the largest wooden structure outside New York City. Its white gingerbread facade complete with red turrets was said to be the inspiration for Emerald City, dreamt up by author L. Frank Baum in *The Wizard of Oz*.

More than a century later, The Del is as splendid as ever. This waterfront Victorian resort includes the original five-story structure plus a new hotel tower and banquet facility. The hotel features 691 rooms and suites with views of the ocean, bay, interior courtyards, or manicured gardens.

Celebrated Honeymoons

When **Joe DiMaggio** married his first wife, actress **Dorothy Arnold**, on November 19, 1939, Marilyn Monroe was still answering to Norma Jean. The famous New York Yankees ball player and his starlet wife were married in the groom's hometown of San Francisco and, according to fellow baseball player Lefty O'Doul, it was the biggest thing to hit the city since the 1906 earthquake. The two honeymooned at The Del, where DiMaggio also celebrated his 25th birthday.

Other famous honeymooners include actors **Hedy Lamarr** and **Gene Markey**, who spent their first days together at The Del in May 1939, as did **Rita Hayworth** and her first husband.

Getting Married at the Hotel del Coronado

The first wedding ceremony performed at The Del took place in the ballroom in 1887, while the hotel was still under construction. The bride

One-Stop Wedding Arrangements

From the time the wedding is booked until the last guest has departed, the staff at the Hotel del Coronado offers one-stop shopping for brides and grooms with more than 80 reputable vendors, from wedding gown boutiques and musicians to photographers and florists, and can coordinate everything on-site for the couple.

and groom happened to be the offspring of two supervising engineers who were employed at the property.

Since then, a spectacular setting and first-class service have become hallmarks of The Del. The **Garden Patio**, situated in the hotel's courtyard, features a small, covered gazebo fashioned after the hotel's main Victorian-style building. It is here where couples exchange vows among the hotel's flora, which includes an array of South American palms. The Garden Patio also is ideal for elegant lawn receptions, not to mention extremely convenient.

Other reception venues include the **Grand Ballroom**, positioned under the hotel's signature turret near the south end of the main lobby. The ballroom offers sweeping waterfront views for up to 1,000 guests. This public room has served as the backdrop for many gala events, including the 1920 ball for the Prince of Wales as well as a 1979 reception for President Jimmy Carter. The **Crown Room** also has had its share of celebrated gatherings, like the fete for Charles Lindbergh in 1927 after he successfully completed his solo flight across the Atlantic. The room, which features a 33-foot ceiling sans pillars, is an elegant venue for wedding celebrations, and can host up to 600 guests.

The **Promenade Deck**, overlooking the Olympic-sized swimming pool and the Pacific Ocean, is perhaps the most spectacular outdoor setting in Southern California. This seaside location, which can house receptions for 300, is a fantastic spot for celebrating. The **Windsor Complex**, which includes the Windsor and Embassy Rooms, is tastefully appointed with views overlooking the Ocean Terrace and poolside promenade. The complex can accommodate 350 guests or be divided into two smaller venues that can accommodate groups of 40 to 70.

The Hotel del Coronado offers a choice of casual-to-elegant restaurants for rehearsal dinners, family gatherings, and post-nuptial celebrations. The **Crown Room** offers a spectacular Sunday brunch and is open for breakfast, lunch, and dinner. The **Prince of Wales Grill** is The Del's latest gastronomic creation, offering candlelit tables for two and floor-to-ceiling windows overlooking the Pacific Ocean. Al fresco dining can be had at the **Ocean Terrace**, a casual bistro for pre-wedding gatherings. For reviewing last minute details, visit the **Palm Court Lounge** overlooking the Garden Patio, which features a live pianist. Two lounges await guests after the bride and groom have made their escape: the **Ocean Terrace Lounge** and the **Promenade Deck Bar** – both overlooking the ocean.

Honeymooning at the Hotel del Coronado

Situated on 33-acres of prime oceanfront property, The Del offers Victorian and contemporary accommodations. Upon arrival, guests are ushered in to the hotel's elegantly appointed **Grand Lobby** where the original bird-cage electric elevator – complete with a 24-hour elevator operator – ferries newlyweds to their historic rooms.

The hotel's guest rooms are housed in three structures: the historic **Victorian Building** and the two contemporary **Ocean Towers**. Each room, classic and nouveau, offers understated elegance with terraces overlooking the ocean, bay, courtyard, or grounds. Those who stay in the Victorian Building enjoy a maze of hallways and hidden staircases that lead to different areas; you can feel the sense of history associated with the building. **The Beach House** is a separate cottage located adjacent to the main building. It features two bedrooms, unobstructed waterfront views, total seclusion from the rest of the world and a price tag to match – $1,300 per night.

Considered an all-inclusive resort, The Del boasts six lighted tennis courts, two heated swimming pools, men's and women's spas and fitness centers, boat house and marina, nine restaurants and lounges, and more than 30 shops and boutiques.

Changing the Course of British History At The Del

History suggests the Prince of Wales, who would later be crowned King Edward VIII of England, first laid eyes on Wallis Spencer Simpson during his 1920 visit to the Hotel del Coronado. In 1936, sixteen years after their brief encounter, Edward would abdicate the throne to marry the twice-divorced American, who was not considered "royal" material by his mum, Queen Mary, or his subjects. After he gave up the throne, he and Wallis Simpson lived a glamorous life as the Duke and Duchess of Windsor.

INN ON MT. ADA

398 Wrigley Rd.
Santa Catalina Island, CA 90704
310/510-2030

Accommodations
$250-$620

Celebrity Guest Register
- *Tracey Nelson & Billy Moses*
- Sally Kellerman
- John Tesh

- Mark Harmon & Pam Dawber
- Harriet Nelson

A History

Chewing gum magnate William Wrigley conducted his life with grandeur. In 1919, he purchased Catalina Island and brought his beloved Chicago Cubs to the remote area for spring training.

Soon after his land acquisition, Wrigley chose the most magnificent slice of land in which to nest. The white-washed Georgian Colonial revival mansion was said to be his wife, Ada's, summer dream house, and the trademark green shutters were her contribution to the design. Covering 7,000 square-feet of space, the home was the most elaborate the islanders had seen. The main floor included arched doorways leading to the den, sun room, living room, drawing room, dining rooms and butler's pantry; a curved staircase disappeared to the second floor where six additional bedrooms could be found.

Perched high above the Pacific Ocean overlooking the small town of Avalon, Wrigley seemed to reign over his tiny principality. He often peered through a high-powered telescope at the baseball diamond below to keep apprised of how his baseball team was doing during the crucial spring training period.

The Wrigley's occupied their summer home for the next 30 years, and after they passed away the estate was donated to the University of Southern California. USC leased the property to the Institute of Marine Coastal Studies as a quasi-campus for cultural and academic studies. In 1985, two local residents signed a 30-year lease and invested more than a million dollars to restore the estate to its original splendor.

Today, Wrigley's estate has been renamed the Inn on Mt. Ada and welcomes weary visitors as an elegant bed and breakfast.

Famous Nuptials

When **Tracy Nelson**, star of such television series as *Square Pegs* and *The Father Dowling Mysteries*, married actor **Billy Moses** (*Mystic Pizza*), the two reserved the entire inn for their July 25, 1987, wedding. The intimate gathering included the bride's uncle, Mark Harmon and wife Pam Dawber, as well as famous brothers Gunnar and Matthew of the band *Nelson*. Guests enjoyed a terrace reception overlooking Avalon as songs by the bride's late father, Ricky Nelson, played in the background.

Getting Married at the Inn on Mt. Ada

Imagine greeting your guests from atop a winding staircase as you graciously welcome mainlanders to your island estate. Well, even if it is not yours to keep, when you marry and celebrate at the Inn on Mt. Ada, the entire mansion becomes the exclusive domain for you and your guests.

Ceremonies are performed in two select areas of the mansion, including the semi-circular **Verandah**, located at the rear of the house and overlooking Avalon and the Pacific Ocean; or inside, where brides descend down the winding staircase to make a most dramatic entrance as guests look on from the Parlor. Both areas can accommodate from 24 seated up to 100 standing.

Receptions also are held outside on the Verandah under umbrella-covered tables or in the elegant **Dining Room**, complete with hardwood floors and a picture window that frames Avalon Harbor. The inn can accommodate 32 seated guests for receptions or 125 standing.

Treat Your Family & Friends In Style!

When reserving the inn for weddings, the tariff includes one night's lodging for up to 16 guests.

Honeymooning at the Inn on Mt. Ada

A stay at the Inn on Mt. Ada is probably equivocal to some of the spectacular gatherings found between the pages of *The Great Gatsby*. The setting is superb, the service impeccable and the surroundings ever so remote – a definite bonus when honeymooning!

After arriving at the Catalina ferry terminal or island airport, just tell any car for hire that you and your beloved are headed to the Inn on Mt. Ada. Not only will they quickly transport you to this grand estate, but the fare is included in your stay as is breakfast, lunch, and dinner.

A tiny circular driveway skirted with colorful flowers leads to the column entryway of the mansion, and once inside the compound, you're made to feel as if you are the guest of honor for the duration of your stay.

There are four bedrooms and two suites each located on the second floor, offering views of the village, the ocean...or both! Each room features period-style antiques, a private bath plus his and her terry cloth robes; some offer separate dressing areas, sitting rooms, fireplaces, and private balconies. Although there are no televisions or phones in the guest rooms, the main parlor provides a television set for those who simply can't do without and a phone is located at the top of the stairs.

Downstairs, guests gather for juice and coffee prior to feasting on a hearty country-style breakfast. A deli lunch is served on the verandah; chilled wine, beer and hors d'oeuvres greet guests after a day of island exploring; and a lavish dinner concludes the day. In between, a supply of soft drinks and snacks are available in the butler's pantry – help yourself! Guests may lounge in any of the public rooms including the club room stocked with board games, the formal library/parlor with its grand piano awaiting a player, the wicker-laden sun porch with a cart full of fresh coffee and baked goods, or the expansive verandah overlooking Avalon and the ocean.

No need to worry about getting around on the island, the inn provides guests with their own electric golf cart to come and go as they please.

Inspired By An Inn

Singer and composer John Tesh used the inn's terrace as the visual setting for the cover of his recent album "Avalon."

LA QUINTA RESORT & CLUB

49-499 Eisenhower Drive
La Quinta, CA 92253
800/598-3828
619/564-4111

Accommodations
$75-$2,100

Celebrity Guest Register

- *Ginger Rogers & Jacques Bergerac*
- Katharine Hepburn
- Robert Taylor
- Joan Crawford
- Frank Capra

- Warren Beatty & Annette Bening
- Sylvester Stallone
- Robert Wagner & Jill St. John
- Clark Gable & Carole Lombard
- Marlene Dietrich

- Greta Garbo & John Gilbert
- Irving Berlin
- Bette Davis
- Jerry Lewis
- Jessica Lange
- Shelley Long
- Errol Flynn & Lili Damita

- Bruce Springsteen
- Clint Eastwood
- Candice Bergen
- Natalie Cole
- Michael Jackson
- Cedric Gibbons & Delores Del Rio
- President Dwight D. Eisenhower

A History

La Quinta Hotel, as it was originally named, was to be Walter H. Morgan's personal oasis. The San Francisco-based businessman was heir to the Morgan Oyster Company, and the distinguished looking Morgan first escaped to the desert in 1921 for health reasons. He purchased 1,400 acres of "Happy Hollow," an area named by the Cahuilla Indians, its original inhabitants. Archaeological studies suggest that the resort stands on the site of an Indian village and burial ground dating back more than 1,000 years.

In 1925, Morgan hired Pasadena architect Gordon Kaufman to build a secluded retreat where guests could be pampered in the privacy of their own "quinta" or country home. In true Spanish tradition, La Quinta was designed around three courtyards that are still present today: the hotel lobby, the service area to the northwest of the lobby, and the interior ovals in the middle of the original 20 casitas. Seventy years later, the sprawling resort now boasts 640 casitas, a 17,000-square-foot ballroom, two new restaurants, a shopping plaza and 25 refreshing pools, plus four golf courses and a tennis club. While the resort has expanded considerably, it's hard to unravel where the old ends and the new begins.

Famous Nuptials

Ginger Rogers and French-born actor **Jacques Bergerac** were introduced in Paris by their mutual friend Evelyn Keyes, best known for her role as Scarlett O'Hara's sister, Suellen, in the 1939 movie classic *Gone With The Wind*. On February 7, 1953, the two tied the knot on La Quinta's sprawling grounds.

Celebrated Guests & Couples

Since its opening in late 1926, La Quinta has continually attracted Hollywood's movers and shakers. **Greta Garbo**, a frequent guest, came with various lovers, including silent screen star **John Gilbert**. She would occupy La Casa, a large casita now used for weddings and receptions, and would take mile-long walks to the nearest store in search of a pack of Camel cigarettes.

Frank Capra first came to know La Quinta in 1934, when he sought seclusion to turn the short story *Night Bus* into the romantic comedy *It Happened One Night,* starring Clark Gable and Claudette Colbert. Capra occupied the San Anselmo casita (room #136) and returned each year to pen classic after classic, including *Mr. Deeds Goes To Town, Lost Horizon, Mr. Smith Goes to Washington,* and other great movies.

It's no secret that Hollywood's most famous bachelor, **Warren Beatty**, became smitten with **Annette Bening**, his leading lady in *Bugsy* who would eventually become his wife. Location shooting took place near La Quinta, and it's rumored that both stars sought refuge – together – in one of the resort's more modern casitas.

A Cool Tune From A Hot Guy

Legend has it that during the 1930s, the December heat at La Quinta inspired frequent guest Irving Berlin to write the classic tune "White Christmas."

Getting Married at La Quinta

La Quinta offers two distinct areas for hosting desert-style weddings. **The Waterfall**, draped in towering palms and blossoming roses, is a unique spot for outdoor weddings. The gentle sound of cascading water is heard as vows are exchanged under the desert sun; the paved area adjacent to The Waterfall can be transformed into a magnificent reception area for celebrations under the stars. **La Casa** was a private home built in the 1920s, and a favorite hideaway for the elusive Greta Garbo. Standing at the top of the tiled stairway overlooking the courtyard, it's easy to imagine the trouser-clad Garbo greeting her guests. Decades since Garbo's time at La Casa, the hacienda-style casita has retained its charm. Intimate weddings and receptions are held indoors at the **Cactus Room** (maximum 60 guests) or in **La Sala** (maximum 65 guests) with most celebrations eventually spilling over into the courtyard.

Other reception areas include the **Frank Capra Room**, which exudes early California charm, accommodating up to 500 guests. The **La Cita Room** offers plush pastel carpets and a spacious breezeway to include outdoor functions, and can hold up to 225 guests. The mission bell atop the **Salon De Fiesta** provides some early California ambiance for one of La Quinta's newer structures. The salon encompasses 17,000 square feet, dividing into 14 separate rooms, and can accommodate groups of 40 or 1,800. The **Salon De Flores**, or "Salon of Flowers," boasts an ample 16,000 square feet with eight separate dividable rooms and a generous reception area. Salon de Flores can accommodate 105 guests up to 1,345. **The**

Tennis Club, built in the 1940s as the Olive Tree Estate, offers one of the most commanding views of the surrounding Santa Rosa Mountains, and can accommodate 180 guests.

The **Adobe Grill**, featuring authentic, regional Mexican dishes, offers a relaxing atmosphere for family introductions. The outdoor terrace overlooks colorful flowers, waterfalls, and The Plaza shopping area. **Morgans** is reminiscent of a roadhouse cafe with brass and glass accents and white tiled floors. Open for breakfast, lunch, or dinner, Morgans features indoor and patio seating as well as creative American cooking, and is ideal for casual gatherings.

Montañas, the site of La Quinta's original 1926 dining room, has been updated to offer more upscale surroundings and features a piano bar. Hand-loomed carpeting, hand-painted tableware, and elegant crystal make this seafood bistro an alluring backdrop for post-rehearsal gatherings. It was on Montañas' terrace that Bette Davis and Paul Henreid toasted one another after completing the motion picture *Now Voyager.*

Honeymooning at La Quinta

Framed by the rugged Santa Rosa Mountains in the Coachella Valley, La Quinta Resort & Club offers an array of antique and modern adobe-style casitas. The whitewashed structures, old and new, reek of old desert charm with tiled roofs, terra-cotta-tiled porches, and vibrant blue wooden shutters that compliment matching doors.

Each casita boasts a minimum of 500 square feet enhanced with Spanish antiques, wood-burning fireplaces, private patios with either mountain or garden views, and oversized bathtubs large enough for two. If you want to celebrate big and, of course, have a budget to match, you may want to consider the **Hacienda Grande** suite. The suite, which means "grand house," features a private pool, double-sided fireplace, and a dining room that seats as many as 20; it also comes with a $2,100 price tag! No worries for the original nutty professor, Jerry Lewis, who recently threw his wife a surprise birthday at the Hacienda Grande suite.

With five championship golf courses, 30 tennis courts, 25 courtyard swimming pools, 30 hot spas and a fitness center, active honeymooners can find plenty to keep busy.

La Quinta's Honeymoon Package
A Romance Package pampers honeymooners with deluxe accommodations, full American breakfast in bed, a bottle of champagne plus chocolate-covered strawberries, and a keepsake La Quinta ceramic tile. Low season rate is $150 (July-September), high season rate $290 (September-May).

LA VALENCIA HOTEL

1132 Prospect Street
La Jolla, CA 92037
800/451-0772
619/454-0771

Accommodations
$175-$1,300

Celebrity Guest Register

- *John Ireland and Joanne Dru*
- Groucho Marx
- Charlton Heston
- Jose Ferrer
- Dorothy McGuire
- Mel Ferrer
- Greta Garbo
- Gregory Peck
- Ginger Rogers
- Lorne Greene
- Jennifer Jones
- Vincent Price

A History

MacArthur Gorton and Roy B. Wiltsie officially opened their 28-room residential creation, La Valencia Apartment-Hotel, on December 15, 1926, with very little fanfare. Designed by Reginald Johnson, the Spanish-style structure, overlooking the famed La Jolla Cove, complemented its seascape surroundings.

Within 24 months, the two completed an expansion that would include an eight-story structure and a total count of 60 hotel-style rooms; a lounge stretching the length of the building would provide unobstructive ocean views; and a new oceanfront restaurant would create culinary masterpieces for diners. A tower, topped with a gold and blue dome, gave the hotel its distinct and unmistakable silhouette.

This time, the grand opening was heralded as the social event of the season, taking place on December 29, 1928. The hotel immediately became host to the wealthy and celebrated, and Hollywood moguls and starlets didn't mind the three hour trek south. From the onset, La Valencia bespoke distinction and glamour, a trait many establishments never acquire.

During World War II, as with many hotels and resorts from the era, La Valencia was transformed from elegant retreat to luxury barracks for servicemen on leave or waiting for their overseas orders. Patriotic La Jollans positioned themselves in the gold-domed tower, scanning the skies for enemy aircraft. As part of the Civil Defense program, the tower was manned 24 hours a day in two hour shifts.

After the war, La Valencia reclaimed its title as the jewel of La Jolla. With the opening of the La Jolla Playhouse, a theater troupe founded by

Gregory Peck, Mel Ferrer, and Dorothy McGuire, a whole new generation of celebrity guests claimed La Valencia for themselves. In 1956, the adjacent Cabrillo Hotel was acquired and incorporated as the West Wing of La Valencia, and the hotel reached a 100-room capacity.

Today, La Valencia Hotel resembles a miniature Spanish castle and is fondly referred to as "the pink lady of La Jolla."

Famous Nuptials

Actor **John Ireland** and actress **Joanne Dru**, who co-starred together in *All The King's Men* and *The Warriors*, were married at La Valencia Hotel on August 7, 1949, in one of the hotel's private ballrooms. The two were attended by actor Mel Ferrer and Barbara Ford, daughter of director John Ford, and famous guests included Gregory Peck.

Famous Honeymooners & Celebrated Guests

While most newlyweds bid farewell to guests for a romantic location, the new **Mr. and Mrs. Ireland** knew that La Jolla was indeed a romantic find! On their wedding night, they attended a play at Gregory Peck's La Jolla Playhouse, and returned to La Valencia Hotel where the groom carried his bride over the threshold!

Few Hollywood luminaries minded motoring down to La Jolla for weekend retreats. In fact, **Greta Garbo** and her lover, actor **John Gilbert**, often escaped to La Valencia Hotel to enjoy a romantic getaway.

Getting Married at La Valencia Hotel

The historic La Valencia Hotel retains its 1920s charm, with a choice of historic locations for both weddings and receptions.

The hotel offers two areas for wedding ceremonies, with spectacular ocean vistas as backdrops. Whether the forecast calls for sunny skies or torrential rains, **La Sala** can still provide dramatic ocean views for your wedding day. Located in the hotel's rustic lobby, couples exchange vows under an arched breezeway, with the faint sound of waves just beyond. La Sala can accommodate up to 50 guests seated plus standing room. The signature pink wrought-iron gate greets guests arriving at the **Garden**, a lush courtyard setting with dazzling views of the ocean. On an alcove overlooking the ocean, couples promise to love, honor, and cherish for a lifetime. The Garden provides an intimate setting for up to 80 seated guests plus additional space for those who wish to stand.

The three reception salons are just as splendid. The **Galeria** is reminiscent of an elegant study with its built-in teak bookcases, conversational sitting areas, and classic bar with French doors leading to the balcony. The Galeria can accommodate up to 75 guests comfortably and is also a regal area to exchange vows. The **Verandah Room and Terrace** gives the feeling of bringing the outdoors inside. The room, which welcomes groups of up to 200, features lush foliage throughout, and the palm trees that extend beyond the floor-to-ceiling windows create a framing for the room. White terrace-style chairs compliment lattice accents to enhance the Mediterranean setting.

The **Mediterranean Room** is a unique setting for pre-wedding gatherings and celebrations. The restaurant features indoor and outdoor dining coupled with Spanish-inspired decor, and offers a weekly Sunday champagne brunch. The setting for **The Tropical Patio** is reflected in the restaurant's name. Sheltered by palm trees and dotted with colorful flowers, diners enjoy a casual setting under the open sky. The Tropical Patio is ideal for bridal lunches or a simple meal for two. **The Whaling Bar** and **Cafe La Rue**, adorned with seafaring trophies and whimsical murals, both are unique spots to share a nightcap. Gather for cappuccinos or cocktails at the **La Valencia Lounge**, located off the lobby, featuring a hand-painted ceiling, panoramic ocean views, and terrace seating.

Create Your Own Theme Wedding

The staff at La Valencia Hotel will assist in creating the wedding of your dreams, including theme weddings. Recently the hotel staged a Renaissance-style ceremony and reception, and has assisted in fulfilling some unusual requests. One such request: a wedding was held on one of the hotel's fire escapes, where months before the groom had popped the question; the rabbi stood above while guests looked on from various hotel windows. Some guests also request that their pets be a part of the ceremony; one made sure his hamster was dressed to the nines, bow tie included!

Honeymooning at La Valencia Hotel

From the moment you step through the towering archway that leads to the lobby, any stress or worry almost magically vanishes. Hidden terraces, palm-shaded patios, and aromatic gardens are hallmarks of the hotel.

Each of the 100 guest rooms and suites have a unique style inspired by the quaint pensions found throughout Europe. Rooms come with a view of either the bustling village of La Jolla, the colorful gardens, or the ocean. Some are especially pampering with whirlpool bathtubs for two, French doors which open up to reveal cool ocean breezes, sleek marble entryways, and enough room to enjoy an extended stay!

MISSION INN
3649 Mission Inn Avenue
Riverside, CA 92501
800/843-7755
909/784-0300

Accommodations
$115-$600

Celebrity Guest Register
- *President & Mrs. Richard Nixon*
- *Bette Davis*
- *Humphrey Bogart*
- Muhammad Ali
- Priscilla Presley
- Jack Benny
- Winona Ryder
- W.C. Fields
- Robert Redford
- Elizabeth Taylor
- Judy Garland

- *President & Mrs. Ronald Reagan*
- *Ray Milland*
- *Constance Bennett*
- *Richard Arlen & Jobyna Ralston*
- Paul Newman & Joanne Woodward
- Raquel Welch
- Amelia Earhart
- Cary Grant
- Oliver Stone
- Martha Stewart
- Anthony Quinn

A History
The Mission Inn's humble beginnings date back to 1876, when it served as a modest two-story, adobe guest cottage. In 1881, Frank Miller, a citrus investor who was raised in the 12-room structure, bought the property from his father.

With the boom of the citrus industry, a new opera house, and the coming of the Southern Pacific Railroad, Miller was convinced the town lacked a certain something – a grand hotel. He persuaded railroad heir Henry Huntington to finance his dream of a palatial, four-story, U-shaped guest wing that would surround his cottage. The original wing opened in 1903, and with various expansions and additions, it would take more than three decades to turn Miller's dream into a reality.

Today the Mission Inn is comprised of four distinct wings: The Mission Wing, The Cloister Wing, The Spanish Wing, and The Rotunda Wing. With its wood-beamed ceilings, wrought-iron accents, hidden palazzos, tiled fountains and arched passageways, the inn resembles a grand Spanish Mission. Guests seem to be transported to another era as well as another continent. Listed on the National Register of Historic Places as well as the Historic Register for the state of California, Riverside County, and the City of Riverside, the Mission Inn has been beautifully preserved after undergoing an extensive renovation just a few years ago.

The inn offers a number of wedding and reception venues, culinary retreats, afternoon tea, and historic accommodations.

Famous Nuptials

When **Richard Nixon** took **Patricia Ryan** as his wife, he was a young deputy city attorney for Whittier, California. Pat was a school teacher at the town's local high school. Because her parents were deceased, Pat did not want her older brothers or her new in-laws to bear the expense of a large, traditional wedding.

Instead the two opted for a small, intimate ceremony at the Mission Inn where they spent weekend afternoons admiring its beauty. The Presidential Suite, where President Theodore Roosevelt stayed during his visit in 1903, when he dedicated the initial structure, served as the ceremony site. While the suite offered an historical setting and undeniable beauty, it was selected by the Nixons because it was the least expensive room the inn had to offer.

The Nixons were married on June 21, 1940, at 3:30 p.m. Afterward, they spent the rest of the day celebrating with friends and family in the long, narrow Spanish Art Gallery. After the reception, the future President and First Lady left for their honeymoon where they spent their wedding night at the Westward Ho in Phoenix, Arizona, before driving on to Mexico.

The St. Francis of Assisi Chapel has hosted many famous brides and grooms, including **Bette Davis** and **William Grant Sherry**; **Constance Bennett**; **Ray Milland**; **Humphrey Bogart**; and **Richard Arlen** and **Jobyna Ralston**, who met while filming the 1927 blockbuster *Wings*.

Celebrated Honeymoons

Future President of the United States **Ronald Reagan** wed actress and future First Lady **Nancy Davis**, on March 4, 1952, in Los Angeles. Actor William Holden and his wife, actress Brenda Marshall, served as best man and matron of honor. The two enjoyed a few days at the Mission Inn before departing for the Arizona Biltmore in Scottsdale, Arizona *(see Arizona Biltmore entry)*.

Getting Married at the Mission Inn

If you've always dreamt of being married in a Spanish castle or Mexican villa, the Mission Inn is the next best place.

The **St. Francis of Assisi Chapel**, which can host up to 150 guests, features a 17th-century gold leaf altar; Tiffany designed, stained-glass windows; and a hand-carved wood ceiling. A much more intimate setting can be found inside the ornate **St. Cecilia Chapel**. It is a perfect location for small family weddings and can accommodate 15 standing guests. For outdoor weddings, **The Gazebo** sits in the lush gardens of **The Court of the Birds**, and can accommodate up to 65 guests.

After the ceremony, the bride and groom can greet well-wishers at the inn's many hidden salons. The most popular settings for receptions include the **Spanish Art Gallery**, draped in hues of burgundy and boasting more than 120 original paintings; a descending marble staircase provides a dramatic entrance for newly married couples and can accommodate up to 150 guests. The **Galleria**, where Bette Davis and William Grant Sherry celebrated with their wedding guests, is conveniently located next to St. Francis of Assisi Chapel and can house up to 250 guests. The Galleria, which reveals one of many Tiffany stained-glass windows found throughout the inn, was originally built as an art gallery and museum. The **Atrio**, an old European-style courtyard located outside both chapels and art galleries, is an ideal spot for pre-reception cocktails and hors d'oeuvres. The **Cloister Music Room**, which can comfortably house 275 people, is reminiscent of a baronial hall found within the confines of a Spanish castle. Inspired by the Mission San Miguel, the Cloister Music Room boasts a wood-beam ceiling, a minstrels' gallery, and pews replicated from London's Westminster Abbey.

Duane's Prime Steaks and Seafood, located in the lower and upper squire arms room, is a traditional chop house and a tasteful setting for rehearsal dinners. The **Mission Inn Restaurant**, adorned with colorful Spanish tiles and ornate wall sconces, is another choice for rehearsal dinners or wedding breakfasts. Guests may dine indoors or al fresco on a bougainvillea-draped courtyard, featuring a collection of bells from the various missions found throughout the United States. The restaurant offers an eclectic menu and has earned a reputation for its fine Sunday brunch. The **Presidential Suite**, where the Nixons were married, has been transformed into a lounge and is ideal for post-rehearsal gatherings.

Oh So Suite!

Honeymooners are swept away with "Suite Memories," featuring overnight accommodations in a luxurious suite; champagne and chocolates upon arrival; dinner for two at the inn's award-winning restaurant, Duane's Prime Steaks and Seafood; two relaxing 30-minute body massages; and a private tour of the hotel. Suite Memories is available for $365 per night.

Honeymooning at the Mission Inn

The Mission Inn's 202 guest rooms and 33 suites provide a sanctuary for newlyweds. With unique architectural facets and priceless antiques, no two rooms are exactly alike: wrought-iron balconies open onto flowered courtyards; tile floors create unique mosaics; leaded and stained glass windows reflect colorful light; and domed ceilings offer roomy surroundings. Historic guided tours are offered daily for a nominal fee, taking visitors on a nostalgic journey. The 70-minute tour tells of the inn's humble beginnings and refers to the many architectural influences found throughout the property. All proceeds benefit the continuous restoration and preservation efforts of the inn.

Couples may choose to take advantage of an Olympic-size, outdoor swimming pool; state-of-the-art health club; masseuse room; and the inn's Museum, which displays an extensive collection of 19th and 20th century artifacts.

That's One Popular Room!

Room 431 is Paul Newman's favorite room as well as Dudley Moore's, and is located in the Rotunda Wing. The Alhambra Suite, atop the Cloister Wing, is where Winona Ryder stayed while filming "How To Make An American Quilt," which was shot on location in nearby Redlands.

OJAI VALLEY INN
Country Club Road
Ojai, CA 93023
800/422-6524
805/646-5511

Accommodations
$195-$600

Celebrity Guest Register
- *Fred MacMurray & June Haver*
- Kevin Costner
- Clark Gable
- Anthony Hopkins
- Loretta Young
- Walt Disney
- Judy Garland
- Bing Crosby
- Oprah Winfrey
- *Jimmy Stewart*
- Michael Douglas
- Bob Hope
- Lana Turner
- Hoagy Carmichael
- President and Mrs. Ronald Reagan
- Paul Newman
- Chi Chi Rodriguez
- Ellen Barkin

A History

Edward Drummond Libbey, a wealthy glass manufacturer and philanthropist from Ohio, had great hopes for the small town of Ojai when he came west in 1906. Besides a renaissance for the then shabby downtown area, Libbey also envisioned a rambling resort for the mountain community.

In 1923, Libbey's vision became a reality when he opened the Ojai Country Club. Designed by Wallace Neff, an architect who catered to the celebrities of the era, the California Spanish Revival-style resort boasted terra-cotta roofs, decorative iron work and tiles, flagstone terraces, and wood corbels. From the beginning, guests enjoyed the seclusion that both the town and inn afforded them. Hidden in the hills above the Pacific Ocean, the inn was a home away from home for the wealthy Hollywood community.

During World War II, the inn assisted the allied effort and was transformed from an exclusive hideaway into a military training camp for a battalion of 1,000 Army troops, later becoming a rest and recuperation facility for the Navy. Two years after the war ended, the property was returned to private ownership and was reopened as the Ojai Valley Inn.

Since its opening in 1923, the Ojai Valley Inn has expanded considerably but has never compromised its architectural charm that has appealed to so many generations. Situated on 220 tree-shaded acres, the inn is a haven for honeymooners wanting nothing but secluded surroundings and time with each other.

Famous Nuptials

Actress **June Haver** and actor **Fred MacMurray** found love together after each experienced their own tragedy. MacMurray, best known as the patriarch in the 1960s television series *My Three Sons*, lost his wife of 17 years to a lengthy illness, and Haver's fiancé was killed in an accident. For her, the loss was so traumatic she temporarily left Hollywood to enter a convent but eventually returned to both acting and dating. On June 28, 1954, June Haver became Mrs. Fred MacMurray at the Ojai Valley Inn. The two enjoyed a small wedding and reception before departing on a honeymoon that would take them to the Grand Canyon in Arizona and Bryce Canyon in Utah.

Celebrated Honeymoons

For years, **Jimmy Stewart**, the soft spoken actor of such classics as *It's A Wonderful Life* and *Mr. Smith Goes To Washington,* was considered by many to be Hollywood's most eligible bachelor. It took a woman as dynamic as **Gloria McLean**, the former daughter-in-law of the Hope diamond owner, to change his status from confirmed bachelor to happily married man. On August 9, 1949, the 41-year-old groom and his bride exchanged vows at the Brentwood Presbyterian Church in the Brentwood neighborhood of Los Angeles.

After a reception at his agent's home, which included such guests as Gary Cooper, Dorothy McGuire, Spencer Tracy, and David Niven, the two enjoyed a few days together at the Ojai Valley Inn before taking an extended honeymoon in Hawaii. And until Gloria's death some 40 years later, the two truly enjoyed a wonderful life... together!

Getting Married at the Ojai Valley Inn

The Ojai Valley Inn offers a secluded and serene setting for weddings and receptions. Ceremonies are held al fresco at **The Hacienda Courtyard** located in the center of the inn's original 1923 structure. The setting is reminiscent of a Spanish-style courtyard surrounded by lush foliage and breathtaking views of the golf course and mountain range. Should weather prove inclement, ceremonies are held indoors in one of three banquet areas. Receptions range from country casual to ultra-elegant. **The Big Red Barn** is part of the working ranch at the inn and a perfect setting for a country-style wedding for groups of up to 300. The barn is available from April through October, and an authentic farmyard of animals adds to the theme. The **Topa Ballroom**, available for groups of up to 350, features floor-to-ceiling pane glass doors with a large, airy foyer extending out toward the Topa Terrace. The **Shangri-La Pavilion**, which welcomes parties of up to 150, is a canopied structure boasting large, picture windows that open up to reveal breathtaking vistas of the golf course's back nine and mountains.

For family introductions and rehearsal dinners, the **Vista Dining Room** is an excellent choice and features foods grown in the inn's own gardens and orchards; panoramic views of the mountains and golf course add to the ambience. A casual outdoor setting can be enjoyed in the shadows of 250-year-old towering oak trees at the **Oak Grille & Terrace**, a relaxing spot to gather with out-of-town guests on the eve of the wedding. **Splashes Grille**, appropriately named because of its close proximity to the inn's pool, is an ideal location for hosting a casual bridal luncheon. **The Club** and **Neff Lounge** are choice gathering areas for unwinding after the rehearsal dinner.

Pamper Yourself

The "Pampering Package" ($303 per night) allows newlyweds the chance to relax after the celebration with luxurious accommodations and in-room massages.

Honeymooning at the Ojai Valley Inn

From the 18-hole championship golf course and full service tennis center to trail blazing on horseback and afternoon hikes, the Ojai Valley Inn offers honeymooners a choice to enjoy sports and nature or to simply relish the relaxing surroundings.

There are 207 spacious guest rooms and suites located in eight separate Spanish-style buildings. Some rooms offer fireplaces and most feature terraces with views of either the mountains or golf course. The historic **Hacienda** building, which features 22 guest rooms, reflects the style and era the inn was built and includes oversized four-poster beds, hand-crafted furniture, Mission armoires, pedestal sinks plus original hardwood floors and hand-painted tiles. Other amenities available to guests include two heated swimming pools, an outdoor Jacuzzi and a health club. A new 31,000 square-foot luxury spa, which has ushered in a new era of pampering at the 74-year-old inn, features private treatment rooms and meditation lofts for newlyweds in need of pampering.

Paradise Found

Director Frank Capra based the mythical Shangri-La from his film "Lost Horizon" on the beauty that surrounds the Ojai Valley Inn.

THE QUEEN MARY
1126 Queens Highway
Long Beach, CA 90802
800/437-2934
562/435-3511

Accommodations
$75-$525

Celebrity Guest Register
- *Elizabeth Taylor & Nicky Hilton*
- Greta Garbo
- Fred Astaire
- Melissa Gilbert & Bruce Boxleitner
- Kirstie Alley & Parker Stevenson
- Jim Carrey
- Duke & Duchess of Windsor
- Charles Durning
- Cary Grant
- Jason Priestly
- *Cyd Charisse & Tony Martin*
- Matthew Broderick
- Queen Elizabeth
- Marlene Dietrich
- Bob Hope
- Clark Gable
- Sir Winston Churchill
- Hugh Hefner
- Spencer Tracy

A History

Once they called her Queen of the Atlantic; a floating city awash in elegance. During her heyday, the Queen Mary was the most elegant ocean liner afloat, and her passenger lists read like volumes of *Who's Who*. With her charming Art Deco decor and spacious first-class suites, the rich and famous considered her the only civilized way to travel.

Built during the early 1930s in Clydebank, Scotland, the Queen Mary, part of the British Cunard fleet, departed on her Maiden Voyage from Southampton, England, on May 27, 1936, and arrived in New York Harbor four days later on June 1. With the outbreak of World War II in 1939, the Queen Mary was instantly transformed from elegant ocean liner into wartime troopship. She served as the seaborne headquarters for Prime Minister Winston Churchill, and while aboard he signed the papers for the D-Day invasion. In 1946, the Queen Mary continued to aid the Allied effort by transporting more than 22,000 war brides and their children to their new homes in America and Canada.

After the war she resumed her status as Queen of the Atlantic. As air travel became increasingly more affordable, the days of transatlantic ocean travel were numbered. In 1967, the Queen Mary sailed from Southampton, England, to Long Beach, California; it would be her final crossing, the end of an era.

Today the Queen Mary's graceful silhouette dominates Long Beach Harbor, where the former ocean liner is permanently berthed as an historic hotel and attraction. The Art Deco era remains timeless within her confines, and guests can relive the elegance of transatlantic travel in the privacy of their own first-class staterooms.

Celebrated Honeymoons

In 1950, **Elizabeth Taylor** and **Nicky Hilton**, heir to the Hilton Hotel empire, were married in a lavish Beverly Hills ceremony. It would be the first of many marriages for the 18-year-old starlet, who at the time was famous for such films as *National Velvet* and *Father of the Bride*. Ironically the newlyweds spent their wedding night at the elegant Breakers Hotel in Long Beach, California – now a retirement home – just across the harbor from where the Queen Mary is now permanently docked.

Days after tying the knot, the couple crossed the Queen Mary's gangway in New York Harbor to begin their honeymoon. While aboard the ship, the newlyweds would have the chef prepare elaborate dinners to enjoy in the privacy of their own suite. It's rumored that Elizabeth often socialized – *alone* – with fellow first-class passengers, the Duke and Duchess of Windsor, while the groom played cards until the early hours of the morning.

After marrying at the Santa Barbara Courthouse in California, actress and dancer **Cyd Charrisse** and husband, singer **Tony Martin**, honeymooned in Carmel and San Francisco before embarking on a grand tour of Europe. They returned from their European honeymoon aboard the Queen Mary on July 6, 1948.

Getting Married aboard the Queen Mary

The **Royal Wedding Chapel**, located on Promenade Deck, originally served as the second-class smoking lounge where a steward's pantry and service bar provided refreshments to the guests from behind the forward bulkhead. When the ship was sailing, the room seated 160 passengers; tables with reversible tops were used for writing and, more often, for playing cards. Today the chapel's elegant doors, which were repositioned from the Sun Deck Verandah Grill, open to reveal rich British brown oak burl walls with walnut pillar accents. The Chapel seats up to 200 guests, and candlelight ceremonies are performed seven days a week, excluding holidays.

Traveling from the wedding site to the reception location is as simple as a stroll down the deck! Each salon recalls the Art Deco era and provides an historic setting for celebrations. The spacious **Grand Salon**, the site of the original first-class dining room, boasts a 33-foot ceiling, dance floor, original artwork, and can accommodate up to 700 guests. The **Queen's Salon** features an elevated stage, marbled fireplaces, Art Deco accents, and can accommodate parties of 400. The **Royal Salon** provides a more intimate setting for groups of up to 160 and is adjoined by the **King's View Room**, which is an ideal location for hosting pre-reception cocktails and hors d'oeuvres. The **Capstan Club**, which can accommodate 130, and the **Britannia Salon**, which can host groups of 480, each feature their own private oceanfront deck for indoor and outdoor affairs. The **Verandah Grill**, located on Sun Deck at the stern of the ship, was once *the* tony a la carte restaurant when the ship was sailing. Today it is used for private receptions and offers sweeping waterfront views, whimiscial decor, and dramatic black carpeting for intimate parties of 100.

The Queen Mary houses three harbor view restaurants for pre-wedding breakfasts, bridal luncheons, and rehearsal dinners. Each bistro boasts 1930s ambiance along with Art Deco splendor, and can be reserved for private parties and gatherings. **Sir Winston's**, a five-star restaurant named for one of the ship's most famous passengers, is an elegant setting for pre-nuptial dinners; the **Chelsea**, specializing in seafood with Mediterranean influences, is another choice setting; the **Promenade Cafe** offers an eclectic menu and is a perfect spot to grab a quick bite while finalizing last minute details; **Champagne Sunday Brunch** is a weekly affair held in the Grand Salon, and a perfect place to gather with out-of-town guests.

> ## Sleep Like The Royals
> *The Hotel Queen Mary offers the "Royal Romance Package," which includes an overnight stay in a deluxe, first-class stateroom and champagne upon arrival for $125 land view, $145 harbor view.*

Romantic Accommodations

Newlyweds can relive the elegance of transatlantic travel without ever leaving port! The **Hotel Queen Mary** houses 365 original first-class staterooms, combining 1930s charm with the most modern conveniences. Each cabin is uniquely appointed with period-style furnishings and original artwork. The extensive corridors, enhanced with rich wood and miles of bold motif carpeting, segue into separate passageways which lead to the thresholds of first-class staterooms. Portholes provide the framing for picturesque views of the harbor and city skyline.

Spacious suites, which vary in size and floor plans, come equipped with one bedroom; former maids' quarters; sitting parlor; foyer; and ample closet space once used for storing steamer trunks. The suites have also been named after their famous occupants: The Churchill Suite, The Windsor Suite, and The Eisenhower Suite. Registered hotel guests also receive the Queen Mary self-guided shipwalk tour free of charge, which takes modern-day passengers from the engine room to the wheel house.

> ## Watch Out For That Golf Ball!
> *When the Queen Mary was sailing, she played hostess to virtually every star of the era: Bob Hope, an avid golfer, would hit golf balls off the Sports Deck during transatlantic crossings; Greta Garbo would often rise very early in the morning to take vigorous walks around Promenade Deck – alone!; and actress Dolores Del Rio was often seen strolling the decks with her Bull Terrier.*

SAN YSIDRO RANCH
900 San Ysidro Lane
Montecito, CA 93108
800/368-6788
805/969-5046

Accommodations
$375-$3,000

Celebrity Guest Register

- *President and Mrs. John Kennedy*
- Clark Gable
- Bing Crosby
- Audrey Hepburn
- Groucho Marx
- *Vivien Leigh & Laurence Olivier*
- Jack Benny
- Phil Collins
- Sophia Loren
- Gloria Swanson

A History

In the early 1700s, the foothills where the San Ysidro Ranch now stands was a way station for Franciscan monks. In 1825, Tomas Olivera, one of many owners, built an adobe, which served as the ranch's main house. Today it is the only structure found on San Ysidro Ranch that remains from the property's early California pioneering days.

In 1883, John Harleigh Johnston and Taylor Goodrich purchased the property to harvest high-quality oranges and lemons. Although mountain fires in the late 1800s nearly claimed their orchards, the men persevered. Sensing a growing popularity among the area resorts, John Harleigh Johnston transformed the working ranch into a small, stylish hotel that could accommodate up to 40 guests at one time, and in 1893, San Ysidro Ranch opened – instantly attracting many wealthy and powerful bluebloods from the East Coast.

In 1935, actor Ronald Colman and his partner, Alvin Weingand, purchased the 540 acres from the Johnston family, setting the stage for many wondrous gatherings. The pair operated the resort as an exclusive hideaway for their clique of actor friends, and soon it became a pied-á-terre of sorts for Hollywood's elite.

Little has changed at the San Ysidro Ranch during the past century. Its rustic charm and sprawling gardens still beckon the rich and famous, yet its carefree style guarantees a stay void of pretense.

Famous Nuptials

At one minute past midnight on August 31, 1940, Ronald Colman and his wife, Benita, hosted a secret wedding for **Vivien Leigh** and **Laurence Olivier** in the ranch's Wedding Garden. Only two days before, Olivier learned he was free to marry Leigh after his divorce became final from British actress Jill Esmond. Although the wedding party was small, it was nevertheless impressive. Garson Kanin, famed director and screenwriter, and future husband of actress Ruth Gordon (*see the Willard Hotel*), served as the best man; Katharine Hepburn, who had been in a script conference with Kanin when he received the news of the pending marriage, was asked to be the maid of honor, though at the time she barely knew either the bride or groom.

After the brief ceremony, Laurence Olivier and the former Miss Leigh honeymooned aboard their hosts' yacht off the shore of Catalina Island.

Celebrated Honeymoons

Few couples have managed to capture the attention of an entire nation the way **John and Jackie Kennedy** did. It was seven years before Camelot that the former playboy took the Bouvier belle as his wife. After an elaborate wedding at the bride's home in Newport, Rhode Island, the Kennedy's left for an extensive honeymoon. The future president and his debutante bride could choose anywhere in the world to honeymoon; for the last leg of their trip they sought seclusion at San Ysidro Ranch. The two rendezvoused in a cottage that has since been renamed "The Kennedy Cottage." Pictures of the President and First Lady still adorn the walls of the reception area, enticing young lovers to create their own Camelot.

Getting Married at San Ysidro Ranch

The lush setting of the **Wedding Garden** lends itself well to ranch-style ceremonies. With a storybook setting for saying "I Do." vows are exchanged amidst a garden of blooming bougainvillea, fragrant flowers, and sweeping views of the nearby mountains. The area accommodates a maximum of 200 guests, providing an intimate setting.

After the ceremony, guests can simply stroll a few yards to the reception. San Ysidro provides a serene and elegant setting for the post-nuptial celebration. **The Hacienda Garden** provides an al fresco setting that can be enhanced with canopies or umbrella-covered tables. The Garden is outlined with stone and colorful flowers and can accommodate up to 150 seated guests. **The Colman Cottage**, named for the ranch's most famous owner, Ronald Colman, can accommodate up to 50 seated guests. This quaint cottage features hardwood floors, an open-beam ceiling, flagstone fireplace, and French doors that open out onto a redwood deck. It lends itself well to rainy days but is equally enchanting for late afternoon celebrations.

There are two restaurants on the ranch. The provincial-style **Stonehouse Restaurant** is perfect for hosting an intimate dinner or a welcoming lunch for arriving guests. Diners can choose to eat indoors or on a cozy terrace overlooking the ranch. Built in 1893, the **Plow and Angel Pub** was the ranch's original wine cellar and is ideal for after rehearsal cocktails and jazz.

All This For You, & A Plaque Too!

Honeymooners receive the star treatment with the "Ranch's Romance Package," which includes a bottle of bubbly and basket of strawberries on arrival, a deluxe cottage, massage á deux, dinner and a horseback ride ($995 Sunday-Thursday). A wooden plaque, featuring the couple's name, graces the outside entry of the honeymoon cabin. What could be more romantic than seeing "Mr. & Mrs." in writing for the first time!

Honeymooning at San Ysidro Ranch

There are 37 bedrooms and suites housed in 21 cozy, yet sophisticated, cottages that are scattered throughout the property. Each chamber features hardwood floors, wood-burning fireplaces, country antiques, handmade quilts or down comforters, stocked refrigerators and plush terry cloth robes.

The resort features a bevy of floral, citrus, herb, and vegetable gardens that guests are welcome to stroll through. Other amenities include two tennis courts, a swimming pool, bocce ball, horseshoes, a sculpture garden and endless acres of trails.

Big Shots Welcome!

Ronald Colman wasn't the first Hollywood actor to acquire a hideaway for the pure pleasure of hosting Hollywood luminaries. Just down the road from the San Ysido Ranch is the Montecito Inn, the hotel Charlie Chaplin built in 1928 for his clique of movie stars and mogul pals.

SONOMA MISSION INN & SPA
18140 Highway 12
Sonoma, CA 95476
800/862-4945
707/938-9000

Accommodations
$320-$740

Celebrity Guest Register
- *Leeza Gibbons*
- Tom Cruise & Nicole Kidman
- *Geena Davis & Renny Harlin*
- Jim Carrey & Lauren Holly

- Goldie Hawn & Kurt Russell
- John Lithgow
- Sylvester Stallone
- Ed Begley, Jr.

A History

The Native Americans were the first to discover the benefits of the natural underground hot mineral waters centuries before the words "spa treatment" were uttered. Dr. T.M. Leavenworth, an eccentric physician from San Francisco, is credited with being the first to develop the hot springs commercially. He built a modest bathhouse and tank on what is now the site of the Sonoma Mission Inn & Spa and created a pioneer health resort for the county. After a violent discussion with his wife, he torched the bathhouse, filled the tank with dirt, and ended his reign in the hot springs industry.

In 1895, a young Englishman named Captain H.E. Boyes acquired the property. While drilling a well he struck 112 degree water at 70 feet and instantly recognized the commercial potential of the hot mineral water. Within five years, the small bathhouse he built gave way to the Boyes Hot Spring Hotel, and soon wealthy San Franciscans began to arrive in droves to "take the waters" at California's finest hot mineral water resort. A 1920s hotel brochure boasted electric lights, running water throughout, masseurs, vaudeville entertainment, the largest mineral water swimming tank, plus cures for rheumatism, stomach, kidney, and nerve troubles!

In 1923, a disastrous fire destroyed the hotel and most of its hot springs. Four years later, the Sonoma Mission Inn rose from the ashes to become one of the finest hotels in Northern California. During the Great Depression, the resort went dark for a number of years and had various uses, including an "R&R" retreat for soldiers during World War II as well as training quarters for professional sports teams.

Today, the Sonoma Mission Inn & Spa is situated on 10 secluded acres and resembles a California mission complete with an arcade and bell tower. The inn has been returned to its 1920s splendor and offers first-class accommodations coupled with a European-style spa for those yearning to be pampered.

Famous Weddings

Academy Award-winning actress **Geena Davis** and action-adventure director **Renny Harlin** were married in 1993 at the Kunde Ranch in nearby Kenwood. The Sonoma Mission Inn & Spa catered portions of the star-studded fête, including a rehearsal dinner for 30 featuring a menu of chilled lobster salad, grilled salmon, Petaluma duck, and a signature creme brulee. The inn also catered the post-rehearsal hoe-down barbecue at a local barn with a menu consisting of ribs, salad, cobbler, and Corona Lite.

Other celebrations included an old-fashioned carnival held at nearby Friedman's Ranch which featured elephant and pony rides, a steel band, and relaxing massages from the inn's staff. Wedding guests, most of whom stayed at the inn, included Lauren Holly, Sylvester Stallone, and Ed Begley Jr. It's been estimated that the newlyweds spent close to $750,000 on their wedding celebration – but you can do it here for a lot less!

Celebrated Honeymoons

After exchanging vows on Valentine's Day in 1991 at the Hotel Bel-Air in Los Angeles, **Steven Meadows** and **Leeza Gibbons**, former correspondent for *Entertainment Tonight* and current host of the *Leeza!* show, headed for California's romantic wine country. During their two-day stay at the Sonoma Mission Inn & Spa, the couple found time to work out, relax, and enjoy the inn's many spa treatments before escaping to their private suite.

Getting Married at Sonoma Mission Inn & Spa

There are two on-site locations to host wedding ceremonies and receptions at the inn: **The Sonoma Valley Room** and **The Tent**. The picturesque Sonoma Valley Room features a dramatic high beamed ceiling, cozy fireplace, and enchanting verandah. The salon can accommodate up to 150 guests and is available Friday through Sunday. The inn's lush front lawn is canopied to create The Tent, and offers an elegant setting for outdoor ceremonies and receptions.

A few miles down the road is **Kunde Ranch**, where Geena Davis and Renny Harlin were married. Sonoma Mission Inn & Spa exclusively coordinates weddings and receptions at this former Kenwood winery. Set in the lush vineyards and hills of the Kunde Estate, the historic ruins of this vintage winery creates a rustic, yet romantic, wedding location.

Sonoma Mission Inn & Spa houses a select number of restaurants for the healthy minded. **The Grille**, which overlooks the main pool and

---

Get The Spa & Wedding Treatment At Sonoma Mission

The Sonoma Mission Inn & Spa offers newlyweds-to-be an all-inclusive "Spa Wedding Package" to revitalize the body and soul before the big stroll down the aisle. For an additional fee, the bride and groom can choose from two stress-free spa treatments, including a bio-energy massage; body scrub; seaweed, herbal or mud wrap; manicure and pedicure; hair and scalp revitalizer; European facial; or make-up application. Also included are the use of the exercise facilities, natural mineral waters, Eucalyptus steam room, and sauna.

gardens, is perfect for al fresco celebrations during the spring and summer months. The Grille features a seasonal menu of Wine Country cuisine, prepared exclusively with fresh locally grown products, and serves an elegant poolside Sunday brunch every week.

The Cafe, the area's oldest continuously operated restaurant, offers a casual setting with cafe-style tables, cozy booths, roadhouse ceiling fans, and an open kitchen. The Cafe also features a separate bar for impromptu wine tastings to be enjoyed with friends and family. The **Sonoma Mission Inn Market**, adjacent to The Cafe, offers an array of specialty food and deli items to bring back to your room for private picnics.

Honeymooning at Sonoma Mission Inn & Spa

The inn houses 200 plush guest rooms and suites in both the original structure and a newer edifice. Of the 70 deluxe Wine Country rooms, 34 offer the warmth of a wood-burning fireplace, where couples can relax after a day of spa treatments; other suites feature private verandahs, spacious floor plans, and total seclusion.

What sets the inn apart from other hotels is the absence of the ordinary; there are special touches in both service and accommodations. Upon arrival, a complimentary bottle of wine awaits each guest, and honeymooners are also sent a bottle of champagne to toast the occasion. Other guest amenities include two lighted championship tennis courts, two swimming pools filled with artesian mineral water, and a number of spa treatments for couples in need of pampering.

Sure, Take My Picture!

Sylvester Stallone, a guest at the Geena Davis-Renny Harlin affair, occupied the inn's Harvest Room. The paparazzi camped out in a vacant lot across from the inn hoping to catch a glimpse of a famous guest – or better yet – the evasive bride and groom. A couple from the San Francisco Bay Area were to be married at 4 p.m. on the front lawn, and as the first chord was struck, a dozen reporters swarmed the wedding believing it was Geena Davis in white. Of course they were fooled, and the other newlyweds became startled when a dozen flashbulbs went off in their faces.

Stallone, who was passing through the area moments before the frenzy, was gracious enough to pose for photos with the groom and groomsmen before heading off to the Kunde Ranch to witness his own friends' wedding.

THE STANFORD INN BY THE SEA
Highway 1 and Comptche-Ukiah Rd.
Mendocino, CA 95460
800/331-8884
707/937-5026

Accommodations
$145-$220

Celebrity Guest Register
- *Kathy Bates*
- Booker T. Washington
- Ted Danson & Mary Steenburgen
- Jill Eichenberg and Michael Tucker
- Richard Dreyfuss
- George Winston
- Raymond Burr
- Alan Alda

A History
While The Stanford Inn by the Sea is more than a century old, its history remains somewhat of a mystery. The inn is situated on the former China Gardens, an area harvested during the 19th century to supply produce to the villagers of Mendocino.

During the early 1980s, the unique structure that occupied the grounds was transformed into a quaint inn. Today, llamas and horses graze under ancient apple trees, the same trees that fed the villagers so many years ago. Although Mendocino is located about 800 miles north of Los Angeles, celebrities arrive regularly to enjoy the coastal views, serene surroundings, and anonymity that the inn provides.

Famous Honeymooners
When **Kathy Bates**, star of such movies as *Misery*, *Delores Claiborne*, and *Titanic*, married **Anthony Campisi** in April 1991, their busy schedules prevented an immediate honeymoon. When time permitted the following December, they escaped to The Stanford Inn by the Sea with their dog, Pip, in tow. As with most honeymooners, the Campisi's stayed to themselves, enjoying breakfast in bed and taking long, enchanted walks along the coast.

Getting Married at The Stanford Inn by the Sea
The inn is ideally suited for very intimate weddings and receptions for groups of up to 100. What is unique about being married at The Stanford Inn is that couples are not restricted to any one place for their celebration. Weddings are held in an array of unusual locations including the rustic **lobby, charming suites**, the **outside deck**, and on the **grounds**. With its island of trees, blooming flowers and ocean views, the **front lawn** is an

especially popular place for exchanging nuptials. Guests are joined by a family of llamas, who hover together behind a fence to witness this human ritual. Other areas include an orchard located in the inn's **Organic Garden**; or for those who seek an out-of-the-ordinary wedding ceremony, the inn will gladly lend their fleet of redwood outrigger canoes for weddings virtually held on the **Big River**!

With the exception of the canoes, receptions can be held at any one of the wedding sites. However, a charming **Cottage**, with a separate driveway and ample parking, lies on the lower end of the property and offers breathtaking views of the rugged coast. The inn's enchanting **dining room** is another popular place for a reception and also boasts views of the ocean.

The owners of the inn are happy to assist with selecting a site for your wedding and reception and can recommend the culinary skills of a local caterer.

Honeymooning at The Stanford Inn by the Sea

Looks can so often be deceiving and, at first glance, The Stanford Inn by the Sea resembles more of a motel than a coastal country inn. Situated across the seaside road is the two-story, 25-room structure encased in natural wood. Each room is its own quaint hideaway filled with country antiques, four-poster or sleigh beds, bouquets of fresh flowers and either a wood-burning fireplace or stove. No room is without a magnificent view of the craggy coast. A breakfast buffet awaits guests each morning, and in the evening a carafe of wine is placed in each room. For honeymooners who simply can't bear to be without the family pet, the innkeepers gladly welcome four-legged guests!

The inn also houses an organic garden; a menagerie of llamas, horses, dogs, cats, deer and swans; a fleet of canoes and kayaks; and bicycles. The aquatic greenhouse, with its draped bougainvillea, flowering hibiscus, and lush tropical plants, also features an indoor swimming pool, spa, and sauna.

Romance On The Big River

During their visit to The Stanford Inn by the Sea, Ted Danson, best-known for his role as Sam Malone on "Cheers," courted his future wife, actress Mary Steenburgen, in one of the inn's redwood outrigger canoes along the Big River.

STONEPINE
150 East Carmel Valley Rd.
Carmel Valley, CA 93924
408/659-2245

Accommodations
$225-$750

Celebrity Guest Register

- *Brooke Shields & Andre Agassi*
- *Harry Hamlin & Nicolette Sheridan*
- Bruce Willis & Demi Moore
- Emma Thompson
- Mick Jagger

- *Dennis Franz*
- Keith Richards
- Arnold Schwarzenegger
- Michelle Phillips

A History

Prior to 1987, when Stonepine extended its hospitality to the public, it was a private estate owned by the same prominent family for more than 55 years.

In 1929, Henry Potter Russell and his wife, the former Helen Crocker of San Francisco banking fame, longed for a quiet hideaway in which to breed thoroughbred horses and raise their family. They discovered a prime piece of property that adjoined the Los Padres National Forest and built the "Double H Ranch," which romantically linked their initials.

The European-style chateau earned a reputation as being the fore-most breeding farm for thoroughbreds west of the Mississippi. Through-out the years, more than 200 champion horses called the Double H Ranch their home, including Kentucky Derby winner Majestic Prince. In 1937, as para-mutual betting was becoming established at such infant race tracks as Santa Anita Park and Del Mar, Henry Russell founded the renowned California Breeders' Association.

In the lower fields, on the banks of the picturesque Carmel River, Helen played hostess at the couple's polo field. Invitational battles with the Pebble Beach and Santa Barbara clubs were held on a regular basis, and the Russell's hosted society's creme de la creme on these grounds, which were later transformed into the present-day Equestrian Center.

The Russell's son, Charles, was as passionate about the Sport of Kings and polo as his parents. When Henry died in 1943, the torch was passed to Charles, who oversaw the ranch and its stable of thoroughbreds. When Charles passed away in 1981, his heirs did not share the same enthusiasm for the family business, and they decided to put the estate on the market.

In 1987, for the first time in its glorious history, the estate was open to the public as a retreat. Since that time, Stonepine has become a mecca for celebrity weddings, honeymoons, and much-needed getaways.

Famous Nuptials

On Saturday, April 19, 1997, the score was love-love for tennis great **Andre Agassi** and model-cum-actress **Brooke Shields** when they tied the knot at St. John's Episcopal Chapel in Monterey, California. The two had met a few years earlier via fax and, because of extremely busy schedules, did not enjoy a vis á vis until a few months later. After that, Agassi and the star of the television sitcom *Suddenly Susan* were inseparable. For her big day, Shields wore a stunning sleeveless, ivory gown with a 16-foot veil trailing behind. After making their union official, the two hosted an elegant reception at Stonepine for about 150 guests, including Judd Nelson and Nastassja Kinski. The newlyweds had rented Stonepine for a total of five days at an estimated cost of $50,000, and spent their wedding night in the Tattinger Suite located in Stonepine's Chateau.

Other famous Stonepine nuptials include former *L.A. Law* star **Harry Hamlin** and *Knott's Landing* vixen **Nicolette Sheridan**, and *NYPD* good guy **Dennis Franz**.

Getting Married at Stonepine

When couples whisper "I Do" at Stonepine, the sky is the limit as to what kind of wedding they desire. Weddings at Stonepine are deemed "exclusive" with the wedding party often converging on the entire estate!

With more than 300 acres, there are a number of places in which to marry and celebrate. The **Cherub-on-the-Swan** garden, where guests are shaded by century-old Italian stone pines, offers a wafting scent of roses as couples recite their vows. The country setting at the **Paddock House**, located near the Equestrian Center, provides an old-fashioned gazebo amid blooming flora and swaying trees.

Post-wedding celebrations are held in a number of places, including the **Chateau's** grand lawns, which can be elegantly tented or remain an open-air venue for afternoon gatherings; the terrace and lawn offer country charm at the **Paddock House**. Both settings are unique, yet Chateau gatherings are reminiscent of yesteryear society parties while the Paddock House provides a remote ranch-like setting. Other open-air venues include the **Chateau Loggia**, sheltered only by an arched colonnade, and the **Chateau Wisteria Terrace**, named for the resplendent vine that clings to the structure. Indoor settings include the **Chateau's Living Room** for cocktails and the **Dining Room** for sit-down dinners.

When money is no object, couples may choose to host a three-day **Estate Exclusive**, which includes the use of the entire grounds. In addition, themed weddings are a specialty at Stonepine, and have included everything from *Gone With The Wind* to *A Day At The Races!* Stonepine can host weddings and receptions for up to 250 people.

Honeymooning at Stonepine

Situated on 330 acres, the country-like setting of Stonepine resembles that of Tuscany, Italy, rather than Northern California. Only the towering oak trees and the effulgent Santa Lucia mountains beyond are reminders that this is in fact the Golden State. Stonepine offers four separate structures, from country quaint to European élan, in which to slumber: the **Chateau**, the **Briar Rose**, the **Gate House**, and the **Paddock House**.

The **Chateau**, the main house, is suggestive of an Italian Villa and features eight distinctively-appointed suites. Two suites are housed on the lower floor, and six are located atop a circular stairway, and segue off a central, arched hallway to maximize privacy. Each Chateau suite includes a private library, ample closet space, a Jacuzzi tub, his and her robes plus bouquets of fresh flowers each day. The secluded **Briar Rose** is a country cottage with its own porch and rose garden and often delights its occupants with glimpses of deer feeding nearby. The perfect honeymoon hideaway, the Briar Rose features a dining room, kitchen, master bedroom, second bedroom and rustic fireplace. The **Gate House** is a mini Spanish-style estate complete with its own guest house, heated swimming pool, and tennis courts! The **Paddock House**, which features four suites, is for those who truly want to feel as if they are a guest at a horse farm. Each room offers country charm plus the convenience of being a stone's throw to the Equestrian Center, for those who desire a horseback honeymoon!

Recreational activities are endless at Stonepine, and include the use of the swimming pool, archery, croquet, bicycling, weight room, nature walks and tennis. The Equestrian Center offers the following services for an additional fee: Western trail rides, English/Western riding lessons, Victorian carriage rides, group hayrides and carriage driving lessons.

Arnold & Emma At Stonepine

Stonepine has the distincition of being the first establishment in the world to host a pregnant man! Strange, but true...by Hollywood standards, anyway. The estate served as the setting for the film "Junior," starring Emma Thompson and Arnold Schwarzenegger, who gave a whole new meaning to the term "motherhood."

Each stay includes breakfast served in the dining room or loggia as well as an evening reception. An a la carte menu is available for lunch, and the estate's signature meal is an elegant five-course dinner served in the formal dining room.

THE WILLOWS HISTORIC PALM SPRINGS INN
412 West Tahquitz Canyon Way
Palm Springs, CA 92262
760/320-0771

Accommodations
$175-$450

Celebrity Guest Register

- *Clark Gable & Carole Lombard*
- Heather Locklear & Richie Sambora
- Albert Einstein

- Josie Bisset & Rob Estes
- Marion Davies
- Brooke Langton

A History
The Willows Historic Palm Springs Inn was once the private oasis of screen-siren Marion Davies, perhaps as well known for her acting as she was for her dalliances with newspaper mogul William Randolph Hearst.

Built in 1927, the villa was originally the winter estate of former U.S. Secretary of the Treasury Samuel Untermyer, the first attorney in the United States to make a million dollar fee for a single case. Untermyer entertained many of the nation's leading artists and public figures from the era, including his close friend Albert Einstein and his wife Elsa.

Untermyer's son, Alvin, and his family resided at the villa following his father's death in 1940, and remained a part of Palm Springs society until the early '50s. After his departure, Marion Davies occupied the estate in 1955, and because of her penchant for alcohol, it is rumored that one of her first remodeling ventures included completely gutting the kitchen in order to install a state-of-the-art bar.

After Davies moved out, the villa experienced various owners. In June 1994, a *for sale* sign hung on the deserted estate awaiting a buyer. Tracy Conrad and Paul Marut stumbled upon the property while vacationing in Palm Springs, and it was love at first sight. The two relocated to the area, began to restore the historic property and opened The Willows Historic Palm Spring Inn for a new generation of luminaries to enjoy.

Today, The Willows is an elegant bed and breakfast nestled at the base of the San Jaquinto Mountains. One look around the Mediterranean-style villa and it's easy to see why Davies may have fled the vastness of Hearst Castle for the more intimate surroundings of The Willows.

Famous Honeymooners

Few Hollywood couples were more in love with one another than **Clark Gable** and **Carole Lombard**. When the two decided to get married in 1939, their main concern was to avoid the press. The two motored with friends to Kingman, Arizona, where a judge quickly pronounced them man and wife. Because of Gable's demanding filming schedule on the set of *Gone With The Wind,* the two had to postpone a honeymoon and head straight back to Los Angeles. At the invitation of Alvin Untermyer, the two spent part of their honeymoon at The Willows.

Getting Married at The Willows Historic Palm Springs Inn

Imagine strolling through the privacy of your own desert villa donning lounging pajamas and feathered mules a la Marion Davies or Carole Lombard. It's more than just a romantic concept because when weddings are held at the inn, the villa becomes the bride and groom's domain. There are two areas where weddings are performed, and each area doubles as a reception site. The **Courtyard**, with its waterfall and abundant foilage, can seat up to 100. If the **Living Room** walls could talk, the stories they might tell! Once the hub for gatherings, today the Living Room is an elegant backdrop for ceremonies and receptions of 100.

Honeymooning at The Willows Historic Palm Springs Inn

Once a mecca for private gatherings, The Willows Historic Palm Springs Inn is a wondrous find for honeymooners who prefer intimate rather than ostentatious. Coated in beige stucco, the two-story Italianesque villa features curved archways, wrought-iron balustrades, vaulted ceilings, and natural hardwood and slate flooring throughout. Two of the eight guest rooms – **Einstein's Garden Room** and **The Marion Davies Room** – are named for their famous occupants. Each chamber is spacious in size, offering private baths; some contain a working fireplace, private balcony, garden patio, and separate outside entrances. Picturesque mountains and colorful gardens are framed by windows and French doors, and the faint sounds of a courtyard waterfall can be heard from nearly every alcove.

If you're interested in an overnight jaunt, the inn provides a gourmet breakfast plus a wine and cheese hour in the evening.

Billy, Isn't That Allison & Amanda By The Pool?

It's not unusual to see one of the stars from television's "Melrose Place" lounging by the pool with a script in hand!

6. Colorado

THE HOTEL JEROME
330 East Main Street
Aspen, CO 81611
800/331-7213
970/920-1000

Accommodations
$160-$1,790

Celebrity Guest Register
- *Don Johnson & Melanie Griffith*
- David Hasselhoff
- Steven Seagal
- Sylvester Stallone
- Paul Simon
- Calvin Klein
- Eddie Van Halen
- Natalie Wood
- Barbra Streisand
- Lana Turner
- Brad Pitt
- Uma Thurman
- Rosie O'Donnell
- Cheech Marin
- Lauren Bacall
- Christie Brinkley
- General Colin Powell
- Liza Minnelli
- Elizabeth Taylor
- John Wayne

A History
When Jerome B. Wheeler, a Civil War hero, built his namesake hotel during the height of Colorado's silver boom in 1889, his plans were to rival the elegant Ritz Hotel in Paris.

In its heyday, The Hotel Jerome may as well have been the Ritz. From the three-story exterior constructed from rich terra-cotta bricks and sandstone to the richly-appointed interiors adorned with elaborate wall coverings and handmade tiles, The Hotel Jerome was pure Victorian splendor. The hotel may have very well conceived the idea of *all-inclusive* – under one roof it was possible to have your horse's teeth attended to, visit your stockbroker, enjoy an osteopathy treatment, savor imported brandies and liquors, have your whiskers trimmed and receive the newest dance instruction!

In 1893, Aspen's bright future quickly dimmed with the demonetization of silver and the crash that followed. Jerome Wheeler fared no better and soon after he lost his hotel to back taxes. The Hotel Jerome was transformed from an elegant hotel to a large, unassuming boarding house. At one time, room and board could be had for as little as $10 a month, but there were barely enough traveling men and steady borders in need of such accommodations.

Throughout the Great Depression, The Hotel Jerome was a gathering spot for the residents of Aspen. Every Sunday evening, people congregated for a fine chicken dinner and music for just 50¢ a person! During World War II, Walter Paepcke secured a 25 year lease on the hotel, and slowly the Jerome began to rise from the ashes. Paepcke turned to Herbert Bayer, his artistic mentor and member of Germany's famed Bauhaus School of Design, who added baths and installed furnishings acquired at auction from another landmark hotel – the Palmer House in Chicago. By the next decade, the matinee idols and screen sirens had discovered Aspen and The Hotel Jerome.

The hotel closed again in the early '60s, and with a leaking roof and faulty wiring, the Jerome was headed for demolition. In late 1984, a local Aspen real estate entrepreneur purchased the hotel and restored The Hotel Jerome to its original Victorian state.

More than a century since Aspen's mining boom, The Hotel Jerome is one of the area's last remaining structures from the fertile era of silver mining and a true testament to those who found, and eventually lost, their fortunes.

Celebrated Gatherings

When **Don Johnson** and **Melanie Griffith** married in 1975, both were virtually unknown to the rest of the world. After a year of marriage, the two went their separate ways. Don went on to earn fame as Crockett on the 1980s television series *Miami Vice*, while Melanie starred in such films as *Something Wild* and *Working Girl*. After more than a decade, the two found love again and decided to get back together.

They hosted an engagement party on December 26, 1988, at The Hotel Jerome and invited 150 of their closest friends, including Sally Fields, Michael Douglas, Donald and Ivana Trump, Kurt Russell and Goldie Hawn, and Cher. The two remarried at the groom's Woody Creek, Colorado, ranch the following year.

Getting Married at The Hotel Jerome

Weddings at The Hotel Jerome recall the era of Victorian elegance with a plethora of stately salons for both ceremonies and receptions.

The **Grand Ballroom** offers a magnificent setting for groups of up to 500. The airy ambiance can be credited to the 16-foot ceilings and series of French doors leading to the outdoor terrace, where a fountain of Mexican origin trickles continuously. With views of the nearby mountains, the **Outdoor Dining Decks** create a spectacular arena for warm weather weddings and receptions of up to 350. The **Antler Bar** lives up to its name with an antler-shaped chandelier serving as the room's centerpiece; high ceilings and turn-of-the-century antiques provide a lodge-like setting for groups of up to 150.

For intimate groups of 125, **Jacob's Corner** is a real treasure featuring dark hardwood floors and a set of balustrades to match. Victorian-style chandeliers are enhanced with wall sconces to create soft lighting, while a series of suspended ceiling fans give the room its saloon feel. With gilded mirrors, crystal chandeliers and a cozy fireplace, **The Century Room** is an elegant venue for groups of up to 125. An intricate wallpaper pattern compliments the various antiques found scattered throughout the room while overstuffed booths and a series of small tables create a casually elegant atmosphere. The **Wheeler Room** is ideal for small groups of 60 or less and features an expansive series of windows, gilded mirrors, a French crystal chandelier and regal hues of burgundy and gold. A number of **one bedroom suites** are also ideal for intimate ceremonies and receptions of up to 30.

While **Jacob's Corner** and **The Century Room** can be reserved for private parties, the two rooms also double as restaurants for hotel guests and are ideal settings for rehearsal dinners. For post-rehearsal gatherings, **The J-Bar** boasts an original 1889 cherry wood bar for preparing such favorites as hot toddies and cocktails.

The staff at The Hotel Jerome provide couples with a highly recommended list of professionals to create a memorable wedding day.

Honeymooning at The Hotel Jerome

Situated at the very core of one of America's top ski resorts, The Hotel Jerome provides winter newlyweds with plenty of powder by day and warm Victorian charm by night.

Upon entering the hotel, the main lobby harkens visitors back to a bygone era with a magnificent relief-carved oak fireplace. Broad, arched hallways lead to 93 guest rooms and suites; 27 rooms are housed in the original hotel and a new wing holds the remaining 66. Each Victorian chamber offers its own unique ambiance with oversized beds, plush down comforters, crocheted duvets, carved armoires and authentic 19th-century furnishings. While guests are transported to another era, they bring with them the comforts of modern amenities such as oversized marble bath tubs or whirlpools for two, and fully stocked mini-bars to be enjoyed after a day on the slopes.

What, He Had Nothing Better To Do?

Legend has it that when Gary Cooper visited the Jerome, he passed his time girl-watching in front of the hotel with some of Aspen's old-timers.

7. Florida

HOTEL INTER-CONTINENTAL MIAMI
100 Chopin Plaza
Miami, FL 33131
800/327-0200
305/577-0348

Accommodations
$259-$2,700

Celebrity Guest Register

- *Jon Secada*
- Gloria Estefan
- President and Mrs. Clinton
- Princess Caroline of Monaco
- President Ronald Reagan
- President Jimmy Carter

A History

Located in the heart of Miami's financial, commercial, and shopping district, the Hotel Inter-Continental Miami is situated on the shores of Biscayne Bay. The 34-story structure towers over neighboring properties and is easily identified by its unique triangular shape.

The hotel opened in 1986 and was immediately applauded for its elegant interiors, which combine antique Florentine and Travertine marble, granites from Brazil and South Africa, rare burnt cedar from Asia's forests and ebony teak from the Orient. The various artwork that graces the hotel often has been a topic of conversation among Miami's art connoisseurs. Among the pieces are *The Spindle*, a sculpture by the late Sir Henry Moore that rises 18 feet into the atrium lobby and weighs 70 tons, creating a dramatic focal point upon entering the hotel.

Since its opening, the regal Hotel Inter-Continental Miami has been a gathering spot for sun-kissed socialites, moguls, dignitaries, and vacationing celebrities.

Famous Nuptials

Miami native **Jon Secada**, former backup singer for Gloria Estefan turned solo artist, married **Maritela Vilar** in March 1997 at the Church of the Little Flower in Coral Gables, Florida. Draped in a traditional white gown, the bride, along with her groom, looked as if they belonged on top of the wedding cake. The two then hosted a lavish midnight reception at the Inter-Continental Hotel Miami, which lasted until 5:30 in the morning. Famous guests included Gloria Estefan and her family.

Getting Married the Hotel Inter-Continental Miami

With the Biscayne Bay as a backdrop, weddings and receptions at the Hotel Inter-Continental Miami are often swank affairs, and the hotel offers four splendid ballrooms in which to host such celebrations. Overlooking Biscayne Bay on the lobby level is the **Bayfront Ballroom** – accommodating up to 500 guests – with large, bayfront windows and hanging chandeliers throughout. A smaller salon, the **Jr. Ballroom**, offers similar appointments for groups of up to 200. Just above on the Mezzanine level are three additional areas to celebrate. The **Grand Ballroom** is alluring for large groups of up to 1,200 with its ultra-high ceiling and a fleet of windows that provides framing of the waterfront view. The expansive **Atrium Mezzanine**, with its elevated glass ceiling and tremendous bay view, is a unique setting for ceremonies, cocktail receptions, and sit-down lunches or dinners. It can accommodate up to 2,500 guests.

The hotel offers a number of casual-to-elegant bistros for entertaining. **Le Pavillon** is strictly for formal gatherings and exemplifies old world elegance with tuxedo-clad waiters and white-glove service. For more casual gatherings such as bridal luncheons, there are three restaurants to select from: **The Royal Palm Court** serves breakfast, lunch, and dinner plus a winning Sunday brunch; the **Oceanside Terrace** offers poolside dining for lunch and cocktails only; and **The Oak Room**, named for its decor of dark oak, features light lunches and happy hour. Members of the wedding party may want to meet up on the eve of the "big day" and toast the newlyweds-to-be at the **Lobby Lounge**.

Couples hosting a wedding and reception at the Hotel Inter-Continental Miami enjoy a complimentary Honeymoon Suite, plus reduced room rates for out-of-town guests.

Honeymooning at the Hotel Inter-Continental Miami

The Hotel Inter-Continental Miami offers a resort-like setting in the midst of a bustling metropolis. There are 644 contemporary-style rooms, including 33 suites. Each room is spacious in design with a cozy sitting area and separate dressing area, and you'll be treated to spectacular views of either Biscayne Bay, the Port of Miami, or the downtown skyline.

A Command Performance For The Commander-in-Chief
In 1986, crews labored around the clock for 10 consecutive days in order to complete the presidential suite in time for then-President Ronald Reagan to inaugurate the room.

Sunbathing takes place on the landscaped **Sun Deck**, which features a swimming pool, panoramic views, and a quarter-mile jogging track. A full-service state-of-the-art health center keeps guests in top shape!

LITTLE PALM ISLAND
28500 Overseas Highway
Little Torch Key, FL 33042
800/343-8567
305/872-2524

Accommodations
$415-$695

Celebrity Guest Register
- *Robert Wagner & Jill St. John*
- Laurence Fishburne
- Joan Lunden
- Senator John Glenn
- Michael Keaton
- Dan Marino
- William Randolph Hearst
- *Luke Perry*
- Charles Kuralt
- Ivana Trump
- Vice President Al Gore
- Drew Barrymore
- David Brinkley

A History
Since its opening in 1988, it seems as if Little Palm Island has redefined the meaning of paradise. The resort, which occupies a small, five-acre tropical island just three miles off the coast in the Lower Florida Keys, offers total privacy and seclusion from the rest of the world.

While the property is less than a decade old, it still has its ties to history. A fishing camp once occupied the resort's grounds and was a secluded haven for Presidential excursions. Presidents Roosevelt, Truman, Kennedy, and Nixon, along with other VIPs, spent time away from the White House in hopes of hooking a prize catch!

Today, Little Palm Island still captivates politicos – and other movers and shakers – who are hoping to catch nothing more than some rest and relaxation. In 1996, readers of *Conde' Nast Traveler* named Little Palm Island one of the Top Ten hotels in the world.

Celebrated Honeymoons

After their 1993 wedding at the Four Seasons Hotel in Beverly Hills *(see page 44)*, actor **Luke Perry**, who rose to fame as the brooding Dylan McKay on the television series *Beverly Hills 90210,* and his wife **Minnie** enjoyed a fall honeymoon at Little Palm Island.

After their 1991 nuptials, actor **Robert Wagner** and actress **Jill St. John** escaped to Little Palm Island to celebrate their new beginning.

Getting Married at Little Palm Island

Little Palm Island offers an intimate setting for weddings and receptions and is best suited for celebrations of smaller proportions. Ceremonies are performed on the resort's private white sandy beach with the gentle sound of surf in the background and towering palms overhead.

For elegant receptions, rehearsal dinners, or pre-nuptial gatherings, **The Dining Room**, which is housed in the original fishing camp lodge, offers island ambiance and award-winning cuisine for its guests. Romantics, who prefer a table for two, can request dinner under the stars at a private table right on the beach with tiki torches blazing nearby.

Honeymooning at Little Palm Island

Honeymooners can forget about arriving at Little Palm Island with old shoes and aluminum cans tied to their bumper. The only way for "just marrieds" to reach the resort is by boat, making the transition from pandemonium to paradise a virtual breeze.

Scattered discreetly among draped bougainvillea, colorful oleander, fragrant hibiscus, and swaying palms are 14 thatched-roof villas. Configured for privacy and seclusion, each villa houses two magnificent ocean-view suites each equipped with a wrap-around sun deck and rope hammocks strung between Jamaican palms. Inside, villas feature a comfortable living room, expansive bedroom with a sitting area, and a king-sized bed draped with mosquito netting to give the effect of island living. A lavishly-equipped dressing area leads to the bathroom, which boasts a whirlpool bath; just beyond, doors lead to a bamboo-fenced, completely private outdoor shower. The only items missing from each suite are a telephone, a television, and an alarm clock, which are virtually banned on the island!

The resort features a spa with a pampering menu that includes massages, facials, pedicures, manicures and various body treatments to be enjoyed in the privacy of your own suite or on the spa's premises.

Each stay includes launch service to and from the island as well as the use of the exercise and sauna room, kayaks and canoes, windsurfers and instruction, Hobie Day sailers, snorkel gear and fishing equipment.

Little Palm Island's Place In Film History

Before Little Palm Island was transformed into a first-class resort, it served as a South Seas movie location for the 1963 film "PT 109," which depicted President Kennedy's World War II experiences.

THE RITZ-CARLTON, PALM BEACH

100 South Ocean Blvd.
Manalapan, FL 33462
800/241-3333
561533-6000

Accommodations
$145-$3,000

Celebrity Guest Register
- Stephen Stills
- Rod Stewart
- Keith Richards
- Ivana Trump
- Mick Jagger
- Christopher Plummer

A History
Since its opening on June 17, 1991, The Ritz-Carlton, Palm Beach, has had its share of rich and famous visitors. While the elegant six-story Mediterranean resort is still in its infancy, its soul is instilled with old traditions of fine amenities and impeccable service that have made all Ritz-Carlton hotels and resorts irresistible to travelers.

Designed as an all-inclusive resort, The Ritz-Carlton, Palm Beach, is situated on a stretch of white sandy beach and boasts three acclaimed restaurants, a fully equipped fitness center and spa, a free-form swimming pool with adjacent cabanas, seven tennis courts, a beauty salon and upscale boutiques. A museum-quality art collection features paintings and objects d'art from the 18th and 19th centuries, which reflect the Romantic Movement – the period following the French Revolution – and feature works from renowned European and American artists.

With all the amenities The Ritz-Carlton, Palm Beach, has to offer, newlyweds may never want to venture off the property!

Famous Nuptials

Stephen Stills, of *Crosby, Stills, Nash & Young* fame, married his children's nanny on May 27, 1996, at The Ritz-Carlton, Palm Beach, the night after the re-formed group (minus Neil Young) launched a 66-city tour. The bride, who wore a simple, ivory gown and carried a bouquet of white lilies, was escorted down the aisle by none other than David Crosby. The 10 minute ceremony, which included about 100 guests, took place at sunset in the hotel's private Dining Room, with the choppy Atlantic Ocean serving as a dramatic backdrop.

A few days later the newlyweds hit the road for a rock 'n' roll honeymoon that would include the remaining 65 cities left on the tour!

Getting Married at The Ritz-Carlton, Palm Beach

With the beach and ocean at your footsteps, it seems only natural to take advantage of Mother Nature by hosting a seaside ceremony. Weddings performed on the white sands in front of the hotel come complete with crashing waves, stretches of unspoiled sand, and curious seagulls. Other outdoor locations include **The Courtyard**, which is surrounded by tropical flowers and plants and perfect for weddings of 50; and the **Pool Terrace**, which can accommodate 300 and offers breathtaking views of the ocean and hotel pool.

The banquet salons are all housed in the resort's north wing, and each features private pre-function reception areas and soundproof walls. **The Ritz-Carlton Ballroom** can accommodate large groups of 500, or can be divided into three separate salons for smaller groups of 150. **The Plaza Ballroom** is better suited for gatherings of up to 180 or can be divided in half for more intimate groups of 90. The elegant rotunda **Atlantic Room** features expansive windows with views of the swimming pool, courtyard, and ocean, and can be reserved for private affairs of 50.

For elegant rehearsal dinners, **The Grill** offers fine dining and nightly entertainment; **The Restaurant** provides a relaxed atmosphere for family introductions, and offers indoor and outdoor dining for breakfast, lunch, and dinner; for poolside cocktails and appetizers, **The Ocean Cafe and Bar** is ideal for enjoying some stress-free moments together; and **The Lobby Lounge** offers traditional afternoon tea by day and live entertainment and cocktails by night.

For those who wish to reap the benefits of the Ritz-Carlton's award-winning cuisine, the hotel offers off-site catering for receptions and gatherings held elsewhere.

Honeymooning at The Ritz-Carlton, Palm Beach

Located on the southern tip of Palm Beach Island in the secluded area of Manalapan, The Ritz-Carlton, Palm Beach, features tastefully-appointed guest rooms and suites with private balconies – many with ocean views – sleek marble baths, and spacious surroundings with 24-hour room service to attend to your every need.

Newlyweds who want to enjoy the Florida sunshine can challenge one another to a game of tennis on one of seven hard and clay courts, or relax beneath a private cabana at the oceanfront swimming pool. Nearby are championship golf courses, scuba diving, fishing, sailing and, of course, those absolutely wonderful Palm Beach boutiques!

8. Georgia

GREYFIELD INN
Cumberland Island, GA
904/261-6408

Accommodations
$320-$350

Celebrity Guest Register
• *John F. Kennedy Jr. & Carolyn Bessett*
• Senator Ted Kennedy
• Caroline Kennedy Schlossberg

• William Kennedy Smith
• Lee Radziwill

A History
Cumberland Island belongs to a cluster of coastal islands located off Georgia's shoreline and is credited with being the largest and southern-most among the archipelago.

During the early 1800s, as with many parts of the south, the island was home to a handful of plantations. After the Confederate Army was defeated during the Civil War, uncertainty and panic swept through the south, and the few plantations that did grace the shores of Cumberland Island were quickly abandoned.

In 1881, Thomas Carnegie, sibling of steel mogul Andrew, and his wife Lucy purchased a piece of the island. They and their nine children, for whom they built four magnificent island mansions, eventually obtained 80 percent of Cumberland for themselves. In 1901, the Carnegies built a Georgian-style mansion as a wedding gift to their daughter Margaret and her bridegroom. The couple christened the 13-room estate Greyfield and made their home there until the 1950s.

A few years later, instead of accepting offers from a number of private companies hoping to turn the land into a commercial resort of non-descript condominiums, the Carnegie heirs donated Cumberland Island to the National Park Service. In the 1960s, Greyfield was opened as an inn by Margaret Carnegie's daughter and her family, who continue to operate it today. It is the only commercial business on the entire island.

Although it has been more than one hundred years since Thomas and Lucy Carnegie discovered Cumberland Island, it remains a timeless treasure from a long forgotten epoch.

Famous Nuptials

On September 21, 1996, women's hearts across the nation were breaking as the news of **John F. Kennedy Jr.**'s impending marriage to former Calvin Klein publicist **Carolyn Besset** was confirmed. Breaking with tradition, JFK Jr. opted for a southern-style wedding rather than a New England affair at the Kennedy Compound. The candlelight ceremony, attended by a handful of friends and relatives, took place inside the quaint, wooden-framed First African Baptist Church, built in 1893 by former slaves. The bride, with her blond tresses elegantly swept back, wore a simple pearl-colored silk slip gown, long gloves, and a tulle veil. The groom, with his dark, good looks, wore a single-breasted midnight-blue suit, white vest and, as a sentimental touch, his father's watch.

After the ceremony, a fleet of pick-up trucks transported the party back to the Greyfield Inn for the reception. Once inside, the couple hosted an elegant sit-down dinner complete with a three-tiered wedding cake. John and Carolyn, along with many of their guests, spent the night at the elegant estate before departing on an exotic Turkish honeymoon.

Getting Married at the Greyfield Inn

With its stately porch and gracious setting, the Greyfield Inn brings to mind the fictional Tara estate from the epic novel *Gone With The Wind*.

Weddings are peppered with Southern hospitality as the island and inn create a secluded scenario for exchanging vows. Ceremonies for up to 100 guests are performed at various areas on the island, including the shores of pristine beaches, under century-old live oak trees draped in Spanish moss, or inside the slave-built First African Baptist Church. For those who wish to marry on the estate there is the beach-front **Gazebo**, ideal for sunset or moonlight ceremonies; the **Front Lawn**, with the imposing mansion creating a striking backdrop; or, should Mother Nature decide to be uncooperative, the parlor-like setting of the inn's **Living Room**.

Receptions are just as extraordinary at the Greyfield Inn with outdoor receptions taking place on the expansive **Front Porch** or under the canopy of live oaks and Spanish moss. Indoor receptions are held by the fireplace in the **Dining Room**, which features antiques from the turn-of-the-century.

Because of the inn's secluded location, the staff can furnish fresh flowers and will also provide a list of mainland services such as clergy, musicians and photographers. Weddings with more than 10 guests require booking the entire inn.

Honeymooning at the Greyfield Inn

A honeymoon to Cumberland Island and the Greyfield Inn is sort of like taking a trip back in time. For starters, only 300 guests are allowed per day on the 18-mile long island and public phones are non-existent. Guests arrive via ferry from Fernandina Beach, Florida, and are greeted by 26 varieties of wild animals, 323 species of birds, and one dirt road traversing the length of the island.

The inn is decorated throughout with Carnegie family heirlooms and antiques. Each of the nine guest rooms in the main house offers its own distinctive features, such as unencumbered views, window seats, spacious parlors, and elegant furnishings. Most rooms share a bath except for the **Library Suite**. Two charming **Cottages**, which are located on the grounds, boast two guest rooms and a private bath, providing honeymooners with the ultimate in privacy. Each sojourn to the Greyfield Inn includes a southern breakfast, picnic lunch, gourmet dinner, cocktail hour, the use of bicycles and a guided island tour or historical outing, plus ferry transportation to the mainland.

Since Cumberland Island has no stores or other commercial distractions, guests are advised to bring such essentials as sunscreen, film, cigarettes, medication and other can't-do-withouts.

9. Hawaii

KONA VILLAGE RESORT
PO Box 1299
Kailua-Kona, HI
800/367-5290
808/325-5555

Accommodations
$425-$710

Celebrity Guest Register

- *Christie Brinkley*
- Candice Bergen
- Sam Elliott & Katherine Ross
- Robin Williams
- Annie Potts

- Michael Crichton
- Harrison Ford
- Kevin Bacon
- Andy Garcia
- Jeff Bridges

A History

For centuries, Ka'upulehu, the ancient village site upon which Kona Village Resort is situated, was a healing center for weary natives. Hawaiians would flock to the bay, which now fronts the resort, to submerge themselves in the refreshing waters of the god Kane. Beneath the bay lies a spring, and many believed you could be cured of any illness as long as you plunged into the water 51 times a day – 25 at sunrise, 25 at sunset, and once to give thanks!

While guests to Kona Village Resort may not take the plunge in the same vein as the villagers, many come from the mainland and neighboring islands simply to rejuvenate. Built in 1967 on 82 acres of oceanfront property, the resort has attracted the rich and famous for more than three decades.

Today, Kona Village Resort continues to provide solitude to those wishing to escape the chaos of city life.

Celebrated Honeymoons

Supermodel **Christie Brinkley** and architect **Peter Cook** exchanged vows September 21, 1996, under a flower-draped gazebo at the bride's rented horse farm in Eastern Long Island's tony Hamptons. The bride, looking radiant as always, wore a floor-length Armani suit for the ceremony while the groom wore a classic black suit by the same designer.

The bridegroom promised to love not only his new bride, but her two children as well. Being a man of his word, Cook whisked Brinkley, along with her two children, to the Big Island for a Hawaiian honeymoon. The foursome retreated to the Kona Village Resort and most likely spent some time with Brinkley's father, who makes his home on the island.

Getting Married at the Kona Village Resort

Kona Village Resort is the ideal place to combine the wedding, reception, and honeymoon. Because of its remote location, the resort is well-suited for small or impromptu celebrations.

Couples often prefer to exchange vows on the **black and white sand beach** that fronts the resort. As rings and promises are exchanged, the sound of swaying palm trees and gentle surf can be heard in the distance. Receptions are hosted nearby in the resort's thatched-roof **Hale Ho'okipa**, or hospitality house, which gracefully opens on to a fragrant garden and lagoon, and can accommodate up to 150 guests.

There are three restaurants sheltered by the resort's signature thatched-roofs for hosting pre-nuptial gatherings or enjoying a romantic tete-a-tete. **Hale Samoa Fine Dining Room** offers casual elegance for special occasions; **Hale Moana** is open for breakfast and dinner, and provides a relaxed atmosphere for either meal; and the al fresco **Hale Moana Terrace** serves a casual buffet lunch overlooking the gardens. An array of lounges are found within the resort for enjoying sunset cocktails and include the **Hale Samoa Terrace**, the oceanfront **Talk Story Beach Bar**, and two poolside watering holes: the **Shipwreck Bar** and the **Bora Bora Bar**.

No request is too big to fulfill at the Kona Village Resort. Couples wishing to marry at the resort are assisted by an experienced wedding coordinator who can assist with everything from applying for a marriage license to the selection of champagne.

Honeymooning at the Kona Village Resort

Upon motoring from the Keahole-Kona International Airport to the Kona Village Resort, guests seem in awe as black lava fields of the Kona Coast are suddenly replaced by a tropical oasis along the water's edge.

Paradise magically unfolds at the resort with the sound of colorful birds, mile-high palm trees, and exotic foliage. Sandy lanes segue to the

125 Polynesian-style *hale,* or bungalows, each protected by thatched roofs. Each hale includes a roomy, king-size bed, a dressing area and bath, a ceiling fan, a refrigerator stocked with complimentary juices and soft drinks, a coffee maker supplied with trademark Kona coffee and sliding doors leading to a lanai.

The omission of in-room phones, televisions, and radios are deliberate rather than an oversight, providing honeymooners with an opportunity for little distraction. "Do Not Disturb" signs are non-existent; instead, a coconut placed at the hale door ensures complete privacy! In addition, each stay includes three meals a day, making the Kona Village Resort a self-contained sanctuary.

There are a plethora of activities to enjoy while in residence at the resort. Endless recreation includes two swimming pools, a Jacuzzi, whirlpool, sunfish sailboats, outrigger canoes, kayaking, snorkeling, tennis courts, and a fitness and massage center. The resort boasts its own helipad, and island helicopter tours depart daily. Nearby is an 18-hole golf course, horseback riding, and scuba diving.

THE LODGE AT KOELE
565-4000 Kameoke Highway
Lana'i City, Hawaii 96763
800/321-4666
808/565-7300

Accommodations
$315-$1,500

Celebrity Guest Register
- *Eva LaRue & John Callahan*
- Billy Crystal
- Carrie Fisher
- Kris Kristofferson
- Emeril Lagasse
- Craig T. Nelson
- Jaclyn Smith

- Kevin Costner
- Michael Douglas
- Gene Hackman
- Cheryl Ladd
- Andrew McCarthy
- Willie Nelson
- Lauralee Bell

A History
Built in 1990, The Lodge at Koele is the sister property to the neighboring Manele Bay Hotel and offers almost total seclusion on the tiny island of Lana'i.

Situated on a former pineapple plantation on the outskirts of Lana'i City, The Lodge at Koele resembles a vintage island plantation with turret wings, peaked roofs, and a generous porch, complete with oversized wicker chairs for endless rocking.

While the hotel offers plush new surroundings, its soul appears to be older than its seven years. Modern-day adventure gives way to such favorite pastimes as lawn bowling and croquet, beer and peanuts are replaced by afternoon tea and scones, and meandering through the Lodge's sprawling gardens is considered by many to be an intense workout.

A sojourn to The Lodge at Koele is indeed a refined way of living, a lifestyle to which most people can easily become accustomed!

Famous Nuptials

While fans of *All My Children* tune in daily to watch the trials and tribulations of Dr. Maria Santos and husband Edmund Grey, few may realize that outside Pine Valley's city limits, actors **Eva LaRue** and **John Callahan** are in fact a real-life twosome. While the two have played husband and wife for three years on television, they finally tied the knot off-screen on November 30, 1996, at The Lodge at Koele.

The bride wore a short white, strappy gown complete with veil, and the groom looked dapper in a black tuxedo sans bow-tie. The two exchanged vows in front of a waterfall and later enjoyed an elaborate picnic lunch with 15 guests beneath an ancient banyan tree.

Getting Married at The Lodge at Koele

Suited for small, intimate weddings and receptions, The Lodge at Koele offers hidden areas in which to be married. There are a number of outdoor locations including three **Gazebos**: one overlooking an ancient reservoir complete with waterfall and age-old banyan trees, one teetering above the blue Pacific Ocean, and yet another overlooking the sprawling grounds. The **Experience at Koele**, the 18-hole championship golf course, also offers stops along the way for exchanging vows, and the **Japanese Garden** offers a unique and picturesque setting as well.

There are a number of areas on the property in which to enjoy picnic receptions. For those who prefer an indoor celebration, the **Octagonal Dining Room** offers a regal setting for post-ceremony celebrations and comes complete with fireplace and expanded windows for parties of 60. The adjacent **Terrace**, ideal for groups of 60, offers al fresco dining with views of the hillside gardens.

Small, intimate weddings are a specialty at The Lodge at Koele. The staff tends to your every request, making the first days of your life together truly unforgettable!

Honeymooning at The Lodge at Koele
Situated 1,700 feet above sea level, temperatures rarely rise above the low 70s at The Lodge at Koele. With a copper-roofed, wooden frame structure and a plantation-style setting, The Lodge houses 102 rooms, creating an exclusive enclave for those who require privacy. Guest chambers are appointed with hand-carved four-poster beds, ceiling fans, oil paintings by local artists, and unobstructed views of the island countryside. The public rooms were designed to encourage conversation with overstuffed furnishings, classical music piped in, and whimsical knick-knacks scattered throughout.

Secluded among century-old towering Cook Island pines, there are many activities here, including world renowned golfing at the **Experience at Koele** designed by Greg Norman, horseback riding, jeep tours, tennis, swimming, lawn games, hiking, and beach and boating activities.

THE MANELE BAY HOTEL
1 Manele Drive, Lana'i City
Hawaii 96763
800/321-4666
808/565-7700

Accommodations $250-$2,000

Celebrity Guest Register
- *Bill Gates*
- *Lisa Kudrow*
- *Prince Alexander von Furstenberg*
- Kevin Bacon
- Laurence Fishburne
- Wayne Gretzsky
- Joe Montana
- Reba McIntire
- Jack Nicklaus
- Randy Travis
- James Woods
- Heather Locklear & Richie Sambora
- *Michelle Pfeiffer & David Kelly*
- *Celine Dion*
- Nicolas Cage
- Dana Delaney
- Helen Hunt
- Gene Hackman
- Troy Aikman
- Tom Selleck
- Oprah Winfrey
- Jack Wagner
- David Bowie & Iman

A History
Although the Manele Bay Hotel is barely out of its infancy, it has managed to capture the attention of this decade's jet set. Built in 1991, the resort offers almost total seclusion on the tiny island of Lana'i.

Situated on a former pineapple plantation, the hotel recalls the days of a more leisurely lifestyle. Dramatically elevated above the blue Pacific and surrounded by lavish gardens, The Manele Bay Hotel boasts commanding views from nearly every angle. The elegant two-story structures feature arcaded loggias, slanted roofs, formal gardens, and multi-level landscaped courtyards.

Since the hotel opened its doors, it has been one of the most sought-after locations on the Hawaiian Islands.

Famous Nuptials

Bill Gates, one of the world's wealthiest men, not to mention the former most eligible bachelor, married **Melinda French** on New Year's Day 1994. The computer mogul, who founded Microsoft, booked every hotel room as guests arrived from around the world to take part in the wedding celebrations. The groom and his bride hosted a rehearsal luau on Hulopo'e Beach, which fronts the Manele Bay Hotel. The nuptials took place on the back tee of the 12th hole at The Challenge at Manele, the resort's championship golf course.

Before flying off to Fiji for an extended honeymoon, the new Mr. & Mrs. William H. Gates III spent a luxurious few nights at The Manele Bay Hotel in one of the butler floor suites, and the two wanted for nothing!

Celebrated Honeymoons

There's never a shortage of celebrity honeymooners at The Manele Bay Hotel. Among those who have jetted here after exchanging "I Do's" include actress **Michelle Pfeiffer** and producer **David Kelly**; *Friends* star **Lisa Kudrow**; **Prince Alexander von Furstenberg**; and singer **Celine Dion**.

Getting Married at The Manele Bay Hotel

If your idea of the perfect wedding includes unspoiled beaches and crashing waves, The Manele Bay Hotel won't disappoint. With four unique wedding sites, the hotel can create a romantic ambience for two or provide large gatherings of 200. Both the **Hawaiian and Bromeliad Gardens** feature tranquil surroundings with serene waterfalls, clear ponds, resplendent flowers, and exotic flora. **The 12th Tee at the Challenge at Manele** offers unencumbered seaside views of Hulopo'e Bay, which is home to the spinner dolphins who are often seen frolicking in the surf. The pristine white sands of **Hulopo'e Beach** provide an endless aisle to the altar; a perfect choice for those who have a fascination for natural wonders.

For elegant receptions, the **Lana'i Conference Center** features an elegant ballroom equipped for up to 240 guests. The room, which can be

Hawaiian Theme Weddings At Manele Bay

Creative touches for weddings are the hotel's forte and include custom leis for both the bride and groom; hula dancers to entertain at the ceremony or reception; and a horse-drawn carriage to make your island getaway!

sub-divided into six smaller venues, features a permanent collection of ancient island artifacts along with breathtaking views of the coastline, beaches, and the neighboring islands of Maui and Kaho'olawe.

Honeymooning at The Manele Bay Hotel

The Manele Bay Hotel is made up of a series of elegant two-story buildings which bring together traditional Hawaiian architecture with Mediterranean elements. The grand lobby leaves a lasting impression with its magnificent views of the coastline below as well as a number of Asian artifacts and paintings by local artists.

Each of the 250 individually decorated guest rooms and suites, which feature furnishings inspired by the Far East, open on to private terraces overlooking sculptured gardens and the blue Pacific. Couples can choose to relax with an array of spa treatments, or enjoy a vigorous workout with state-of-the art health facilities, personal fitness training, and customized workouts. There are also tennis courts, a golf course, and an oceanfront swimming pool for couples who enjoy a little competition!

PRINCEVILLE RESORT

P.O. Box 3069
Kauai, HI 96722
800/826-4400
808/826-9644

Accommodations
$340-$3,500

Celebrity Guest Register
- *Leanza Cornett*
- Reba McIntire
- Oprah Winfrey
- Clint Eastwood
- Michael Crichhton
- *Vice President & Mrs. Al Gore*
- John Tesh & Connie Selleca
- Janet Jackson
- Melissa Ethridge
- Loni Anderson

A History

The Princeville Plantation on the island of Kauai, where the Princeville Resort now stands, was transformed from a sugar cane field to a cattle ranch around the turn-of-the-century. For years, cattle grazed on the area known as the *pu'u* or mountain, and it would be some time before tourists began arriving to enjoy the warm Hawaiian sun.

In 1969, an investment group purchased 11,000 acres of the former plantation and received state zoning to develop a community that would include residential neighborhoods, a resort, and a 27-hole golf course. Two years later, the Makai Golf course was completed along with several homes, and commuter flights soon began arriving at the Princeville Airport.

The Princeville Resort opened in 1985, on the breathtaking cliffside at Pu'u Poa Point. From 1985 to 1992, the resort enjoyed a wealth of visitors and earned the status as one of the premier resorts on the island of Kauai. That would all change on September 11, 1992, when Princeville was hit by one of the most devastating hurricanes in Hawaiian history. With wind speeds measuring 175 miles per hour and wind gusts of 227 miles per hour, Hurricane Iniki (translated "piercing wind") wiped out 90-95 percent of the island's homes and condominiums, and caused $1.2 billion of damage in less than six hours.

The Princeville Resort was transformed from a first-class retreat into a community shelter, housing most of the North Shore residents during the devastating storm. The resort suffered a considerable amount of damage as well and was closed for more than a year as it underwent an extensive renovation.

The Princeville Resort reopened on October 15, 1993, and within a short time was hailed by readers of *Condé Nast Traveler* as one of "The Best Places to Stay in the World."

Famous Nuptials

Leanza Cornett, former Miss America (1992) and reporter for *Entertainment Tonight*, wed aspiring actor **Mark Steiunes** on July 22, 1995, under a trellis on a stretch of beach in front of the Princeville Resort. The groom donned a traditional tuxedo, while the bride wore a simple white sleeveless dress and chiffon veil sans shoes. After the ceremony, family and friends enjoyed a traditional Hawaiian luau complete with leis, native dancers, and breathtaking island views.

Celebrated Occasions

Many have accused **Vice President Al Gore** of being somewhat boring, but they certainly can't label him unromantic. In May 1995, he and wife **Tipper** spent a week on the island of Kauai and celebrated their 25th wedding anniversary at the Princeville Resort. Together, with Secret Service agents trailing close behind, the two jogged, snorkeled, played tennis, and hiked around the tropical island.

Getting Married at the Princeville Resort

Couples planning a Hawaiian wedding often envision fragrant flowers, endless white sand beaches, spectacular sunsets, and a blanket of blue Pacific. The Princeville Resort offers both indoor and outdoor settings for island-bound couples wanting to wed, celebrate, and honeymoon all in one location.

With two beachfront locations for wedding ceremonies, the Princeville Resort is a popular destination for mainland brides and grooms. A stretch of pristine velvety sand extends effortlessly to meet the Pacific Ocean practically at the hotel's doorstep. Couples exchange vows under a floral-covered trellis with waves gently crashing at their feet. The **Beach Gardens**, located near the hotel's swimming pool and just steps away from the shore, overlooks Hanalei Bay and is perfect for both ceremonies and receptions of up to 400. The **Makana Terrace** offers more intimate surroundings for groups of up to 70, and pairs ocean vistas with spectacular views of the famed Bali Hai.

Get Married On The Beach, Hawaiian-Style

The staff can assist in arranging a beachfront wedding for those who truly want the Hawaiian experience. Other arrangements can be handled through the hotel, including flowers, leis, wedding cake design, and more.

Located on the hotel's eighth floor are two salons designed especially for wedding receptions. With an 18th-century Renaissance ambiance, the **Grand Ballroom** features suspended chandeliers, expansive ceilings, and floor-to-ceiling windows. Magnificent views of the waterfront await groups of up to 500, and the room can be divided into four smaller venues for more intimate gatherings. Adjacent to the ballroom is the lanai setting of **Hanalei Bay Terrace**, which embraces the tropical feel of the Hawaiian islands. Only partly enclosed, the room offers spectacular vistas of the ocean and gardens for groups of up to 200.

Rehearsal dinners take on a casual island feel at the Princeville Resort as each restaurant offers views of Hanalei Bay. **La Cascata**, with its terra-cotta floors, trompe l'oeil paintings, and ocean views, is popular for pre-wedding dinners. **Cafe Hanalei and Terrace** is another unique choice for pre-wedding dinners, but is even more ideal for gathering with guests for al fresco Sunday brunch. Adjacent to the lobby is **The Living Room**, where guests unwind with cocktails, afternoon tea, and unbelievable sunset views. For ultra-casual dining, the **Beach Restaurant and Bar** serves poolside lunches and snacks, and features a traditional Hawaiian Luau twice a week.

Honeymooning at the Princeville Resort

The tiered Princeville Resort is molded along the side of a cliff overlooking Hanalei Bay and the famed "Bali Hai" on Kauai's north shore.

The elegant resort features 252 guest rooms and suites, including seven **Executive Suites**, two **Presidential Suites**, and one very private **Royal Suite**. Guest rooms are ample in size and tastefully appointed in hues of cream with pale green accents. Each room is positioned to overlook the oceanfront, pool area, golf course, or gardens, and features original oil paintings and prints. Newlyweds can relax at the oceanfront swimming pool or enjoy a vigorous workout at the state-of-the-art fitness center. There are also two renowned golf courses: the 18-hole **Prince Course**, which has been rated number one in Hawaii by *Golf Digest*, and the 27-hole **Makai Course**.

What's An Entourage Without A Chef?

Janet Jackson, who recently visited the resort, is not known for her light traveling. In addition to packing an absolutely fabulous wardrobe, she also carted along her own chef.

RENAISSANCE WAILEA BEACH RESORT
3550 Wailea Alanui Drive
Maui, HI 96753
800/992-4532
808/879-4900

Accommodations
$175-$2,700

Celebrity Guest Register
• *Heather Locklear & Richie Sambora*
• Cindy Crawford
• Nicolette Sheridan
• Debbie Reynolds

• Harrison Ford
• Paul Simon
• Penny Marshall
• Dustin Hoffman

- Kareem Abdul Jabar
- Lloyd Bridges
- Ozzie Ozborne
- Claudia Schiffer

A History

When the Renaissance Wailea Beach Resort opened in 1978, it was one of the first resort hotels to grace the Maui shoreline.

As an island pioneer, the resort claimed 15 pristine acres fronting one of Maui's most beautiful crescent-shaped beaches. Dotted with tall palms, tropical gardens, and green rolling acres, the Renaissance Wailea Beach Resort has been a haven for Hollywood types since opening day.

Today, the Renaissance Wailea Beach Resort is a renowned enclave for enjoying first-class service and surroundings.

Famous Honeymooners

In December 1994, actress **Heather Locklear** and **Richie Sambora**, member of the rock group *Bon Jovi*, were married at The American Cathedral in Paris. The two hosted a lavish reception at the landmark *Ritz Hotel* immediately following for their friends and family who made the trek from the states. The bride, a native California girl, must have yearned for some fun in the sun. With the ink barely dry on the marriage license, the two said *au revoir* to the City of Light and headed back to the United States for an island honeymoon at the Renaissance Wailea Beach Resort.

Getting Married at The Renaissance Wailea Beach Resort

Swaying palm trees, conch shells, waterfront beauty, and a remote location create a romantic recipe for tropical weddings and honeymoons at The Renaissance Wailea Beach Resort.

While the hotel offers a choice of indoor and outdoor settings, there is no denying that al fresco celebrations are what attracts brides and grooms to the resort. Each venue serves as both wedding and reception sites, offering couples and their guests complete privacy. **The Luau Gardens** are ideal for island-style celebrations and feature a sprawling patch of landscaped lawn with the Pacific Ocean as a backdrop, and can accommodate up to 400 guests. The **Makena Lawn** at **Makena Point**, a serene spot for groups of up to 300, overlooks the ocean and features an expansive lawn framed by coconut palms, graceful ferns, and fragrant hibiscus. The **Maui Onion Poolside** offers a roomy deck which overlooks the resort's pool, and is surrounded by towering palm trees for groups up to 270 people. For smaller, more intimate celebrations, there are three adjacent **Lanais** nearby, each sheltered by flora trellises for receptions of up to 60 guests.

Indoor celebrations are just as enchanting at the resort and include the contemporary **Wailea Ballroom**, which can accommodate parties of up to 400 or be divided into two separate rooms for smaller occasions. The ballroom boasts a 12-foot-high ceiling, recessed lighting and elegant hues of cream. The **Wailea Terrace**, for smaller groups of up to 120, offers expansive panoramic views of the ocean and tropical gardens. For those who want both an indoor and outdoor setting, the **Renaissance Pavilion** is a mobile structure which can be set up in any of the outside areas. The Pavilion, a spacious venue for groups of up to 600, is elegantly appointed with French doors, a towering 21-foot-high ceiling, mood lighting, and mesh gabled ends for catching trade winds.

There are an array of casual to elegant restaurants for pre- and post-wedding celebrations. With contemporary Japanese decor, the intimate **Hana Gion** lends itself to a more non-traditional celebration with a sushi bar being the focal point for gatherings. The casual, open-air **Palm Court** is surrounded by gardens and boasts panoramic island views. Located on the third floor of the hotel, Palm Court is ideal for enjoying a leisurely meal with out-of-town guests. Poolside dining is enjoyed at the very casual **Maui Onion** featuring lush gardens and cascading waterfalls – a perfect spot for reviewing last-minute details. The open-air **Sunset Terrace Lounge** offers breathtaking views for sipping early evening cocktails.

The staff at The Renaissance Wailea Beach Resort is accustomed to arranging weddings, receptions, and honeymoon stays for mainland newlyweds. A wedding coordinator will be assigned to assure your day – and stay – are unforgettable, and will assist in the necessary preparations.

Honeymooning at the Renaissance Wailea Beach Resort

A honeymoon at the Renaissance Wailea Beach Resort is equivalent to a sojourn in paradise. Upon arrival, guests are greeted with a fresh flower lei before being whisked off to the privacy of their own deluxe guest room. The resort's distinctive t-shaped design offers views of either the Pacific Ocean or Mt. Haleakula from every vantage point. There are 311 guest rooms and 10 suites appointed in contemporary island decor offering spacious lanais and sitting areas. The 26-room **Mokapu Beach Club**, located in an exclusive two-story building just steps from the resort's crescent-shaped beach, offers such pampering amenities as private check-in, in-room continental breakfast served on a private lanai, plush terry robes, and access to a private swimming pool and beach cabanas.

Other unique services available to guests include traditional Hawaiian craft classes and demonstrations, massage therapy, two swimming pools, tennis and basketball courts plus such classic games as ping-pong and shuffleboard.

Celebrity guests who stay at the Renaissance Wailea Beach Resort usually prefer to rest their heads in the 3,000 square-foot **Aloha Suite**!

THE ROYAL HAWAIIAN

2259 Kalakaua Avenue
Honolulu, HI 96815
800/782-9488
808/923-7311

Accommodations
$275-$1,200

Celebrity Guest Register
- *John Wayne*
- Clark Gable
- J.D. Rockefeller
- Norma Talmadge
- Peter Lawford
- George Burns & Gracie Allen

- *Henry Ford*
- Mary Pickford & Douglas Fairbanks
- Al Jolson
- Shirley Temple
- Charlie Chaplin
- President Franklin D. Roosevelt

A History

Honolulu's famed Royal Hawaiian hotel was the brainchild of William P. Roth, a San Francisco stockbroker and son-in-law of Captain William Matson, founder of the Hawaii-based Matson Navigation Company. Roth saw the hotel as a way to complement his father-in-law's fleet of ocean liners which traveled to and from the mainland.

Construction got underway in the summer of 1926, and was orchestrated by the architectural firm of Warren and Wetmore of New York. The six-story, 400-room building resembled a Spanish-Moorish castle, a design that came into vogue during Rudolph Valentino's reign on the big screen. Four million dollars and 18 months later, the legendary "Pink Palace" was ready to welcome wealthy American travelers.

The Royal Hawaiian opened on February 1, 1927, with a black-tie gala celebration for 1,200 people. The first registered guest was Princess Kawananakoa, who might have been crowned queen had the monarchy survived. From day one guests arrived in droves, bringing with them numerous steamer trunks, servants, and even Rolls Royces, which would be stashed in the hold during ocean voyages.

The first two years were glorious for The Royal Hawaiian, and guests felt as if they had discovered paradise. All that would change temporarily with the stock market crash of 1929, when many Americans went to bed millionaires only to awaken more destitute than their servants. The Great Depression and World War II would also dampen island fever in the years to come.

During the war, Waikiki Beach was surrounded by barbed wire and a month after the bombing of Pearl Harbor, the Royal Hawaiian was leased to the United States Navy as a rest and recreation center for those serving the Pacific Fleet. After the war, the hotel was returned to Matson, who spent nearly $2 million renovating the property to its original pre-war grandeur. Eventually the hotel was acquired by ITT Sheraton in the 1960s, and although the corporation no longer owns the property, it continues to manage it under its current proprietors.

Carrying on a 70-year tradition of excellence, The Royal Hawaiian is as striking as ever with its trademark pink facade and prime beachfront location.

Celebrated Honeymoons

On November 1, 1954, actor **John Wayne** married **Pilar Palett** at the former home of King Kamehameha II in Kailua, Kona, on the Big Island of Hawaii. The bride looked striking in a pink organdy cocktail dress as director John Farrow escorted her down the aisle. After the reception, the newlyweds flew to the neighboring island of Oahu where they honeymooned at The Royal Hawaiian.

Other famous honeymooners include industrialist **Henry Ford** and his first wife, **Anne**, who also stayed at the hotel during part of their honeymoon.

Getting Married at The Royal Hawaiian

The one criteria for an island wedding is there must be a view! Of course, each ceremony and reception location at The Royal Hawaiian offers endless ocean vistas and understated elegance.

Wedding ceremonies of up to 2,000 are generally held outdoors in the **Coconut Grove**, amid fragrant flowers and lush foliage. After the ceremony, it takes just a simple stroll through the grounds to reach your reception salon. The elegant **Monarch Room** opens up onto a lanai which spills out onto the lawn and has a capacity to seat up to 500 guests for celebrations. The posh and sophisticated **Regency Room**, adorned with crystal chandeliers and regal appointments, can open up to create a large, airy room for 220, or be divided into three separate salons for smaller functions of 75. With a private ocean terrace overlooking Waikiki Beach, the **Lurline Room** is truly unbeatable for small receptions of up to 60. Sheltered by the hotel's pink walls, the **Ocean Lawn**, which can seat up to 1,200 guests for receptions, overlooks the blue waters of Oahu and can be illuminated with twinkle lights or tiki torches to create an evening glow.

For elegant simplicity, the **Surf Room** is ideal for rehearsal dinners or post-wedding Sunday brunches and features the most breathtaking views of Waikiki Beach. For post-rehearsal gatherings, the circular **Mai Tai Bar**, where the drink of the same name was perfected, also overlooks Oahu's sandy shores as well as Diamond Head and features terrace seating. The

Beach Club Cafe provides a relaxing atmosphere for enjoying mid-day snacks and umbrella-garnished drinks.

The Royal Hawaiian offers wedding packages that include a ceremony, clergy, music, flowers, photography, champagne and wedding cake ranging in price from $1,525-$1,925 inclusive.

Honeymooning at The Royal Hawaiian

While The Royal Hawaiian offers a new, modern structure in the form of the **Royal Towers**, it's the charm of the historic main building that sets it apart from neighboring hotels. The original guest rooms offer old-world charm with high ceilings and walk-in closets enmeshed with the comforts of modern amenities; vistas of the Pacific Ocean, nearby Diamond Head, the hotel swimming pool, or the interior gardens are viewed from large windows or private lanais.

Guests are greeted with fresh-flower leis upon arrival and warm banana bread is placed in each room to welcome hungry travelers. Other amenities include a private sunbathing area along the beach, plus a swimming pool that is open from sunrise to sunset.

Have Your Very Own Waikiki Wedding!

When Bing Crosby serenaded movie goers with "Sweet Leilani" from the hit movie "Waikiki Wedding," it garnished an Oscar for the best film song of 1937. It also helped to lure romantics to the island of Oahu, and may have been responsible for many a sold-out night at The Royal Hawaiian.

10. Idaho

SUN VALLEY RESORT
1 Sun Valley Road
Sun Valley, ID 83353
800/894-9932
208/622-3700

Accommodations
$89- $1,000

Celebrity Guest Register

- *Groucho Marx*
- Brooke Shields
- Katarina Witt
- Gary Cooper
- Clark Gable
- Sonja Henie
- Errol Flynn
- Oksana Baiul
- Ernest Hemingway
- Paul Newman
- Clint Eastwood
- Judy Garland
- Marilyn Monroe
- Nancy Kerrigan
- Mary Lou Retton

A History

Long before ski bums and bunnies were traversing down the slopes of Sun Valley, the area's first inhabitants, the Shoshone and Bannock Indians, wintered on this once desolate landscape. As seasons changed and years evaporated, the tribes were replaced by miners and sheepherders, who congregated to the area. Eventually, businessman, diplomat, and former New York Governor Averell Harriman discovered Sun Valley for himself, claiming it was the true American Shangri-La.

As a member of the board of directors for the Union Pacific Railroad, Harriman was looking for a way to attract passenger traffic into the west. An avid skier, Harriman was greatly impressed by the resorts nestled in the Swiss Alps and was determined to develop America's premiere grand destination ski resort. In 1935, he hired Count Felix Schaffgotsch of Austria to scout the American west and northwest, and gave him only one instruction – the resort must be near a Union Pacific rail line.

Frustrated at not finding any suitable prospects, the Count was close to abandoning his search when he learned of Ketchum, Idaho. He enthusiastically wired Harriman, who joined him in Idaho. Within days, he purchased the 4,300-acre Brass Ranch and began creating his lodge. Next he recruited Steve Hannagan, the public relations guru who helped transform Miami Beach from a sand dune into a rave resort, to publicize the area. It was Hannagan who coined the name Sun Valley, and both he and Harriman agreed the resort should be elegantly-appointed where guests would "rough it" in style.

The finished product was remarkable, with a glass-enclosed swimming pool, gourmet fare, unsurpassed service, and nightly entertainment. The concoction of a gorgeous setting, dream resort, and country elegance did not change the fact that Idaho was about as isolated as one could get! Hannagan needed to put the right spin on Sun Valley in order to attract the proper clientele. He looked to Hollywood for help, and when the resort hosted its grand opening, starlets were flown in for the occasion. What took Mother Nature countless years to cultivate and Averell Harriman a decade to create became an instant success.

Since its 1936 debut, Sun Valley Resort has expanded to become one of the most sought-after destinations in the region for both winter and summer frolicking.

Famous Nuptials

Groucho Marx, the cigar-chomping comedian who rose to fame as a member of the Marx Brothers comedy team, wed model **Eden Harford** on July 17, 1954, at Sun Valley Resort. The wedding was delayed by a few hours as the bride and bridegroom scrambled to get a marriage license, which they had to obtain in Twin Falls, located more than 80 miles away.

When it came time for the wedding, the only witness was Groucho's 7-year-old daughter, Melinda. The bride, who at 24 years of age was quite a bit younger than her 58-year-old fiancé, wore a light green organdy dress which offset the white chrysanthemums she carried. After making it official, the two, along with Melinda, stayed on a few extra days at the resort.

Getting Married at Sun Valley Resort

Whether it's an al fresco wedding atop a snow-covered mountain or a spring ceremony near a lake, Sun Valley Resort offers a number of natural settings for saying "I Do." Each ceremony is tailored to the couple's request, and the incredible vistas are included at no charge.

Afterwards, receptions are held indoors at either the historic **Sun Valley Lodge** or the more conventional **Sun Valley Inn Conference Center**. The Sun Valley Lodge offers some fabulous settings for both ceremonies and receptions. The picturesque **Sage Room** is ideal for groups of up to 40; the celestial **Sun Room**, with its breathtaking views of the surrounding mountains, is showered by the sun's rays during the day and illuminated by a galaxy of stars at night, and can easily accommodate groups of up to 50. The **Sun Valley Inn Conference Center** offers more modern facilities with the capacity to divide ballrooms into smaller arenas. There are five banquet rooms: the **Ram Dining Room, Convention Center, Limelight, Continental**, and the **Walnut Room** – suitable for receptions of 40 to 1,100, and varying in size and decor.

For rustic rehearsal dinners, there are a number of restaurants available. For winter weddings, a pre-nuptial gathering is a must at the **Trail Creek Cabin**, where the entire party can be chauffeured to and fro in a sleigh! A favorite with the Hollywood jet set, Trail Creek Cabin is located two miles east of Sun Valley, and is uniquely built from logs and rock. For steaks and seafood, the **Ram Restaurant and Bar** and **Gretchen's Restaurant** offer a charming setting and panoramic views. For an ultra-elegant meal, the **Lodge Dining Room** offers French and Continental cuisine and a lavish Sunday brunch for post-wedding goodbyes. For hot toddies in the evening, the casual **Duchin Bar & Lounge** features dancing, cocktails, and nightly entertainment.

Because of its remote location, Sun Valley Resort is the ideal location in which to host a wedding and reception, and spend the first few days of a honeymoon.

Honeymooning at Sun Valley Resort

Sun Valley Resort offers all the élan and elegance of a European resort, without forgetting its American roots. Honeymooners who have an appetite for skiing, hiking, fishing, horseback riding, golfing, whitewater rafting or other outdoor activities will assume they've arrived in paradise!

There are four lodges, each distinctive in design, in which to slumber after a day of exploring. Each lodge is its own mini-resort, offering various amenities within its confines. The original **Sun Valley Lodge**, built in 1936, features charming spacious suites with terraces overlooking the terrain. The **Deluxe Lodge Apartments** and **Wildflower Condominiums** offer large one, two, and three-bedroom units each with its own kitchenette, living room, and breakfast nook. The **Village Condominiums** also offer one, two, and three-bedroom accommodations, and form a horseshoe around the heart of the Village, placing guests in the center of activity and within walking distance to practically everything.

There are six **cottages** dotted throughout the resort, which are perhaps the most splendid. Each cottage offers total privacy and feature one to three bedrooms, kitchens, dining rooms, sitting areas and unencumbered views of either the sprawling grounds or the resort's lake.

Hemingway's Favorite Piece Of Idaho

Novelist Ernest Hemingway was so taken with Sun Valley Resort that he used this inspiring piece of American landscape in creating the classic novel "For Whom The Bell Tolls." In fact, Papa, as he was fondly called, penned the majority of his novel from Room 206 in the Sun Valley Lodge, which has since been renamed in his honor.

11. Illinois

THE DRAKE HOTEL
140 E. Walton Place
Chicago, IL 60611
800/445-8867
312/787-2200

Accommodations
$275-$1,000

Celebrity Guest Register

- *Gloria Swanson*
- *Gene Siskel*
- Sinclair Lewis
- Bill Murray
- Daryl Hannah
- Gary Sinese
- Shaquile O'Neal
- John Goodman
- Richard Gere
- *Roger Ebert*
- Amelia Earhart
- Princess Grace Kelly
- Dustin Hoffman
- John F. Kennedy Jr.
- John Malkovich
- Aretha Franklin
- Julia Roberts
- Dan Aykroyd

A History
Chicago pioneer Ben Marshall was a flamboyant and ingenious architect who was instrumental in shaping the infamous Chicago skyline along Lake Shore Drive. A bit of an egoist, his continuous motto was "I can build a better one," a promise he kept when hotelier John Burroughs Drake commissioned him to build a magnificent establishment bearing his name.

In 1917, Marshall had the vision to foresee that the Near North Side would evolve into the city's most prominent area and would therefore be the ideal location for The Drake. With an eye for detail, Marshall borrowed elements found in Italian palaces to create the 13-story, limestone structure. Once the exterior was completed, Marshall worked feverishly on the appointments for the public rooms, a task he didn't take lightly.

With a final tab of $10 million, The Drake was ready to open, and Marshall chose New Year's Eve 1920 in which to host its debut. The original 700 rooms were serviced by 900 employees, and while the hotel was owned and managed by The Drake family, Ben Marshall kept a watchful eye on its every operation, from decor and entertainment to the efficiency of service.

The Drake family lost control of the hotel in 1933, and the Kirkeby chain leased it for the next 10 years, maintaining the property for military lodging. In 1943, The Drake was returned to the Marshall family; Ben Marshall's niece, Katharine, and her husband Edward Brashears, took over the operation, keeping Ben Marshall's dream for The Drake alive. After World War II, with fewer soldiers in need of a hostelry, the hotel was refurbished to its original splendor.

Today, The Drake looks as regal as it did the day it opened, and is a gathering spot for a medley of dignitaries, celebrities, and noteworthy guests visiting Chicago.

Famous Nuptials

In the early 1930s, actress **Gloria Swanson**, whose most famous role may have been that of real-life mistress to Joseph Kennedy, the patriarch of the famous Kennedy clan, was not only engaged at The Drake, but married there as well. Legend has it that Ms. Swanson's husband-to-be proposed to her at the hotel and, because he had to leave town immediately on an urgent trip, the two decided to tie the knot the very next day. Because everything was last-minute, the bride did not have a proper dress, so she called a boutique across the street and picked one from a dozen or so modeled. The two were married in one of the hotel's suites and, because she was a local gal, her family was able to attend as well.

While the film critics for both the *Chicago Tribune* and *Chicago Sun-Times* can't always agree on Hollywood's latest blockbuster, they do share the same tastes when it comes to wedding sites. Both **Gene Siskel** and **Roger Ebert** married their wives at the The Drake, giving the hotel a two thumbs up!

Getting Married at The Drake

It's easy to presume that with a reputation for orchestrating state dinners for this century's most notable dignitaries, including Emperor Hirohito of Japan and Queen Elizabeth II of England, weddings within The Drake's confines must be simply spectacular. And, of course, they are.

The hotel offers four major banquet rooms where society's creme de la creme have dined, mingled, and danced late into the night. The magnificent **Gold Coast Room** looks as though it belongs in a palace with an endless number of crystal chandeliers, slick marble floors, enormously high ceilings, expansive windows that overlook the famous Lake Shore Drive as well as Lake Michigan. Italianate columns, covered in gold-leaf vines, appear to effortlessly support the room. This elegant salon is ideal for large, grandiose weddings and receptions, accommodating up to 700 guests.

In contrast is **The Grand Ballroom**, showcasing Georgian-style architecture and appointments, which welcomes groups of 600. The ballroom features a mezzanine, an ideal locale for exchanging vows while guests admire from below, mirrored French doors, regal chandeliers, floor-to-ceiling windows, and a floating parquet dance floor that puts a bounce in each step! Reminiscent of the Louis XVI period, the **French Room** features square columns adorned with a ribbon relief, large windows framing Lake Michigan as well as Michigan Avenue and Lake Shore Drive, and crystal chandeliers creating soft light throughout. The French Room, one of the city's most popular reception venues, welcomes groups of up to 450.

The ultra-private **Club International** is a blueprint of Haddon Hall, an English manor located in Derbyshire, and a notable example of medieval architecture. The room boasts a rich oak finish, walls of palm plaster, a scroll-pattern relief graces the ceiling, and a Gothic opened-hearth fireplace adds a touch of warmth to the room. Club International seats up to 150, and use of the facility requires a membership.

Pre-nuptial gatherings run the gamut from nostalgic to refined. The cozy **Cape Cod Room**, established in 1933, is a real "joint" and ideal for breaking the ice with the in-laws, where red-checked tablecloths drape the tables and copper pots hang overhead. The **Oak Terrace** is named for the soft wood that graces its interior, and is ideal for upscale dinners or a fabulous Sunday Brunch. The elegant **Palm Court** is located in the hotel's upper lobby where afternoon tea and evening cocktails are enhanced with the trickling sound of an indoor fountain. The entire wedding party can meet for a late-night supper and cocktails at **Coq d'Or**, which emulates a pub-like atmosphere.

Honeymooning at The Drake

More than 75 years since its opening, The Drake is still a symbol of white-glove elegance, and honeymooners, along with other guests, are treated as if they are indeed royalty.

The hotel lobby makes a lasting impression with its rows of crystal chandeliers, floral centerpieces, and sweeping ceiling. Above are 535 spacious guest rooms and suites with either views of Lake Michigan or the spectacular Chicago skyline. Rooms feature awning-striped wall coverings, king-size beds, and sitting areas, while suites offer separate bedrooms and living area. Guests awake to a medley of fresh fruit in the morning and end the day with a decadent chocolate placed upon their pillow.

In addition to being centrally located in the heart of Chicago, The Drake also features its own state-of-the-art health center and a shopping arcade with an array of boutiques and services.

Another First At The Drake

The Chicago radio station WGN aired one of its first broadcasts from atop The Drake, where the famous big bands from the era played in the elegant Gold Coast Room.

12. Louisiana

OMNI ROYAL ORLEANS
621 St. Louis Street
New Orleans, LA 70140
800/843-6664
504/529-5333

Accommodations
$210-$730

Celebrity Guest Register
•James Carville & Mary Matalin
• Bette Midler
• Barbra Streisand
• Richard Simmons

• Farrah Fawcett
• Jerry Seinfeld
• Diana Ross
• Don Rickles

A History
The Omni Royal Orleans hotel has been a New Orleans fixture since 1960, but it is the ghost of the old St. Louis Hotel that still lingers at 621 St. Louis Street.

New Orleans, like many other southern cities, prospered during the early 1800s both in population and wealth. Prior to the arrival of the St. Louis Hotel in the mid-1830s, the city offered nothing more than cramped hotels and overcrowded boarding houses to accommodate visiting businessmen and their belles. The St. Louis Hotel was a welcomed addition to the bustling town and cost a then-staggering $1 million to build. With its splendid accommodations and two enormous ballrooms, there is no denying it was well worth every penny.

In 1841, a fire swept through the hotel, partially destroying the building. Workers labored night and day to reconstruct the St. Louis and created an even more majestic building designed in the Roman Revival style. With all its grandeur, the St. Louis was popular with sophisticated travelers because of its close proximity to places like the French Opera House, the Place d'Armes, and Jackson Square.

With the onset of the Civil War, the St. Louis was eventually transformed into a hospital for both Confederate and Union troops. Following the war, the hotel was purchased by the state government and was the gathering spot for the Carpetbagger Legislature. Sadly, in 1915, the antebellum structure that once dominated the social scene of the French Quarter was destroyed by a hurricane – only a few stone arches withstood the wrath of Mother Nature.

Until the 1960 arrival of the Omni Royal Orleans, 621 St. Louis Street remained void of any structure. Today, as with its glory years, the site is once again the hub of social activity.

Famous Nuptials

Mary Matalin, political advisor to President George Bush, and **James Carville**, political advisor to President Bill Clinton, gave credence to the theory that politics makes strange bedfellows! The two were married in a civil ceremony beneath the crystal chandeliers of Omni Royal Orleans' Grand Salon on Thanksgiving Day 1993.

Following the candlelight service, crowds queued up along the avenue to watch the wedding party march to the beat of a traditional Dixieland jazz street parade, which ended with a reception at Arnaud's restaurant.

Getting Married at the Omni Royal Orleans

With the lively French Quarter as a backdrop, weddings and receptions at the Omni Royal Orleans can be as whimsical as a day at Mardi Gras, or more refined as an afternoon garden party, depending on the style of the newlyweds.

In addition to the ballrooms, there are a number of outdoor settings to say "I Do." The **Royal Garden Terrace Patio** offers a courtyard setting complete with center fountain and brick patio, and up to 200 guests can witness the vows. The unique **Pool Terrace**, located atop the roof, allows couples to overlook the French Quarter and Mississippi River while taking the biggest plunge of their lives...literally right next to the swimming pool! Indoor venues include the **Royal Garden Terrace**, for celebrations of up to 200, which features floor-to-ceiling French doors that open onto the adjoining patio with lush greenery. The **Grand Salon**, with candelabra-like chandeliers, carved molding accents and mural-type mirrors, is ideal for parties of 700 or, when divided into smaller arenas, can accommodate anywhere from 25-400.

The **Esplanade Complex**, located on the lobby level, features a stunning arched skylight which casts mood lighting on the room day or night, and can accommodate up to 150 guests. The **Vieux Carré Suite**, with its rectangular configuration, opens up onto classic wrought-iron terraces that gaze down upon the French Quarter. The Vieux Carré Suite can accommodate up to 200 guests, or be divided into smaller venues for celebrations of fewer than 50.

The English-style **Rib Room** is ideal for rehearsal dinners or for gathering with out-of-towners for Sunday brunch, and features expansive windows that open onto the public promenade of Royal Street. People watching is an art form in New Orleans and **The Touche Bar**, a sidewalk cafe, provides diners with front row seats. By day the quaint bistro is ideal for enjoying a leisurely lunch while going over wedding details, and by night The Touche Bar emerges as a sophisticated spot for enjoying mint juleps.

With its drawing room ambiance and flaming coffee menu, afternoons and late evenings are especially enjoyable in the **Esplanade Lounge**. The seasonal **La Riviera** (April-October), hidden on the hotel's rooftop, serves superb breakfasts and light luncheons while offering sweeping views of the French Quarter and Mississippi River.

Added amenities for newlyweds hosting a wedding and reception at the hotel include a silver cake knife for slicing the wedding cake, a complimentary honeymoon suite on the wedding night, plus a private dinner for two behind closed doors!

Honeymooning at the Omni Royal Orleans

New Orleans is the ideal setting for storybook romances. After all, it was to this southern seaside city that Rhett Butler brought his bride, Scarlett O'Hara, for their honeymoon in the classic saga *Gone With The Wind.*

The building features the architectural influences of New Orleans Creole with a French-style facade accented with Spanish wrought-iron balconies, which together create a paradoxical intrigue of the old South. Upon arrival, honeymooners encounter a graceful marble stairway, which leads to the elegant lobby complete with fresh-cut flowers, crystal chandeliers, and brass appointments. There are 346 guest rooms and suites, offering four-poster beds, original artwork, and striking views of the French Quarter. Honeymoon suites feature expansive rooms and whirlpool baths.

The Omni Royal Orleans is near many attractions and curiosities, including Bourbon Street, Jackson Square, and the French Market.

THE PONTCHARTRAIN

2031 St. Charles Avenue
New Orleans, LA 70140
800/777-6193
504/524-0581 ˙

Accommodations
$120-$600

Celebrity Guest Register
- *Rita Hayworth & Prince Aly Khan*
- Tom Cruise
- Truman Capote
- Jack Benny
- Carol Channing
- Frank Sinatra
- Yul Brenner

- Jerry Seinfeld
- Tyrone Power
- Anne Rice
- Richard Burton
- Ethel Merman
- Jose Ferrer

A History
In 1927, businessman E. Lysle Aschanggenburg opened a luxurious residential hotel in New Orleans' Garden District. In keeping with the city's French influence, he named the hotel in honor of Count de Pontchartrain from the court of Louis XVI.

With its brick facade and striking Moorish-style architecture, The Pontchartrain sheltered many influential people of the era. For 14 years, it was considered the grand "guest house" of New Orleans, but in 1941, the hotel converted a portion of the apartments into hotel rooms. The timing proved essential as the conversion was finished at the onset of World War II, when hotel rooms were as much in demand as silk stockings.

Even during these lean times, guests were treated to luxurious accommodations. The hotel lobby featured a barrel-vaulted ceiling supported by marble columns imported from Italy. A glass-enclosed courtyard encased with 18th-century Georgian gates imported from London was a refuge for weary travelers, where original artwork graced the walls.

For many years, The Pontchartrain was the tallest commercial building in the city's Garden District, and up until 1990, the hotel continued to house permanent residents. Today, the hotel remains a testimonial to the elegance and charm of a bygone era.

Celebrated Gatherings
Just a few weeks prior to their marriage, **Rita Hayworth** and her third husband, **Prince Aly Khan**, enjoyed a hush-hush New Orleans rendezvous

at The Pontchartrain. It remained a quiet getaway most likely because the two were not married – at least to one another – and the Prince already had a wife! Hayworth, the star of such classics as *Gilda* and *The Lady From Shanghai*, was twice-divorced (her second husband was film genius Orson Welles) and Catholic. In order to marry her prince, she desperately needed the approval of his Muslim father, Aga Khan III.

Her future father-in-law finally relented and gave his permission for a French Riviera wedding. On May 27, 1949, with scores of reporters looking on, the bride, dressed in a simple light-colored dress, matching hat, and black gloves, became a princess in less than eight minutes!

Getting Married at The Pontchartrain

Weddings and receptions at The Pontchartrain can be described as elegant without being ostentatious. Venues include **The Garden Courts I & II**, which are popular backdrops for ceremonies and receptions; one court features a glass-enclosed courtyard, while the other mirrors a sidewalk cafe setting as passersby parade along St. Charles Avenue. Both Garden Courtyards can accommodate intimate groups of 20. The elegant **Patio Room** is a light, airy venue enhanced with the soft lighting of gas lantern chandeliers, and is ideal for parties of up to 100.

Named for its ornate centerpiece, **The Fountain Room** is a serene setting for celebrations of up to 75, and features skylights, brick-covered walls, and a living room setting. **The Founder's Room** features high ceilings and classic wood paneling, and offers a regal setting for groups of up to 75. The elegant **Penthouse Garden and Terrace** is an extremely private suite located atop the hotel and features a roomy 2,000 square-feet, a split-level balcony overlooking the city, a living room and dining room, plus two bedrooms for hosting out-of-town guests. The **Penthouse** can accommodate up to 45 people for a celebration. The modern **Grand Court** offers high ceilings, recessed lighting, and muted hues for receptions of up to 250 guests, or can be divided into two salons for smaller groups of 75-125.

No Need To Go To Paris To Eat At The Eiffel Tower

Perhaps the most unique setting for a soiree is "The Eiffel Tour," which can accommodate up to 500 guests. The structure, which was once the restaurant atop the famed Parisian landmark, was taken apart piece by piece in 1981 because its weight was causing the actual tower to sag. It was shipped to New Orleans where it has been reassembled at The Pontchartrain. The trés chic salon features floor-to-ceiling plate glass walls which are enclosed by a 30-foot domed ceiling; the effect is truly magnificent.

Elegant surroundings and Creole delicacies are hallmarks of the **Caribbean Room**, a wondrous gathering spot for pre-nuptial dinners. Decorated in a cozy French-provincial motif, the sunny **Cafe Pontchartrain** is a celebrated spot for family breakfasts, lunches, and leisurely dinners, and is the chosen breakfast nook for the city's politicians and civic leaders. For enjoying an after-dinner aperitif or cocktail, the **Bayou Bar**, a favorite of Frank Sinatra, features exquisite canvas murals by noted artist Charles Reinike.

Honeymooning at The Pontchartrain

Honeymooning at The Pontchartrain can be compared to slumbering in a small European-style hotel, where service is personal and no two rooms are alike.

Guests motoring up St. Charles Avenue immediately notice the five ornate gas lamp posts which frame the hotel's entrance, and are duplicates of the ones in Paris' Place Vendome. Inside, the hotel lobby retains its original 1920s decor as admirers sweep through the room.

There are 58 guest rooms and 46 suites, many named for their famous residents. Each room is uniquely appointed with period-style furnishings and are accompanied with views of the Garden District. The spacious suites are even more elegant with full kitchens or kitchenettes, separate living rooms and bedrooms, entertainment/dining areas, and balconies. The **Grand Suite** was a favorite of actresses Mary Martin, Helen Hayes, Joan Fontaine, Carol Channing and many other luminaries.

Good Setting For Weddings... And Mystery Novesls!

The Pontchartrain and The Cafe are the settings for a portion of mystery writer Anne Rice's critically-acclaimed novel "The Witching Hour."

13. Massachusetts

BOSTON HARBOR HOTEL
70 Rowes Wharf
Boston, MA 02110
800/752-7077
617/439-7000

Accommodations
$170-$1,600

Celebrity Guest Register

• *Dennis Hopper*	• Forest Whitaker
• Madonna	• Billy Joel
• Liza Minnelli	• Natalie Cole
• Ted Turner & Jane Fonda	• Tyne Daly
• Sharon Gless	• Lauren Hutton
• Shaquille O'Neal	• Alan Alda
• Carly Simon	• Roseanne
• Paul Newman	• Julio Iglesias

A History
    The Boston Harbor Hotel opened in August 1987, and is considered by New England standards a new "in" gathering spot.
    Nonetheless, the site of the hotel is steeped with history dating back to the mid-1600s when a proctective battery known as the Sconce, or South Battery, was constructed. During the 1760s, John Rowe constructed one of two wharfs at the site of the old Battery. The other wharf, owned by Charles Apthorp, was confiscated when he backed the wrong side during the American Revolution. Rowe's fleet of ships sailed the ocean collecting such goods as silk stockings, ribbons, linens, woolens, English taffetas and salt, which stocked his shop and warehouses. One of Rowe's more famous expeditions came in 1773, when his tea ship had its

entire cargo dumped in the harbor during the infamous Boston Tea Party.

Through the 1800s, the wharf thrived as trade merchants sailed to and from Boston Harbor. The city's urban waterfront began a slow decline during the 1930s as Rowes Wharf slowly began to rot and ramshackle sheds dotted the docksides. Maritime activity nearly came to a halt, and not until the 1960s did a need for urban renewal become painfully evident.

For the next three decades, Boston Harbor slowly rose from the ashes to become a premiere, urban waterfront location, with the Boston Harbor Hotel playing a pivotal role as the wharf's elegant centerpiece.

Celebrated Nuptials

Dennis Hopper, who starred in the 1960s cult classic *Easy Rider* as well as dozens of other films including *Hoosiers, Blue Velvet, The River's Edge* and *Rebel Without A Cause*, just to name a few, married **Victoria Duffy** on April 12, 1996. The bride, who wore an elegant satin gown and traditional veil, is a native of Massachusettes and selected Boston's Old South Church to seal the deal with Hopper. Afterwards, the two hosted a dinner for 50 at the Boston Harbor Hotel to celebrate, and famous guests included the groom's longtime pals Warren Beatty and Jack Nicholson.

Getting Married at the Boston Harbor Hotel

The Boston Harbor Hotel is a perfect locale for those who want the convenience of a big city wedding yet have always imagined a breathtaking setting.

Fairytale weddings are held on the wharf inside **The Gazebo**, a glass circular structure capped with a dome ceiling, which can accommodate up to 125 guests. After being pronounced husband and wife, couples can choose from three venues in which to celebrate. **The Wharf Room**, a spectacular ballroom boasting floor-to-ceiling windows on three sides of the room, overlooks the famous Boston Harbor and is ideal for larger groups of 350. The bi-level **Foster's Rotunda** is located in the center of the hotel occupying the ninth floor, featuring an outside terrace overlooking the harbor, and the 10th floor, with captivating views of the city skyline. Foster's Rotunda can accommodate groups of up to 150. For small, intimate celebrations, the **Presidential Suite** offers an elegant setting with unencumbered views from the top of the 16th floor, and is ideal for up to 10 people.

Pre-nuptial feasts are a specialty at **Rowes Wharf Restaurant**, a magnificent setting with two private dining rooms offering sweeping views of Boston Harbor. The restaurant is open for breakfast, lunch, and dinner and serves an excellent Sunday brunch. For more casual gatherings, **Rowes Wharf Bar** offers traditional pub food, fine ales, and spirits. The **Harborview Lounge** is ideal for an afternoon bridesmaids' tea or evening cocktails. For seasonal, outdoor dining, **Rowes Walk Cafe** overlooks the harbor and the wharf esplanade, and serves lunch and dinner from May to September.

Honeymooning at the Boston Harbor Hotel

Honeymooners with an appreciation for history will truly enjoy a stay at the Boston Harbor Hotel. Within steps is an oasis of cultural activity, from the New England Aquarium and Faneuil Hall Marketplace to the historic Freedom Trail and the home of Paul Revere.

The hotel itself is extraordinary in its design and decor. French doors open to reveal an elegantly appointed lobby adorned with carved woodwork, crown moldings, Chippendale furnishings, and the aroma of freshly-cut flowers. A fine art collection, which could rival almost any museum, includes an authentic map designed by Captain John Smith in 1614, which was used to guide the Pilgrims to Plymouth Rock.

After exploring the city, newlyweds can retreat to one of 230 guest rooms and suites, each featuring large windows framing either the Boston Harbor or the city's silhouette. Other features include Chippendale furnishings, sitting areas, and such homey touches as plush robes and slippers as well as umbrellas for strolls in the rain. Other amenities include a whirlpool and sauna room, spa treatments, and an excercise room.

For those arriving at Logan International Airport, a seven-minute ferry service, which deposits guests at the hotel dock, is available.

Madonna's Boston Gym

There are some things a material girl just can't do without. During her stay at the Boston Harbor Hotel, Madonna transformed one of the guest rooms into her very own state-of-the-art gym!

THE RITZ-CARLTON, BOSTON

15 Arlington Street
Boston, MA 02117
800/241-3333
617/536-5700

Accommodations
$355 - $1,000

Celebrity Guest Register

- *Caroline Kennedy Schlossberg*
- Jason Alexander
- Lena Horne
- Tyra Banks
- David Brinkley
- Gary Cooper
- Danny DeVito
- Albert Einstein
- Kelsey Grammer
- Alfred Hitchcock
- Tom Jones
- B.B. King
- Jay Leno
- General Colin Powell
- Frank Sinatra
- John Wayne
- Prince Charles
- Lauren Bacall
- Lucille Ball
- Christie Brinkley
- Truman Capote
- Walter Cronkite
- Michael Douglas
- Judy Garland
- David Hasselhoff
- Whitney Houston
- Eartha Kitt
- John Cougar Melloncamp
- Princess Grace Kelly
- Andrew Shue
- Steven Spielberg
- Mimi Rogers

A History

Edward N. Wyner, a Boston real estate developer, had a vision of constructing a luxury apartment building at Arlington and Newbury Streets overlooking the city's Public Garden. After being approached by a local politician, who pleaded that the city was in more need of an elegant hotel rather than apartment dwellings, Wyner obliged and obtained the rights to The Ritz-Carlton name for his establishment. On May 18, 1927, The Ritz-Carlton, Boston, opened its doors.

From the beginning, Wyner was determined that his hotel would emulate the high standards that he so admired at the original Ritz Hotel in Paris. He granted rooms only to those patrons found listed in the *Social Register, Standard's and Poor's Directory of Executives,* or *Who's Who in America.* However, money or importance did not always play a factor in guaranteeing a reservation; if Wyner did not approve of a person's conduct or attitude, they were immediately shown the door regardless of their status. During his 34-year tenure, this self-imposed policy rarely allowed exceptions, and when Wyner died in 1961, an era died with him.

Throughout the years, the hotel cultivated a great appreciation for the arts. Because Boston was considered a trial city for Broadway plays, the hotel hosted a number of writers, producers, directors, and actors. Tennessee Williams wrote new material for *A Streetcar Named Desire* at the hotel, and Oscar Hammerstein wrote the lyrics to *Edelweiss* during an overnight sojourn. Many more literary and musical masterpieces were conceived at the hotel.

Today, The Ritz-Carlton, Boston, is still the one of the city's most luxurious hotels, and a magnet for celebrities, artists, and dignitaries of all ages. With a fashionable address, breathtaking views, and central location, it's no wonder The Ritz-Carlton, Boston, is still as magnificent as the day it opened.

Celebrate Honeymoons

Caroline Kennedy, former first daughter of the United States, married **Ed Schlossberg** on July 19, 1986. The nuptials were held at The Church of Victory in Centerville, Massachusetts, and Senator Ted Kennedy did the honors of giving the bride away. Caroline's mother, Jacqueline Kennedy Onassis, helped plan the elegant affair that included a Kennedy-style reception at the family's home in nearby Hynannis Port. After an evening of dancing, feasting, and toasting, the couple said their goodbyes and headed for The Ritz-Carlton, Boston, to spend their wedding night.

Getting Married at The Ritz-Carlton, Boston

The Ritz-Carlton, Boston, has always been the hub of social activity for the rich, famous and aspiring. The Grand and Petite Ballrooms have been graced with many famous faces during the hotel's history, providing newlyweds with a lasting impression of their wedding day.

The Grand Ballroom, so named for its spacious surroundings, offers picturesque views of the Public Garden. Brides descend from the grand staircase on the second level to the Ballroom below, where vows are exchanged in an elegant milieu. The two-story high salon is surrounded on three sides by a terrace, and can accommodate up to 500 guests. **The Petite Ballroom**, which can host up to 150 guests, is located in The Carlton Wing and offers expansive windows and views of the Public Garden. **The Ritz** and **Carlton Rooms**, both boasting bay windows with vistas of the Back Bay and historic Commonwealth Avenue, can easily be combined to accommodate larger parties of up to 200; separately The Ritz Room holds up to 70 guests, while The Carlton Room welcomes groups of 60. **The French** and **Adam Rooms** both overlook Newbury Street; used jointly, the rooms can hold up to 170 guests. Individually, The French Room can accommodate up to 70 people while The Adam Room can host up to 100 guests. The third floor also has a number of small rooms ideal for rehearsal dinners and intimate receptions.

The Dining Room, with views of the Public Garden, is an excellent choice for rehearsal dinners or post-wedding brunches; live piano music adds the finishing touch. Less formal dining can be found at **The Cafe**, a quaint romantic bistro situated along Newbury Street, and an ideal spot for sharing casual family meals. Tuxedoed waitstaff attend to your every need at **The Roof**, an al fresco grill located atop the 17th floor. With magnificent views of the Public Garden, The Roof is considered the best location for sunset dining, and is a seasonal venue. For those with a taste for fine living, **The Lounge** offers caviar by the ounce, champagne, fine cigars and decadent desserts, weekend jazz and afternoon tea. Resembling an intimate drawing room, The Lounge provides a relaxing atmosphere for going over last-minute wedding details. For those who enjoy an upscale club-like atmosphere, **The Bar** is the perfect place to gather after the rehearsal dinner.

At The Ritz-Carlton, Boston, each bride and groom are made to feel as if they are the hotel's only client. Wedding planning and coordination is provided by the hotel's professional catering staff, who will assist with everything from cake selection to transportation.

Honeymooning at The Ritz-Carlton, Boston

The Ritz-Carlton, Boston, is ideal for honeymooners longing for a metropolitan setting coupled with a bit of New England charm. There are 239 guest rooms and 39 elegant suites; each room features classic French provincial furnishings and distinctive works of art. Some windows open up to reveal beautiful views of the Public Garden and Beacon Hill, while others offer vistas of the Charles River and historic Commonwealth Avenue or Newbury Street. Most of the 39 luxury suites feature working fireplaces for those cold Boston nights and elevated, four-poster beds.

Where Celebrity Pets Are All The Rage

The Ritz-Carlton, Boston, has had its share of noteworthy guests, not all of them human. Famous felines and celebrity canines include Lassie, Rin Tin Tin, and that finicky cat Morris!

14. Michigan

THE RITZ-CARLTON, DEARBORN
300 Town Center Drive
Dearborn, MI 48126
800/241-3333
313/441-2000

Accommodations
$120-$225

Celebrity Guest Register

- *Tom Arnold*
- Hugh Grant
- Joan Cusack
- Chris Farley
- Joey Lawrence
- Arnold Schwarzenegger

A History

As with any hotel that bears The Ritz-Carlton insignia, the Dearborn property meets the high standards set forth by the establishment's namesake, Cesar Ritz.

Opened in 1989, The Ritz-Carlton, Dearborn, is situated in an affluent suburb of Detroit and is ideal for newlyweds who want to shop till they drop. Situated on nearly seven acres, the hotel faces the Fairlane Town Center, the state's largest shopping mall, which boasts 220 specialty shops! Auto enthusiasts and history buffs will also delight in being just minutes from the Henry Ford Museum, Greenfield Village, the Wright brothers cycle shop, Harvey Firestone's farm and Noah Webster's home.

Although The Ritz-Carlton, Dearborn has only been open less than a decade, it has become a Midwestern sanctuary for celebrities visiting the Detroit area, and pampers every guest who crosses its threshold.

Famous Nuptials

When actor **Tom Arnold** (*McHale's Navy, True Lies, Nine Months*) married college co-ed **Julie Champnella** on July 22, 1995, the comedic actor decided his wedding would not become a Hollywood production. The wedding and reception took place at The Ritz-Carlton, Dearborn, not far from where the bride was raised. The ceremony blended the Christian faith of the bride with that of her Jewish groom, and featured 16 attendants, a maid of honor, and best man Chris Farley.

After pronouncing the two husband and wife, 500 guests enjoyed a five-course sit-down dinner and nibbled on an eight-tiered wedding cake laced with dozens of edible flowers. After the celebration, the new Mr. and Mrs. Arnold cruised the Atlantic Ocean on a private yacht.

Getting Married at The Ritz-Carlton, Dearborn

The Ritz-Carlton, Dearborn offers elegant surroundings for both wedding ceremonies and celebrations. There are two regal ballrooms where couples can exchange vows and host a post-nuptial reception.

The **Presidential Ballroom**, with its muted hues, crystal chandeliers, and carved woodwork, can accommodate parties of 20 to 12,000 and can be sub-divided to create seven separate salons. A pre-reception foyer allows guests to mingle prior to being seated for lunch or dinner, and the newlyweds can make their much-anticipated entrance through its grand doors. The smaller **Plaza Ballroom**, for groups of up to 350, mirrors its larger counterpart with the same elegant decor and pre-reception foyer, and can be divided into two separate ballrooms for smaller celebrations.

For pre-nuptial gatherings, the hotel features **The Grill**. An ideal spot for rehearsal dinners, The Grill should also be considered for a family Sunday Brunch after a Saturday evening celebration, and is open for breakfast and lunch as well. For catching up with out-of-town bridesmaids, **The Lobby Lounge** offers a leisurely afternoon tea by day, and refreshing cocktails by night.

Luxuriate On Your Own Private Floor

Guests desiring additional privacy may wish to stay on The Ritz-Carlton Club Floor, accessed by a special elevator key. In addition to personal concierge service, guests enjoy the exclusive use of a private lounge where complimentary continental breakfast, afternoon tea, hors d'oeuvres, beverages and cocktails are served.

Honeymooning at The Ritz-Carlton, Dearborn

A honeymoon to the "motor city" may not at first appear to be a recipe for romance, but honeymooners planning on being in the area couldn't pick a more romantic hotel.

The hotel features 308 guest rooms and suites housed on 11 floors. With an array of 18th and 19th-century art and antiques displayed throughout, the hotel takes on an old world ambience. Each room mimics the classic Ritz-Carlton style, from the marble-coated bathrooms to the custom fabrics draped throughout. Amenities enjoyed by guests include a heated indoor swimming pool, an executive fitness center, and 24-hour room service for those newlyweds who simply lose track of time!

15. Mississippi

MONMOUTH PLANTATION
36 Melrose
Natchez, MS 39120
800/828-4531
601/442-5852

Accommodations
$120-$225

Celebrity Guest Register
- *Donna Rice*
- Jefferson Davis
- Joanne Dru
- President and Mrs. Clinton

- Rob Reiner
- James Woods
- Alec Baldwin
- Carol Lawrence

A History
John Hankinson, a native of Monmouth County, New Jersey, came south in 1818 to Natchez to serve as the area's postmaster. Shortly after his arrival, he built a Federal-style brick home which he fondly called Monmouth, named for his home county.

In 1826, General John Quitman, a transplanted northerner who served in the Mexican War, purchased the estate as a wedding gift to his bride, Eliza. The plantation was located among some of the finest estates in the South, and as far as Quitman was concerned, it announced to his fellow Southerners that he had finally arrived. With his lovely wife, nine children, and scores of servants, Monmouth Plantation became a place for well-respected Southerners to gather.

During his tenure at Monmouth Plantation, Quitman made drastic changes to the estate. He eventually altered the facade of the home from its original Federal-style brick design to its current Greek Revival structure with scored and plastered walls; he added a green house; built additional slave quarters; and added a brick barn and stables. The General died in 1858 of National Hotel Disease, a strange outbreak similar to Legionnaire's Disease of the mid-1970s, and his wife, Eliza died a year later. Their grown children, who occupied the estate, barely escaped the wrath of the Civil War.

In July 1863, Yankee troops occupied the town of Natchez with soldiers encamped on the grounds of Monmouth Plantation. Because of his Northern upbringing, General Quitman's family was viewed as traitors by the Yankee occupants, who had little desire to spare the plantation. They pillaged the mansion, raided the garden until it was barren, and butchered the property's towering oak trees for firewood. When they were through, the plantation offered nothing more than a weed infested field and a dilapidated home. The children were so despondent that they temporarily fled following the end of the war.

The mansion stayed in the family until 1914, when General Quitman's grandchildren sold the estate to Mrs. Annie Gwin, who set up a dairy farm on the grounds and eventually leased the mansion out when she remarried. By the 1970s, a blanket of litter polluted the deserted estate, sheets of paint were peeling from the mansion's gracious front columns, and weeds grew thick across the grounds.

In 1977, a Los Angeles couple fell in love with Monmouth Plantation and purchased the estate. They painstakingly restored the home to its original antebellum grandeur, and acquired many items that once belonged to General Quitman and his family, including china and the family bible.

Today, Monmouth Plantation has come full circle and is once again the pride of the south!

Famous Nuptials

Donna Rice enjoyed her 15 minutes of fame when a photographer spotted her and 1988 Presidential candidate and U.S. Senator Gary Hart aboard a yacht ironically christened *The Monkey Business*. Within days, the very married Senator Hart disappeared from the political arena while Donna Rice went on to promote *No Excuses Jeans*.

Fast forward to May 27, 1994, when Donna Rice became Mrs. **Jack Hughes**, wife of a corporate vice president, at Monmouth Plantation. The two exchanged vows under the wisteria-draped pergola in the Rose Garden with the bride wearing a traditional gown and veil. The two had hoped for a garden reception, but unexpected rain forced the celebration inside. Nevertheless, both the newlyweds and their guests enjoyed the day, rain and all!

Getting Married at Monmouth Plantation

A wedding at Monmouth Plantation is ideal for couples wishing to recreate a 19th-century epoch. It's easy to imagine the bride-to-be escorted down the aisle in her hoop skirt and rustling petticoat ready to live happily ever after.

Whether you are in search of a period-style wedding or an elegant 20th-century affair, Monmouth Plantation combines history with romance to create a breathtaking setting in which to exchange vows. Ceremonies are held either al fresco in the **Rose Garden**, which accommodates up to 100, or in the mansion's stately **Parlor**, ideal for parties of 50. White wooden chairs fill the garden, which overlooks a serene pond and foot bridge, as couples say "I Do" under a wisteria-draped pergola. A much more formal setting is enjoyed in the antique-filled Parlor, which is dramatically illuminated with gas chandeliers.

Receptions are a return to the antebellum South, with garden parties and mint juleps! The **Rose Garden** features an elegant salon with an outdoor terrace where guests mingle among the fragrant garden. A stately reception salon awaits newlyweds who wish to celebrate inside the mansion. The salon, with its roaring fireplace, features a set of French doors which open up onto a brick courtyard to create additional seating. The courtyard, with its fountain centerpiece and garden vistas, can be tented for afternoon parties. The mansion can accommodate up to 100 guests for receptions.

The mansion's dining room is an ideal place to host an unforgettable rehearsal dinner and offers a five-course candlelight dinner served on fine china and antique silver.

Honeymooning at Monmouth Plantation

Whatever stress or anxiety newlyweds arrive with at Monmouth Plantation quickly evaporates as couples are transported to another era within the confines of the antebellum estate.

There are 26 rooms and suites, each featuring private baths, located in either the Greek Revival mansion or in the two-story brick **Plantation House**, which originally served as slave quarters. Each room features a view of the courtyard or gardens. Guest rooms recreate the elegance of the 19th-century with original antiques, canopied beds, sitting areas, and fireplaces. The secluded Plantation House, with its garden location, is ideal for honeymooners and features oversized whirlpool tubs.

Romantic strolls are enjoyed on pebble paths traversing the 26 acres of landscaped gardens. Colorful flowers, moss-draped oak trees, and Mississippi songbirds create a hideaway for country picnics – all this without ever stepping foot off the estate.

Honeymooners are greeted with chilled champagne on arrival, and each guest awakes to a Southern breakfast in the main dining room.

Hollywood In Mississippi

During the filming of Ghosts of Mississippi, much of the cast and crew stayed at Monmouth Plantation, including director Rob Reiner, Alec Baldwin, and James Woods, who received an Academy Award nomination as Best Supporting Actor. In fact, the estate was used for location filming as a country club and included exterior shots of the front of the mansion as well as the courtyard.

16. Nevada

THE ALADDIN HOTEL & CASINO
3667 Las Vegas Blvd. South
Las Vegas, NV 89109
800/634-3424
702/734-3583

Accommodations
$65-$350

Celebrity Guest Register

- *Elvis & Priscilla Presley*
- Roseanne
- Jon Bon Jovi
- Dwight Yoakam
- Toni Braxton
- Bryan Ferry
- Trisha Yearwood
- Patti LaBelle
- Neil Diamond
- Frank Sinatra
- Martin Lawrence
- Danny Elfman
- Eddie Vedder
- Stevie Nicks
- Jack Nicholson
- Alanis Morrissette
- Jerry Lee Lewis
- Sade

A History

The Aladdin Hotel was born from the disastrous Tallyho, an English Tudor-styled hotel with a country club ambiance. The hotel was missing one essential component – a casino! Founder Edwin Lowe was convinced that the ample amount of tourists pouring into Las Vegas each week were doing so because of the warm climate and year-round activities available, not because of the legal gambling. Lowe's Tallyho resort opened in February 1963 and subsequently closed its doors before the year's end.

Lowe was soon relieved of the financial burdens that come with owning an empty hotel when an Indiana-based realty firm took over the responsibility. Following in Lowe's footsteps, the new owners also decided to run the hotel without a casino, and within months it was put on the auction block. Several offers were made on the property during the next two years, but none panned out.

Enter Milton Prell, a man who made a name for himself when he built and ran the highly successful Sahara Hotel just a few blocks away. Prell had left Las Vegas in 1961 to run his own consulting firm in Beverly Hills, but returned a few years later, purchasing the dismal Tallyho for an estimated $16 million.

Prell transformed the English manor into a Middle Eastern oasis known as the Aladdin, a name that brings to mind magic and mystery. Prell worked some of his own magic on the hotel by renovating the existing rooms and public areas, adding a 500-seat theatre, a lounge, a 150-seat gourmet restaurant, and, of course, a casino. All of this was completed in the record time of just three months, so the hotel could make its midnight debut on April 1, 1966.

For more than three decades, the Aladdin has had a magical effect on the Las Vegas Strip, and any traces of the ill-fated Tallyho have long since vanished.

Famous Nuptials

When **Elvis Presley** decided to marry his longtime sweetheart **Priscilla**, it was Viva Las Vegas all the way! Elvis' manager, Colonel Tom Parker, oversaw the wedding preparations including the "everything pink" theme requested by the bride. Elvis had a long-standing friendship with Milton Prell, owner of the Aladdin, and decided to have his wedding in Prell's private hotel suite on May 1, 1967. Prell arranged for the couple to get their license at the county courthouse at 2 a.m. in order to avoid both a medley of fans and the paparazzi, but more than 10,000 fans descended on the hotel; at the last minute, a press room was set up for working media.

The bride, who wore a white empire dress, heavy eye make-up, and a bouffant-style 'do, was the poster child for '60s fashion, while the groom sported his signature coif. The couple recited their vows before a dozen family and friends, and after a few toasts and congratulations, the newlyweds boarded Frank Sinatra's private jet and headed back to their rented Palm Springs, California, home. Four weeks later, the two hosted a formal reception at the groom's Graceland home in Memphis, Tennessee.

Getting Married at The Aladdin

While there is no wedding chapel on the premises of the Aladdin, a mere drive down the famed Las Vegas Strip will reveal wedding chapel after wedding chapel, either free standing or within a neighboring hotel.

However, wedding ceremonies can still be enjoyed within the Aladdin's **Imperial Ballroom**, which divides into six separate areas to host both the wedding and a reception just next door. The ballroom, which can accommodate up to 500 guests, features crystal chandeliers, high ceilings, and a pre-reception area. **Salons A** through **D** are also available for weddings and receptions, offering similar appointments.

For impromptu wedding celebrations that require nothing more than a reservation, the Aladdin offers a number of restaurants. **Fisherman's Port** resembles a seaside setting with a menu to match; for a Far East getaway, **Sun Sun** specializes in Chinese, Vietnamese, and Korean fare; and, for a more formal setting, **Wellingtons** is a traditional steak house offering an assortment of prime cuts. The hotel also features a coffee shop, diner, and traditional Las Vegas-style buffet.

Honeymooning at The Aladdin

Arriving under an awning of millions of lights, honeymooners have to keep focused in order to reach their room at the Aladdin. At every turn there are dice rolling, wheels turning, and slots spinning, making it incredibly easy to get caught up in the frenzy when someone nearby bellows *jackpot*! However, the great thing about the Aladdin, as well as the rest of Las Vegas, is that it's a 24-hour playground, and the tables, slots, and other casino games will be there whenever the urge strikes.

The Aladdin rises 19 stories above the Strip and houses 1,100 rooms, including 42 suites, 29 lanai suites overlooking the swimming pool, two super suites, plus two penthouse suites. Standard rooms are adequately appointed with queen or king-sized beds and a small sitting area, and all rooms are soundproof so that the only noise that is audible is yours.

There are two outdoor pools for sunning and swimming, three lighted tennis courts, an arcade, a number of shops and, of course, the action-packed casino. In addition, there is live entertainment in the **Aladdin Lounge**, with as many as four different acts each week.

GOLDEN NUGGET

129 East Fremont Street
Las Vegas, NV 89125
800/634-3454
702/385-7111

Accommodations
$59-$375

Celebrity Guest Register

- *Demi Moore & Bruce Willis*
- Dean Martin
- Paul Anka
- Bob Hope
- Nicolas Cage

- Frank Sinatra
- Sammy Davis Jr.
- Judy Garland
- Eddie Fisher
- Liberace

A History

On a hot, balmy night in August 1946, the Golden Nugget opened its doors in what was then a little-known town in Nevada's Mojave desert.

Prior to the arrival of such establishments as the Golden Nugget, Las Vegas was nothing more than a dust bowl. That all changed in the mid-1940s, when a new era of tourism and opportunity was ushered in. The Golden Nugget, with its crystal chandeliers, imported marble floors, and a restaurant that served haute cuisine, was a dramatic departure from its neighboring rough and tumble sawdust joints that lined Fremont Street in the downtown district.

In those early years, the Golden Nugget was mainly a gambling hall for tourists and locals hoping to strike it rich with a roll of the dice, pull of a handle, or shuffle of the deck. In the early 1970s, the Golden Nugget began a metamorphosis from gambling hall to grand resort and casino with the addition of three hotel towers, a lavish spa and salon, and an array of culinary destinations. Although the action began to shift to the hipper area known as the Las Vegas Strip, the Golden Nugget remained a treasure for those who preferred the comforts of downtown.

While the Las Vegas Strip is still preferred by many of today's tourists, attention is once again being paid to the downtown area with the opening of the Fremont Street Experience, a four-block covered pedestrian walkway with a 90-foot high celestial vault centerpiece.

Throughout its 50-year history, the Golden Nugget has remained a pivotal icon of the ever-changing Las Vegas skyline.

Famous Nuptials

When actor **Bruce Willis** proposed marriage to actress **Demi Moore**, it was no indecent proposal. But when news broke of their spontaneous Las Vegas wedding, the Hollywood gossips were speechless. After all, Willis, the star of the action-adventure *Die Hard* movies, was the party boy of Hollywood, and Moore, the star of *About Last Night, Indecent Proposal,* and *A Few Good Men* was a bit more grounded. The two, who had dated a little more than a year, flew to Las Vegas for a boxing match, and at the last minute applied for a marriage license.

They were married on November 21, 1987, in Suite 7-A at the Golden Nugget, the same room they were staying in. The bride donned a purple Victorian dress and made her entrance from the suite's staircase; at the bottom awaited the anxious groom wearing a suit and t-shirt. A few weeks later they married again on a Hollywood sound stage; this time it was a more traditional affair with bridesmaids, a white wedding dress, and scores of friends to witness!

Getting Married at the Golden Nugget

While there are hordes of wedding chapels on nearly every corner, you won't find one inside the Golden Nugget. However, there are 12 banquet salons for celebrations of five to 500, which are popular locations for both weddings and receptions. The two most sought-after locations both overlook the tropical swimming pool area and provide a dynamic setting for toasting newlyweds. Each ballroom features crystal chandeliers, high ceilings, and mood lighting. Instead of a banquet room, weddings and receptions can be hosted inside a spacious suite a la Bruce and Demi.

The hotel also offers a number of dining options, including the Italian-countryside setting of **Stefano's** or the lively ambiance of **Lillie Langtry's**. More casual surroundings are enjoyed at the popular **California Pizza Kitchen**, the charming **Carson Street Cafe** and, of course, the **Buffet**, a Las Vegas tradition found at most any hotel and casino.

Honeymooning at the Golden Nugget

With a 36,000-square-foot casino open 24 hours a day, a Las Vegas honeymoon can be distracting for newlyweds. He likes the excitement of craps while she prefers the odds at blackjack, and both the bride and groom have spent the day in the company of a dealer rather than each other.

Fortunately, the Golden Nugget offers activities for spouses to enjoy together. **The Grand Court**, housed in the **Spa Tower**, is a relaxing spa that features whirlpool baths, massage rooms, and a grand whirlpool bath where exhausted newlyweds are able to rejuvenate. Tanning side-by-side can also be enjoyed at the hotel **swimming pool**, surrounded by lush palm trees.

Couples may choose to spend more time in their rooms rather than at the roulette table. The Golden Nugget offers 1,907 rooms – including one and two-bedroom suites, 27 luxury apartments, and six Penthouse Suites – sheltered under three towers. Rooms run the gamut from standard to stupendous, depending on the style chosen.

If you'd like to be pampered, register at the lavish Spa, where pedicures, massages, and mineral baths are just an elevator ride away!

> ## The Mirage Empire
> *At the tender age of 30, Steve Wynn, chairman of the board and chief executive officer of Mirage Resorts, was able to parlay his entrepreneurial dealings by entertaining a real estate transaction with the enigmatic Howard Hughes. The 1972 business deal allowed Wynn to begin a major investment with Golden Nugget, Inc., which owned the Golden Nugget and has since been reorganized under the umbrella corporation of Mirage Resorts. In addition to the Golden Nugget, Wynn's Las Vegas hotel and casino empire now include The Mirage, Treasure Island, Bellagio, and the Beau Rivage in Biloxi, Mississippi.*

RIVIERA HOTEL & CASINO

2901 Las Vegas Blvd. South
Las Vegas, NV 89109
800/634-6753
702/734-5110

Accommodations
$59-$300

Celebrity Guest Register

- *Tony Curtis*
- Natalie Cole
- David Copperfield
- Rodney Dangerfield
- Pauly Shore
- Barry Manilow
- Steve Martin
- Woody Allen
- Vikki Carr
- Harry Belafonte
- Liberace
- Jerry Seinfeld
- Garry Shandling
- Frank Sinatra
- Tony Bennett
- Dolly Parton
- Joan Rivers
- Olivia Newton-John
- Dean Martin
- Johnny Mathis
- Xavier Cugat
- Barbra Streisand

A History

When the new $10 million Riviera Hotel opened its doors on April 20, 1955, "I Like Ike" was the political catch phrase, a hip-swiveling Elvis Presley was about to make music history, and a flamboyant pianist with a flair for flash was slicing the ribbon on the new Las Vegas resort.

The resort was the town's first high-rise hotel boasting a nine-story tower, 300 guest rooms, and a neo-modern facade that contrasted with the town's typical frontier-style architecture, a trend which dominated the Las Vegas Strip at that time. The event drew rave reviews from Hollywood columnists, and with the opening, "no vacancy" signs hung at the entrance to every hotel and motel in the city. Although considered extremely modest by today's standards, the hotel casino was viewed as state-of-the-art with 18 gaming tables and 116 slot machines.

With a "keeping up with the Jones'" attitude presently sweeping Las Vegas, the Riviera has expanded considerably in order to compete with the newer and bigger themed-resort hotels and casinos. However, to the delight of many long-time visitors, the Riviera still retains a vintage Vegas charm.

Famous Nuptials

Actress Jamie Lee Curtis' papa, **Tony Curtis**, made a name for himself by appearing in hit films such as *Some Like It Hot*, *Spartacus*, and *Francis, The Talking Mule*. He and Jamie Lee's mother, actress Janet Leigh (*Psycho*), were quite the item before eventually divorcing *(see Waldorf-Astoria)*. He took another gamble on love and married **Christine Kaufman** on February 8, 1963, at the Riviera Hotel. When that marriage ended, he returned to Las Vegas in 1968 to try again at "happily ever after" with model Leslie Allen; the two exchanged vows at the Sahara Hotel and Casino.

Tie The Knot In America's Wedding Capital

The Riviera can assist with wedding and reception preparations. Since Las Vegas is considered to be America's "Wedding Capital," there is never a shortage of photographers, florists, limousine companies, and bridal boutiques nearby. The staff at the Riviera can recommend a number of services to complete your wedding preparations.

Getting Married at the Riviera

Las Vegas-style weddings tend to be impromptu events fueled by a combination of bright lights, high stakes, and the constant flow of adrenaline. When the mood strikes, the staff at the **Riviera Wedding Chapel** is prepared. The modest chapel seats up to 50 guests and offers all of the necessary services such as clergy, flowers, photography, and music.

Receptions require a bit more planning, and while the Riviera offers a number of banquet rooms, many appeal more to the conventioneer than the blushing bride. However, there are two rooms that are ideal for hosting a wedding reception: the **Grande Ballroom**, with its crystal chandeliers, expansive ceilings, and muted hues, is ideal for parties of up to 250, while the **Top of the Riv Ballroom** has panoramic views of the Las Vegas Strip – illuminated by millions of neon and glittering lights – creating a striking backdrop for evening weddings. The Top of the Riv Ballroom can accommodate up to 300 guests, and is miles above the noise of the casino!

For those who just wish to celebrate on a smaller scale in one of the hotel's restaurants, there are a number of choices. **Kristofer's**, with a Mediterranean motif, fine steaks, and seafood, is the Riviera's showpiece; **Ric' Shaw** offers casual dining with a Far East ambiance; and the quaint **Ristorante Italiano** captures the spirit of Italy both in ambiance and cuisine. The hotel also offers a food court, 24-hour coffee shop, a classic Vegas-style buffet, and three cocktail lounges.

Honeymooning at the Riviera

Positioned in the heart of the Las Vegas Strip, a Riviera honeymoon is sure to be filled with non-stop action!

There are 2,075 guest rooms including 158 suites located in the **Monte Carlo Tower, Monaco Tower, Mediterranean Tower North** and **South, San Remo Tower** and the **Beckett Wing.** Each tower offers an abundance of rooms, ranging from the nicely-appointed deluxe rooms to a spacious two-bedroom penthouse suite. As the only tower offering both a honeymoon suite and a fantasy suite, the Mediterranean Tower North will especially appeal to newlyweds.

In addition to 100,000 square feet of casino space, the hotel also features an Olympic-sized swimming pool with a pool deck lounge and courtyard, two lighted tennis courts, his and her's health spas and exercise rooms, an arcade of shops and live entertainment nightly.

Ol' Blue Eyes At The Riviera

Once again, Frank Sinatra did things his way when he filled in at the last minute for an under-the-weather Liza Minnelli back in 1980. The legendary crooner refused to accept any compensation from the hotel management for his three-day engagement, which would have netted him quite a sum!

17. New Mexico

THE BISHOP'S LODGE

Bishop's Lodge Road
(3 1/2 miles north of the Plaza)
Santa Fe, NM 87504
505/983-6377

Accommodations
$95-$435

Celebrity Guest Register
- *Phil Donahue*
- Oprah Winfrey
- Robert Conrad
- Michael Keaton
- Kris Kristofferson

- *Polly Draper*
- Shirley MacLaine
- Steven Seagal
- Tom Brokaw
- Michael Crichton

A History

The land on which the Bishop's Lodge sits, the Canoncito del Rio de Tesuque, can be traced back to 1540, when Francisco Vasques de Coronado led an expedition of Spanish conquistadors north from Mexico in search of the Seven Cities of Cibola. Instead of discovering a land made of gold, all they found were adobe Indian villages and pueblos stacked one on top of the other.

During the next three and a half centuries, the area would belong to various Mexican and Spanish owners. During the early 1850s, a young French missionary priest, Jean Baptiste Lamy, purchased a small piece of land along the Little Tesuque stream, just a few miles north of Santa Fe. An irrigation system was already in place and the land was rich for producing crops. The lodge – Villa Pintoresca – was built on a small hill that overlooked the desert plains, and the result was a blend of traditional Hispanic New Mexican architecture and old world European design.

Adobe walls were laid upon stone foundations and were sealed with mud plaster; wooden gables jetted out of the shingled, pitched roof; and a graceful steeple bearing a humble wooden cross atop its spire rose above the roof.

When Lamy died in 1888, the Catholic Church retained ownership until 1909, when Archbishop John B. Pitaval sold the 152.8 acres stipulating that the chapel was to be maintained by the new owner at his own expense for the use and benefit of the resident Catholics to worship.

On June 5, 1915, members of the famous Pulitzer publishing company bought the ranch and added two new lodges and a carriage house. Three years later, James R. Thorpe purchased the ranch and formed The Bishop's Lodge Corporation, and Lamy's retreat was transformed into an elegant resort.

The Bishop's Lodge, still owned and operated by the Thorpe family, has retained its charm from the days of Jean Baptiste Lamy. It is a first-class resort for those seeking seclusion.

Celebrated Honeymoons

Phil Donahue, former talk show host and author, married first wife **Margaret Cooney** in 1958. The wedding took place in Albuquerque, New Mexico, and friends and family gathered at the nearby Alvarado Hotel to celebrate. Afterwards the new Mr. and Mrs. Donahue motored to Santa Fe for a honeymoon at The Bishop's Lodge.

Polly Draper, who played the career-minded Ellen on the television drama *thirtysomething*, also honeymooned at The Bishop's Lodge with her bridegroom, **Michael Wolfe**.

Getting Married at The Bishop's Lodge

There are no limits to planning a wedding at The Bishop's Lodge. Ceremonies are performed in a number of unique places, including the original **Chapel** built by Bishop Lamy. A winding stone staircase leads to the unimposing Chapel, whose doors open up to reveal a modest altar. The Chapel provides an intimate setting for groups of 12. The covered **Verandah**, located just beyond the Chapel's doors, is surrounded by a number of fruit trees and lilac bushes and can host up to 50 guests. There are a number of natural settings throughout the property, and ceremonies are even performed on horseback!

Receptions run the gamut at The Bishop's Lodge, from rustic to refined. The **Main Lodge** houses four reception rooms, including the **Thunderbird Room**, featuring a high ceiling and a grand copper-hooded fireplace, for groups up to 175. Carved woods, freesias, and expansive windows grace the elegant **Sunset Room**, which can accommodate groups of up to 85. The light and airy **Main Dining Room**, ideal for groups of up to 85, features a high-beamed ceiling, suspended lanterns, a copper-hooded fireplace, and life-size murals. With a wood-beamed ceiling, Mexican lanterns made from tin and a wooden balustrade, **El Charro** offers intimate surroundings for groups of 75. Situated in a valley surrounded by towering trees is the **Pool Terrace and Deck** for groups of up to 300. A canopy covers the adjacent lawn for buffet-style receptions while cozy tables encircle the swimming pool, which is illuminated in the evening with an array of floating candles.

There are a number of secluded outdoor areas that are equally enchanting. For reenacting the days of the Old West, casual gatherings are a natural at the **Mesa Vista**, where guests dine on redwood picnic tables that overlook the mountains. Mesa Vista can accommodate up to 175 guests. Raised high above the ground overlooking the nearby mountains and desert plains, guests socialize under umbrella-covered tables on the **Firelight Terrace**, available for groups of 125.

The Bishop's Lodge Restaurant is the only restaurant on the premises and is open for breakfast, lunch, and dinner. The restaurant is ideal for gathering with family and friends on the eve of the wedding to enjoy authentic Southwestern fare. Afterwards, retreat to **El Rincon**, a delightful, al fresco corner bar offering sunset views.

For brides and grooms who need to unwind, the staff will even arrange for a relaxing pre-wedding massage!

Honeymooning at The Bishop's Lodge

Located just three miles from Santa Fe's landmark Plaza, The Bishop's Lodge offers honeymooners secluded country charm in the shadows of lovely Santa Fe. Located on 1,000 acres of rolling piñon and juniper foothills, the property is blanketed with tall cottonwoods and towering oak trees and is adjacent to the Santa Fe National Forest.

Eleven buildings, which are scattered throughout the property, shelter the 68 guest rooms and 20 suites. The **North** and **South Lodges** are the oldest, dating back before World War I; the remaining nine lodges have been added throughout the years with the most recent addition in 1994. Rooms vary with amenities and may include sitting areas, fireplaces, patios, decks or wet bars. There are a number of seasonal activities available for couples who enjoy the great outdoors, including horseback riding, tennis, skeet and trap shooting, and nature walks. The lodge also offers a heated outdoor swimming pool, an indoor whirlpool and sauna, and an exercise room.

The lodge offers both the **European Plan** (accommodations only) and the **Modified American Plan** (breakfast with a choice of lunch or dinner) for those who never desire to wander elsewhere!

The Bishop's Story

Willa Cather's novel, Death Comes For The Archbishop, depicts the life of The Bishop Lodge's original owner, Bishop Jean Baptiste Lamy.

LA FONDA

On The Plaza
100 E. San Francisco
Santa Fe, NM
800/523-5002
505/982-5511

Accommodations
$174-$500

Celebrity Guest Register

- *Zsa Zsa Gabor & Conrad Hilton*
- Tommy Lee Jones
- Goldie Hawn & Kurt Russell
- Matthew Broderick
- Christopher Lloyd
- Mickey Rourke
- Gene Hackman
- Lou Diamond Phillips
- Jack Palance
- Jacqueline Kennedy Onassis
- President George Bush
- Matt Dillon
- Vincent Price
- Demi Moore
- Eileen Brennan
- Larry Hagman
- Diane Keaton
- Shirley MacLaine
- Jane Fonda
- Willem DeFoe
- Richard Chamberlain
- Robert De Niro

A History

When the town of Santa Fe was officially founded in the early 1600s, an inn – or *fonda* – was already established. Two centuries later, Captain William Becknell completed his first successful trading expedition from Missouri to Sante Fe, which marked the beginning of the commerce route commonly known as the Santa Fe Trail. As he and the other trappers, traders, mountain men, soldiers, gamblers and opportunists journeyed west across the desert plains, there was always an empty bed and warm hospitality waiting for them at the hotel, located literally at the end of the trail.

The original structure, which had many names during its history, burned to the ground in 1913. Seven years later architect Isaac Hamilton

Rapp designed a new hotel in the Pueblo Revival style, and the inn opened on December 30, 1922. The first few years of operation were a struggle, but by 1928 it was evident that an expansion was necessary to accommodate the many guests who flocked to the hotel.

The Fred Harvey organization, operators of La Fonda, hired architect John Gaw Meem to expand and renovate the property. At the same time, Mary Colter, a renowned designer best known for her work at the Grand Canyon's El Tovar, was commissioned to refurbish the hotel in the Southwestern style. Her authentic touches – tin and glass light fixtures, Navajo blankets, Spanish serapes, pueblo pottery and Apache blankets – still dominate the interior of La Fonda, creating a distinctive style emulated by contemporary designers throughout the world.

While names, structures, and interiors have taken on different forms during the hotel's history, the changing hues that dramatically tinge the skies and nearby mountain ranges at sunrise and sunset have remained constant. La Fonda offers an historic setting enhanced by Southwestern influences, and is a perfect place for couples to begin their life together "at the end of the Santa Fe Trail."

Famous Nuptials

Zsa Zsa Gabor and hotel tycoon **Conrad Hilton** were married during a civil ceremony before a Santa Fe judge in April 1942, just a few months after being introduced at the famed Ciro's restaurant in Los Angeles. After the brief nuptials, the newlyweds enjoyed a lavish reception at La Fonda before jetting off to Chicago for their honeymoon.

Getting Married at La Fonda

A wedding at La Fonda is not only a celebration of love, it's a celebration of Southwestern heritage. The **Ballroom** and **banquet salons** pay homage to the Native Americans that once roamed the plains. Each room takes on the feel of its own individual style with such features as kiva fireplaces, carved corbels, sand-painted ceiling murals, Native American artwork, handmade tin and stained glass chandeliers, just to name a few.

The Ballroom can be divided into two separate areas, one for wedding ceremonies and the other for receptions. For large receptions, the Ballroom can be opened up to create one salon, and can accommodate up to 750 guests. Smaller venues include the **New Mexican Room**, which holds up to 200 guests; the **Santa Fe Room**, with its Spanish tile floor, is ideal for pre-reception cocktails of 100; the **Stiha Room**, which can host groups of 70; and the **Coronado Room**, which is ideal for small ceremonies of 60 or less.

La Plazuela is an ideal spot for rehearsal dinners and features a skylit courtyard, festive color scheme, and authentic New Mexican cuisine. The open-air **Bell Tower Bar**, located on the rooftop, offers magnificent vistas of the mountains, and is a perfect spot for couples to enjoy some stress-free time together.

Honeymooning at La Fonda

La Fonda offers honeymooners a choice of 153 guest rooms and suites, each uniquely appointed. While each room offers authentic touches such as colorful hand-decorated wooden furniture, paintings by local Pueblo Indian artists, balconies, arched adobe doorways and fireplaces, no two rooms are identical. The carved details and embellishments around all the wooden doors and windows were done decades before by a passing wood carver who lent his craftsmanship to the hotel in exchange for room and board.

Jackie O At La Fonda

*Whether Jackie Kennedy Onassis wanted attention or not, she always managed to captivate those around her, even while performing the most mundane tasks. While lunching at La Fonda's **French Pastry Shop** during the 1980s, Jackie appeared to be the only one enjoying her meal; it seemed everyone else's food grew cold as they sat entranced by her presence.*

18. New York

THE ALGONQUIN HOTEL
59 West 44th Street
New York, NY 10036
800/228-3000
212/840-6800

Accommodations
$245-$600

Celebrity Guest Register
- *Orson Welles*
- Maya Angelou
- Douglas Fairbanks, Sr. & Jr.
- Barbra Streisand
- Helen Hayes
- Angela Lansbury
- Anthony Hopkins
- Harry Connick, Jr.
- Boris Karloff
- Jeremy Irons
- Ella Fitzgerald
- Brooke Shields
- Glenn Close
- Geena Davis
- Ethel Barrymore
- Susan Sarandon
- Gore Vidal
- Liza Minnelli
- Laurence Olivier
- Sinclair Lewis

A History

On November 22, 1902, a small hotel built of red brick and limestone opened its doors at one of the most toniest addresses New York City had to offer. For a few years it was known as The Puritan, but that changed in 1907 when legendary manager Frank Case bought the place. He felt the hotel's name evoked a strait-laced, dull image, and immediatley replaced it with a name he felt was more indigenous to the American culture. The Algonquin Hotel was born.

Case played a pivotal role in positioning the hotel at the core of New York's literary and theatrical life. He was fond of actors and writers, and welcomed women guests from the beginning, while other establishments shunned female clientele. Three Nobel laureates were regular guests at The Algonquin: Sinclair Lewis, who offered to buy the place; William Faulkner, who drafted his Nobel acceptance speech at the hotel in 1950; and most recently Derek Walcott.

The famous Algonquin Round Table, established by *Vanity Fair* writers Dorothy Parker, Robert Benchley, and Robert E. Sherwood, set the standard for literary style and wit, influencing such young writers as Fitzgerald and Hemingway. Arnold Ross, legendary editor and friend of the Round Table, launched *The New Yorker* magazine on February 21, 1925, with funding he secured through contacts he met at the hotel.

Today, nearing a century since its opening, The Algonquin Hotel still captivates the rich, the famous, and the up and coming, and sports as much personality as the many guests who have entered its doors.

Celebrated Honeymoons

When **Orson Welles** married **Virginia Fall** in 1934, he was a talented unemployed actor. The two young lovers secretly eloped without either of their parents' knowledge. When the bride's father was informed days later, a New Jersey church wedding was immediately staged. After the celebration, young Orson Welles and his new wife headed across the river to New York City, where they spent their wedding night at The Algonquin Hotel.

Getting Married at The Algonquin Hotel

The Algonquin Hotel is a New York City landmark, and offers a unique ambiance for exchanging vows and hosting receptions. Whether it's a celebration for 20 or 120, at The Algonquin yours will be the only event taking place.

The hotel offers three private function areas for weddings and receptions. Both **The Helen Hayes Room**, named for the famous actress, and **The Library**, welcome intimate groups of 20 or less. Each room resembles a study with rich wood paneling and plush carpeting, and are perfect for smaller celebrations or rehearsal dinners. **The Gallery** features understated elegance with crown molding, gold framed mirrors, and a wood-burning fireplace and can accommodate up to 150 guests.

Fine linen, rich brocade, and sparkling crystal are hallmarks of **The Rose Room**, the restaurant where the famous Algonquin Round Table congregated. The Rose Room is open daily for dinner, and is an ideal gathering spot for family introductions and rehearsal dinners. **The Oak Room** is a lunch venue by day and a sophisticated cabaret by night, and an excellent spot for unwinding with out-of-town guests over dinner and live music. **The Blue Bar** is an ideal spot to grab cocktails and appetizers, while the hotel **Lobby** provides conversational settings ideal for finalizing last-minute details while lingering over a cup of coffee or tea.

Honeymooning at The Algonquin Hotel

The Algonquin Hotel is for couples with an appreciation for charm and nostalgia. Located in the heart of midtown Manhattan, it's just a short walk to such New York attractions as Times Square, Rockefeller Center, the savvy Fifth Avenue Shops, and the Broadway theaters.

Upon check-in, guests are greeted by Matilda, the resident cat, who meanders throughout the lobby. There are 142 guest rooms and 23 suites, evoking memories of an English country home with large armoires and window seats overlooking the city. The one and two bedroom suites feature foyers and living areas, and include memorabilia related to the hotel's many famous guests, from Dorothy Parker to James Thurber.

All guests are treated to a complimentary continental breakfast in the lobby plus a copy of – what else – *The New Yorker!*

The Musicians' & Writers' Choice!

The Algonquin has been a haven for literati and musicians since its opening day. Alan Jay Lerner and Frederick Loewe are credited with writing "My Fair Lady" at the hotel, and New York City was treated to the talents of Harry Connick, Jr. when he made his cabaret debut at The Algonquin in 1989.

THE PLAZA HOTEL

768 Fifth Avenue at Central Park South
New York, NY 10019
800/527-4727
212/759-3000

Accommodations
$260-$15,000

Celebrity Guest Register

- *Eddie Murphy*
- Howard Stern
- Barbra Streisand
- Paul McCartney
- Ernest Hemingway

- *Donald Trump & Marla Maples*
- Brooke Shields
- Elizabeth Taylor
- George Harrison
- F. Scott Fitzgerald

- Robert Redford
- Liza Minnelli
- Macaulay Culkin
- Chris O'Donnell
- Frank Lloyd Wright

- Jane Fonda
- George M. Cohan
- Al Pacino
- Richard Gere
- Alfred Hitchcock

A History

The Plaza Hotel is perhaps as much a New York landmark as the Statue of Liberty.

The original Plaza Hotel opened in 1890 on the former site of the New York Skating Club. In 1905 the property was jointly purchased by financier Bernhard Beinecke, hotelier Fred Sterry, and Harry S. Black, the president of Fuller Construction Company. Their immediate plans for the hotel became evident when the 15-year-old Plaza was quickly demolished in order to make room for a larger and grander Plaza Hotel.

The trio commissioned renowned architect Henry James Hardenbergh to design The Plaza with all the prestige and glory of a French Chateau. In the meantime, Beinecke, Sterry, and Black headed to Europe to scour the continent in search of the finest furniture, accessories, and adornments in which to properly furnish New York's grandest hotel. Their purchases included, among other things, sleek marble slabs to coat the lobby floor, exclusively designed Irish linens, and Swiss embroidered organdy curtains. They also placed the largest single order in history for gold-encrusted china from L. Straus & Sons and purchased more than 1,650 crystal chandeliers! When the new Plaza Hotel opened in 1907, people gasped at the final $12 million price tag, a staggering sum for the era.

When the hotel opened its doors, 90 percent of its guests were permanent residents who enjoyed the luxury of having both an urban dwelling and a country manor. The very first residents to sign the register and occupy their own suite of rooms were the very wealthy Mr. and Mrs. Alfred Gwynne Vanderbilt. Eventually the focus shifted more towards short-term stays as dignataries and debutantes, famous and infamous checked in to the swank surroundings afforded by The Plaza.

In the last 90 years, the hotel has gone through several owners, including the imposing Conrad Hilton as well as yuppie tycoon Donald Trump. With its French Renaissance design and exclusive Fifth Avenue address, The Plaza remains a New York City landmark and is one of the last elegant buildings from its era.

Famous Nuptials

When you're the bride of millionaire **Donald Trump**, the word "budget" is seldom part of your vocabulary. Just ask former model **Marla**

Maples who became Mrs. Donald Trump on December 20, 1993, at her husband's Plaza Hotel. The guest list included 1,000 of the couple's closest friends and associates; the menu consisted of medallions of lobster, beluga caviar, and rack of lamb; the nine-tier, 6 1/2 foot high wedding cake was covered in sugar ivy vines, roses, lilies and other candy flora; and the bride donned a flawless 20-carat pear-shaped tiarra courtesy of Harry Winston Jewels! The ceremony took place in the elegant Grand Ballroom, with the reception and celebration spilling onto the Terrace Room and Palm Court.

Eddie Murphy may have played a pseudo *Beverly Hills Cop* in the movie by the same name, but when it came time to tie the knot, he was definitely a New York City groom. He and model **Nicole Mitchell** married on March 18, 1993, inside the Grand Ballroom of the Plaza Hotel. The bride wore a traditional off-the-shoulder white gown, but later changed into a body-hugging sequined dress for the reception, which took place in the Terrace Room and Palm Court. The guest list included more than 600 family, friends, and celebrity guests.

Getting Married at The Plaza

When it comes to weddings and receptions, nothing is more grand than a Plaza celebration. Brides seeking simplicity should look elsewhere, for nothing at The Plaza is without embellishment, from the decor to the food presentation.

There are five magnificent ballrooms capable of accommodating anywhere from five to 1000 guests. The **Grand Ballroom**, the hotel's pièce de résistance, is lavish. The salon features an extraordinarily high ceiling adorned with a single, yet very ornate, crystal chandelier; colonnades festooned with billowy drapes; a center balustrade that divides at the parquet dance floor; and gilded accents throughout. The remaining four salons – **Baroque Room**, **Terrace Room**, **White and Gold Room**, and **Louis XV Room** – are each regally appointed with silk wall coverings and murals, antique crystal chandeliers, gilded accents, and sweeping ceilings.

For pre-nuptial celebrations, The Plaza provides an elegant backdrop for even the most simple of gatherings. **The Edwardian Room**, named for its turn-of-the-century decor, offers a sophisticated setting coupled with a classical dinner menu, while **The Oak Room** is reminiscent of a 1930s men's club with a steak and chops menu to match. People watching is a favorite pastime at **The Palm Court**, where New York's finest gather to enjoy live classical music over Sunday brunch and afternoon tea. **The Oyster Bar**, with an English pub feel, offers a casual atmosphere for lunch and dinner. For after-dinner drinks, **The Oak Bar** is a favorite watering hole for theater goers and literary types.

Honeymooning at The Plaza

A Plaza honeymoon is a sophisticated retreat steeped not only in history, but luxury as well. Looming 19 stories above New York's famed Central Park, The Plaza features more than 805 French-style rooms, 96 suites and 16 ultra-deluxe suites. Among the hotel's grandest accommodations – not to mention the most expensive – are those suites which have been named for their famous occupants: the **Vanderbilt Suite**, **Astor Suite**, and **Frank Lloyd Wright Suite** (he lived in this room for six years, from 1953-1959, during the construction of the Guggenheim Museum).

The Plaza's Film Credits

In 1958, when director Alfred Hitchcock began shooting "North by Northwest" in the Plaza's Oak Bar, it marked the hotel's entrance into the movies. Since making its movie debut, The Plaza has been the backdrop for countless films, including "The Way We Were," "The Great Gatsby," "Funny Girl," "Scent of a Woman," "Cotton Club," "Barefoot in the Park," "Plaza Suite," "Arthur," "Home Alone II," both "Crocodile Dundee" movies – just to name a few.

THE RITZ-CARLTON, NEW YORK

112 Central Park South
New York, NY 10019
800/241-3333
212/757-1900

Accommodations
$325-$4,000

Celebrity Guest Register

- *Liam Neeson & Natasha Richardson*
- *Douglas Fairbanks & Mary Pickford*
- Warren Beatty
- Barbra Streisand
- Bono
- Mick Jagger
- David Letterman
- Jim Carrey
- Bette Midler
- Kim Basinger
- Johnny Depp
- *John Barrymore*
- Brooke Shields
- Steve Martin
- Geena Davis
- Jerry Garcia
- Vanessa Williams
- Mel Gibson
- Christian Slater
- Roseanne
- Winona Ryder
- Al Pacino

A History

Celebrated Europen hotelier Cesar Ritz crossed the Atlantic in 1910 to open his first American property, the famed Ritz-Carlton in Manhattan. With first-class accommodations, blueblood guests, and a host of gala events, it was to many the "miracle on 46th Street" and Madison Avenue. The Ritz-Carlton, New York, didn't follow trends, it set them! In fact, Chef Louis Diat invented the popular potato and leek soup, Vichyssoise, at this address. After World War II, the hotel closed, and eventually the building was razed in the early 1950s. It would be more than three decades before The Ritz-Carlton carved another niche in the Big Apple.

In 1982, The Ritz-Carlton, New York, opened at the former site of The Navarro Hotel on Central Park South. The building was once the home of Consul General de Navarro of Spain. During the 1920s, the building expanded upward and opened as an apartment hotel in 1928. It would remain The Navarro Hotel for the next 54 years before being transformed into the elegant Ritz-Carlton.

Today, The Ritz-Carlton, New York, emulates the standards set by its founder, Cesar Ritz. Guests are given the highest level of service and comfort at one of New York City's most prestigious addresses.

Famous Nuptials

John Barrymore, grandfather of Drew Barrymore and a member of one of the greatest acting families of all time, married poet **Michael Strange** at The Ritz-Carlton, New York, in 1921. The only guests present were the groom's famous siblings, Lionel and Ethel Barrymore.

Famous Honeymooners

During the 1920s, **Mary Pickford** and **Douglas Fairbanks** were equivalent to, if not more famous than, Bruce Willis and Demi Moore, Maria Shriver and Arnold Schwarzenegger or Tom Cruise and Nicole Kidman. Wherever they went, the press hounded them and they were always willing to oblige as was expected of stars from their era. When the two married in 1920, they spent a couple of days at The Ritz-Carlton, New York, before departing on a European honeymoon.

Celebrated Occasions

Irish-born actor **Liam Neeson** was once considered one of Hollywood's most eligble bachelors. Best known for his portrayal of Oscar Shindler in the Academy Award-winning film, *Shindler's List*, Neeson kept company with many beautiful women. However, only actress **Natasha Richardson** managed to capture his heart for good. The two attended an engagement party in their honor at The Ritz-Carlton, New York, which was attended by many of Hollywood's "A" list.

Shortly before the big day, Richardson was treated to a surpirse bridal shower also hosted at The Ritz-Carlton, New York. Guests included Mia Farrow and the bride's mum, British actress Vanessa Redgrave, plus a few other celebrity chums.

Getting Married at The Ritz-Carlton, New York

The Ritz-Carlton, New York, is ideally suited for small, elegant affairs. The name alone guarantees the highest level of service as well as the poshest of surroundings.

The hotel offers four private function areas for weddings and receptions for gatherings of 10 to 150. **The Ritz-Carlton Suite**, located on the 23rd floor, is larger than most homes and can accommodate up to 50 people. Elegantly-appointed with a marble foyer and a fireplace, there's also a separate living room and dining room, four balconies which overlook Central Park, and a separate pantry. A few floors down on the 16th floor is **The Club**, with a wrap-around balcony, panoramic city views, and a cozy fireplace. The living room-style setting creates a warm yet refined ambiance and can accommodate up to 60 guests. **The Park Suites**, located on the second floor, boasts large picture windows that frame Central Park, and can hold up to 70 guests.

Fantino, the hotel's award-winning restaurant, serves contemporary Italian cuisine, making it an ideal choice for rehearsal dinners. The bistro features traditional European decor and is enhanced with two fireplaces and tables adorned with china designed by the late Gianni Versace. With enough room for 150 guests, it shouldn't be overlooked for wedding receptions and ceremonies. The **Fantino Bar** is a wonderful spot to mingle after the rehearsal dinner, and is located adjacent to the restaurant.

New York's Ritzy Honeymoon Deal

The Special Occasion Honeymoon Weekend Package, priced at $745 per night, includes overnight accommodations in a suite overlooking Central Park, a bottle of Ritz champagne with two Ritz-Carlton champagne flutes to toast, chocolate covered strawberries, continental breakfast, valet parking and use of The Fitness Center.

Honeymooning at The Ritz-Carlton, New York

The Ritz-Carlton, New York, is considered the hub of sophistication. Travel 15 minutes in any direction, and you'll arrive at some of the world's most renowned museums, cultural centers, and exclusive shopping districts.

The Ritz-Carlton, New York, houses 214 guest rooms, including 10 one and two-bedroom suites, plus an on-site fitness center. Traditional European decor creates an understated elegance that has become the hallmark of The Ritz-Carlton empire. Many rooms offer breathtaking views of Central Park as well as the unmistakable New York City skyline, and many offer Italian marble bathrooms and his and her matching terry cloth robes. The **Ritz-Carlton Suite** offers the ultimate in privacy with its own separate elevator key access.

Where The Boss Toasts His Anniversary

Who would have guessed that America's blue-collered crooner, Bruce Springsteen, is also a romantic at heart? The Boss and his wife, former E Street Band back-up singer Patti Scalfia, were spotted enjoying an anniversary champagne toast in the hotel's bar.

THE ST. REGIS
2 East 55th St. at Fifth Avenue
New York, NY 10022
800/759-4500
212/753-4500

Accommodations
$455-5,000

Celebrity Guest Register
• *Lorraine Bracco & Edward James Olmos*
• *Michael Kennedy & Vicki Gifford*
• Frank Gifford
• Mary Pickford & Douglas Fairbanks
• Jackie Kennedy Onassis
• *Faye Wray*
• Salvador Dali
• Howard Cosell
• Marlene Dietrich
• Cecil Beaton

A History
When millionaire John Jacob Astor opened The St. Regis Hotel in 1904, it was the tallest building to grace the New York City skyline. Designed in the Beaux Arts fashion, the 18-story building was hailed by *The Architectural Record* as "a new and higher standard for the construction and decoration of hotels."

It was not uncommon in those days for the wealthy to occupy suites of rooms at upscale hotels for their city dwelling, while maintaining a country estate for weekend entertaining. Astor, a blueblood by birth, catered to this sophisticated way of life and made sure his guests wanted for nothing. The rooms were filled with priceless antiques, European tapestries, Oriental rugs, and anything else that reeked of money and taste.

In 1927, a new wing was added, making The St. Regis even more grand – a task some thought impossible. As the hotel approaches its centennial anniversary, it has undeniably retained its elegant stature as one of New York City's premier hotels.

Famous Nuptials

In March 1981, **Michael Kennedy**, son of Ethel and the late Robert Kennedy, married **Vicki Gifford**, daughter of football great turned commentator Frank Gifford, at St. Ignatius Loyola Roman Catholic Church in Manhattan. Afterwards, a lavish reception for 200 was held on the The St. Regis Roof and included the groom's aunt, Jackie Kennedy Onassis, along with the rest of the Kennedy clan. A sentimental touch came when the groom toasted his bride with a goblet borrowed from his parents' 1950 wedding. Later, the new Mr. and Mrs. Michael Kennedy enjoyed a honeymoon in Sun Valley, Idaho, and Tahiti.

Other famous St. Regis brides and grooms include the union of actress **Lorraine Bracco**, star of *Goodfellas,* and actor/activist **Edward James Olmos**, star of *American Me* and *Blade Runner,* on January 28, 1994. **Faye Wray**, best-known as the damsel in distress in the original *King Kong,* also married at the hotel in the 1940s.

Getting Married at The St. Regis

With such an opulent setting, The St. Regis provides the perfect locale for elegant celebrations. There are an array of exquisite salons that provide a breathtaking backdrop for both wedding ceremonies and receptions.

A tromp l'oeil painting featuring white clouds against a radiant blue sky make the ceiling of **The St. Regis Roof** seem almost transparent. Magnificent chandeliers hang suspended from the ceiling while paned French doors open onto a terrace that overlooks the city below. The St. Regis Roof, located on the 20th floor of the hotel, can accommodate groups of up to 500 for cocktails or 250 for a dinner dance. The second floor of the hotel features a number of ballrooms and small salons, including the two **Louis XVI Suites**, which are flanked in dark, rich wood offset by gleaming crystal chandeliers. Separately, the rooms can host from 30 to 125 people; when combined the suites can hold 200.

The regally-appointed **Versailles Room**, available for groups of up to 250, mimics a palace setting with a hand-carved ceiling, gilded embellishments, and ornate chandeliers. Rich woods, stacked bookshelves, and a roaring fireplace are hallmarks of the **Library**, an intimate salon that can accommodate up to 80 guests. Adorned in Louis XIV furnishings, the ornate **Fontainebleau Room** awaits the elegant bride with brilliant crystal chandeliers and dramatically high ceilings. The salon can accommodate up to 200 guests, and an equally elegant foyer sets the mood for cocktail hour.

Rehearsal dinners are nothing less than spectacular at the award-winning **Lespinasse**. Best described as understated elegance, the restaurant features cream-colored walls and Louis XIV-style decor. It is one of the best (and most expensive) restaurants in New York. The stately **King Cole Bar and Lounge**, where the Bloody Mary originated, is perfect for after-dinner drinks and cigars. Tea and crumpets arrive on Limoges China and Tiffany & Co. silver at **The Astor Court**, an elegant setting for gathering with bridesmaids.

Where weddings are concerned, no detail is left to chance at The St. Regis. Every couple is assigned an attentive wedding coordinator to see to the major and minor details, and a number of excellent sources are available through the hotel.

Honeymooning at The St. Regis

Summoning a butler at any hour of the night is a skill honed by the very rich – and those who stay at The St. Regis. Most folks have never actually encountered a maître d'étage, the French pronunciation for butler, yet after having one at your disposal 24 hours a day at The St. Regis, it's quite easy to get accustomed to! A butler performs any task requested, from uncorking a bottle of Dom Perignon at midnight to pouring the first cup of coffee of the day, all while wearing white glove and tails!

Aside from the extraordinarily attentive service, there are 222 rooms and 91 suites soaring 20 stories above Manhattan. Each room is spacious in size with silk wall coverings, mahogany furnishings, fresh-cut flowers, and picturesque windows. The bathrooms resemble small apartments with sleek Italian marble, gold fixtures, and a bathtub and shower with room enough for two.

Could The Guests Have Been His Inspiration?

Salvador Dali, renowned artist of the surrealist movement, made his home at The St. Regis for nearly 25 years.

TARRYTOWN HOUSE
East Sunnyside Lane
Tarrytown, NY 10591
800/553-8118
914/591-8200

Accommodations
$99-$149

Celebrity Guest Register
- *Bonnie Raitt & Michael O'Keefe*
- Paul Newman
- Steven Spielberg
- Bette Davis
- Burt Reynolds
- Jack Lemmon
- Kirk Douglas
- Woody Allen
- Christopher Reeve
- Gregory Peck
- Burt Lancaster
- Raquel Welch
- Sylvester Stallone

A History
The sprawling grounds of Tarrytown House conjure up images of afternoon croquet parties, debutante balls, and a refined society that has long since vanished. Within the gates of Tarrytown House, this forgotten lifestyle has been triumphantly recaptured.

Tarrytown House is actually comprised of two magnificent mansions: the **King House** and the **Biddle Mansion**. The King House, the smaller of the two mansions, is a white columned Georgian Revival home built in 1840. In 1900, the Vice President of the Baltimore and Ohio Railroad Company, Thomas M. King, bought the mansion, which still bears his name more than a century later. The neighboring estate, now referred to as the Biddle Mansion, was built during the same era, and at one time both estates shared the same owner. In 1905, William R. Harris, founder of the American Tobacco Company, took possession of the stone mansion and spent the next seven years rebuilding the estate using granite taken from the nearby hills.

Eventually the two neighbors would become in-laws when Thomas King's son, Frederick, married William Harris' daughter, Sybil; the newlyweds resided at the King House until Sybil's death in 1955. Harris sold the stone mansion to tobacco heiress Mary Duke Biddle in 1921, and it soon became the gathering spot for New York society. After Biddle's death in 1960, both mansions were used as a consulate for the Republic of Mali.

The estates of Tarrytown House, which now include additional buildings for hotel and conference use, share the 26 acres along the

Hudson River and can be savored by those who have a taste for the good life, but not the budget!

Famous Nuptials

Grammy Award-winning singer **Bonnie Raitt** married actor **Michael O'Keefe** (*The Great Santini, The Slugger's Wife*) in May 1991, at the Union Church in nearby Pocantico Hills. The bride, dressed in a traditional wedding gown, was given away by her father, stage actor John Raitt, who donned a Scottish kilt for the occasion. After the ceremony, the bride and groom were introduced to their guests as "Mr. & Mrs." at Tarrytown House. Guests included Daryl Hannah, Wynonna Judd, and Jackson Browne.

Celebrated Honeymoons

Bonnie Raitt and **Michael O'Keefe** didn't have to travel far to find privacy on their wedding night. After bidding guests farewell, the newly-weds retreated to their charming suite in the King House at Tarrytown.

Getting Married at Tarrytown House

With two magnificent estates as a backdrop, weddings at Tarrytown House recall the era of the Great Gatsby.

The **King House** offers four intimate salons for weddings, ceremonies, and receptions, each appointed with elegant furnishings reflecting the stately Georgian Revival architecture of the mid-1800s. Hues of navy, burgundy, and gold create an elegant motif throughout and gracefully complement the ornately paneled libraries and 19th-century salons. A series of paned windows and French doors overlook the cultivated grounds. The **Grand Salon**, the largest of the mansion's public rooms, can accommodate up to 40 guests; the **Library**, **Manor**, and **Butler** salons can accommodate from 10-24 guests. The **Outside Terrace**, which encircles the mansion, provides an elegant setting for exchanging vows or hosting pre-reception cocktails.

The **Biddle Mansion** is truly the centerpiece of Tarrytown House. With its stone exterior and manicured grounds, The Mansion boasts four elegant venues for intimate dining or receptions. The **Mary Duke Ballroom**, an addition built in 1994, complements the original 19th-century structure with 12-foot windows, a roaring fireplace and a spiral staircase, and is perfect for galas of up to 350 guests. The **Winter Palace** can host up to 175 guests, and features floor-to-ceiling windows, a raised marble dance floor and expansive outdoor terraces. The adjoining **West Terrace** overlooks the Hudson River, and is an ideal choice, weather permitting, for ceremonies or cocktail receptions. Elegant wall sconces frame a wood-burning fireplace inside the elegant **Garden Room**, which can accommodate up to 56 guests; the **Music Room** also features a cozy fireplace, crystal chandelier, and muted hues for groups of 48; and the **Sun Porch**, perhaps the most charming of all the salons, allows guests to view the gardens and Hudson River through floor-to-ceiling paned-glass windows. The Sun Porch can house up to 45 guests, and would be an ideal choice for brisk or rainy days.

Wedding ceremonies may also be held al fresco on the estate's grounds. Packages are available and can be tailored to create the wedding of your dreams.

Honeymooning at Tarrytown House

Staying at Tarrytown House is like accepting a weekend invitation at a country estate.

In order for newlyweds to reach their room, first they must drive through the soaring iron gates, pass the carriage house, and meander through the grounds before arriving at their door. There are 138 guest rooms housed in modern structures that complement the 19th-century mansions. A glass-roofed atrium adjoins the **Fairfield House** with the **Westchester** and **Rockland Houses**; each building offers rooms with views of the Hudson River, manicured lawns, or gardens.

The **King House** offers 10 rooms that transport guests to a more refined era. Sleeping chambers are spacious in size and feature hardwood floors, period-style furnishings, and French doors that open onto a private balcony overlooking the Hudson River.

Down the hill is the **Stone Cottage**, a former guest house once used to accommodate weekend visitors. The cottage has been divided into three separate guest rooms and, because of its location, offers newlyweds the ultimate in privacy. The **Biddle Mansion** offers no sleeping accommodations.

Honeymoon In The Shadow Of Sleepy Hollow

Legend has it that author Washington Irving wrote the classic "Legend of Sleepy Hollow" on the banks of the Hudson River where Tarrytown House presently overlooks. It doesn't take a vivid imagination to picture the Headless Horseman galloping along the embankment on a moonlit night.

THE WALDORF-ASTORIA
301 Park Avenue
(Between 49th and 50th Streets)
New York, NY 10022
800/WALDORF
212/355-3000

Accommodations
$300-$6,500

Celebrity Guest Register
- *William Randolph Hearst*
- *Tony Curtis & Janet Leigh*
- Bob Hope
- Princess Grace Kelly
- Burt Reynolds
- Frank Sinatra
- Warren Beatty
- *Joan Crawford & Franchot Tone*
- *President and Mrs. John F. Kennedy*
- Arthur Ashe
- Arnold Palmer
- Liza Minnelli
- Duke and Duchess of Windsor
- Gregory Peck

A History
In 1893, millionaire William Waldorf Astor launched a 13-story hotel at Fifth Avenue near 34th Street. Built by renowned architect Henry Janeway Hardenbergh, The Waldorf boasted the opulence of a European mansion with the warmth and comfort of a private residence.

The hotel immediately appealed to Astor's rich and famous friends, and soon New York's most distinguished families were hosting lavish dinner parties not at their Park Avenue penthouses, but at The Waldorf. In 1897, The Waldorf was joined by the adjacent 17-story Astoria Hotel, built by William Waldorf Astor's cousin, John Jacob Astor IV. Together the Astor cousins built a corridor to connect the two buildings, which were joined together as one to become The Waldorf-Astoria.

In 1929, after decades of hosting internationally celebrated visitors, The Waldorf-Astoria closed its doors in order to make room for another landmark – the Empire State Building. The following year construction began on a new Waldorf-Astoria further north and over on Park Avenue, as construction workers labored to create the world's biggest hotel – an endeavor that piqued the public's curiosity on a daily basis. No one was quite prepared on October 1, 1931, when the new Waldorf-Astoria was unveiled at a grand opening gala. Thousands of onlookers gazed down Park Avenue as stately rugbearers ceremoniously laid 50 red carpets in front of the main entrance. The hotel, which stretched all the way from Park Avenue to Lexington Avenue, soared 42 floors above midtown

Manhattan and boasted 2,200 rooms. Indeed, it was the largest hotel in the world at the time.

The elegant Waldorf-Astoria, which includes the residential and transient Waldorf Towers, embraces the Art Deco style that has become synonymous with the '20s and '30s. More than a century since its original opening, The Waldorf-Astoria offers unparalleled luxury enhanced with impeccable hospitality at one of Manhattan's most discriminating addresses.

Famous Nuptials

Publishing tycoon **William Randolph Hearst** married Brooklyn-born **Millicent Wilson** on April 28, 1903, at Grace Church in New York City. Because her roots were closer to blue collar than blueblood, the groom's mother did not find her a suitable mate for her son. Regardless, Hearst married his Brooklyn sweetheart, and the two hosted a post-nuptial breakfast for 30 relatives and friends at The Waldorf-Astoria.

Celebrated Honeymoons

Joan Crawford and actor **Franchot Tone** were married by the mayor of Englewood Cliffs, New Jersey, in a quick, simple service on October 11, 1935. Because the bride savored elegance, only The Waldorf-Astoria would suffice for a proper honeymoon. The new Mr. & Mrs. Tone enjoyed their first few days as husband and wife in one of the hotel's lavish suites.

Tony Curtis and **Janet Leigh** also honeymooned at the Waldorf-Astoria in the 1950s, and **John** and **Jackie Kennedy** spent their wedding night here as well.

Getting Married at The Waldorf-Astoria

The Waldorf-Astoria has hosted many brides and grooms over the years. There are 25 elegant Art Deco ballrooms and salons that can accommodate intimate gatherings of 10 or gala celebrations of 1,500. Many of the rooms are named or famous guests, such as the **John Jacob Astor Salon**, the **Cole Porter Suite**, the **Duke of Windsor Suite**, and the **Vanderbilt Suite**. The most popular backdrops for weddings and receptions are the **Grand Ballroom, Hilton** and **Empire Rooms**, the **Starlight Roof**, the **Basildon Room** and the **Presidential Suite**.

The **Grand Ballroom**, an Art Deco masterpiece that rises from the third to the seventh floors, has the distinction of housing the only two-tiered ballroom in New York and the only four-story ballroom in the world! A 10-foot wide crystal chandelier, which hangs from the 41-foot high ceiling, serves as the ballroom's focal point, while an additional 17 crystal chandeliers are suspended throughout. The Grand Ballroom can accommodate up to 1,500 guests, and has been the gathering place for kings and queens, presidents and dignitaries. The **Hilton** and **Empire Rooms** have also been returned to their 1930s splendor, and are located to the north and south of the hotel's Park Avenue lobby. The Hilton Room, originally named the Wedgewood Room, features the original nickel silver balustrade that surrounds the maple dance floor. The Empire Room, formerly named the Sert Room after the large murals of Jose Mario Sert, gleams with elegant crystal chandeliers. Elaborate carved and etched mirror panels stretch from the floor to the ceiling and a rich motif carpet of ribbons and bows frames the room.

The elegant **Starlight Roof** is a spectacular setting for ceremonies and receptions of up to 400 guests, and features a blue-and-white color scheme to create the illusion of a starlit sky. The smaller **Basildon Room** is adorned with original murals which originally graced an English castle of the same name. The **Presidential Suite** features 3,100 square feet of elegance and can accommodate intimate parties of 50.

For an elegant family gathering or rehearsal dinner, the **Peacock Alley** offers superb surroundings; the **Bull & Bear** is an ideal place for the groom and his friends to gather for hearty steaks and cocktails; for casual pre-wedding gatherings, **Oscar's** offers an informal, garden cafe setting; **Inagiku**, an outpost of one of Japan's best restaurants, is a unique venue for rehearsal dinners; and the club-like atmosphere of **Sir Harry's Bar** is a perfect place to unwind with the wedding party.

Couples who host receptions of 100 or more guests receive complimentary wedding night accommodations in a magnificent suite that includes an elegant champagne breakfast in bed the following morning.

Honeymooning at The Waldorf-Astoria

The Waldorf-Astoria, a name recognized around the world, provides newlyweds with opulent surroundings and excellent service. There are 1,380 guest rooms, including 200 suites, located at Park Avenue between 49th and 50th Streets. Each room is individually decorated and features original Art Deco touches. Within walking distance are some of New York City's finest shops, art galleries, and theaters, but with all the amenities The Waldorf-Astoria has to offer, couples may never have the urge to leave the premises.

Sinatra's Start At The Waldorf

The Empire Room, which was once the premier entertainment club in New York, takes credit for launching Frank Sinatra's singing career in the 1930s.

19. South Carolina

THE MILLS HOUSE HOTEL
115 Meeting Street
Charleston, SC 29401
800/874-9600
803/577-2400

Accommodations
$130-$600

Celebrity Guest Register
- *Timothy Hutton & Debra Winger*
- President Gerald Ford
- Hal Holbrook
- Robert E. Lee
- Garth Brooks
- James Taylor
- President Ronald Reagan
- Princess Caroline of Monaco
- Elizabeth Taylor
- Beverly Sills
- President Theodore Roosevelt
- Eddie Vedder
- Tom Berenger
- Lee Majors

A History
During the 1830s, the south embodied grandeur and refined living. It was during this period that Charleston thrived as a bustling seaport in the southern belly of the United States.

Otis Mills, a local businessman and entrepreneur, played a pivotal role in the shaping of Charleston. One of his many dreams was to create a luxury hotel for visiting dignitaries. He purchased the former St. Mary Hotel at the corner of Meeting and Queen Streets and for 10 years leased the site to the United States Government to use as a courthouse. In 1846, he began to make renovations and additions to the property and re-opened it later that year as The Mansion Hotel. In 1852, Mills decided to create an establishment worthy of bearing his name, and commissioned architect John Earle to restructure the building.

Earle was instrumental in the hotel's design and creation; the goal was to reflect graceful southern living. Drastic changes included the addition of two stories and several wings enhanced with such adornments as heavy cornices, terra-cotta window pediments, a balcony enclosed by ornate cast iron, imposing columns and stuccoed walls fashioned after New York brownstones. Inside, elaborate embellishments included ceiling moldings, marble mantels, a grand marble staircase with mahogany rails, thousands of dollars worth of furnishings, and running water and steam heat throughout – a major coup for its time.

The new hotel opened in 1853, and was known throughout the region as "the finest hotel south of New York City." This antebellum grandeur would last less than a decade as the war between the states changed the face of the south forever. When the Confederate Army surrendered in 1865, The Mills House was one of the few buildings left standing. Although the war may have ended, the South was waging yet another battle: severe economic depression. Rumors circulated that Otis Mills cashed in all his assets to help "the cause," and during this time his dream hotel sadly slipped from his grasp.

In the years that followed, the hotel began a slow decline, and what was once considered the South's crown jewel was nothing more than an eyesore. In 1967, a group of investors purchased the dilapidated hotel and began the tedious task of restoring it to its original grandeur.

Today, The Mills House Hotel is the epitome of 19th-century southern living; a lifestyle that can only be found between the pages of an epic novel or portrayed in a Hollywood drama.

Celebrated Honeymoons

When news leaked out that actress **Debra Winger** (*An Officer And A Gentleman, Forget Paris*) married actor **Timothy Hutton** (*Taps, Ordinary People*) even Hollywood insiders were taken aback by the union. Few people knew the two were dating, let alone a serious item. They married in the winter of 1986, along the Big Sur coast in northern California.

The groom had to leave immediately for Charleston, South Carolina, where he was to begin filming *Made In Heaven*, in which his new bride made a cameo appearance. Most of the cast were staying at The Mills House Hotel, including Hutton, and Debra Winger, who was juggling a hectic schedule of her own, made the trek to South Carolina to spend a brief honeymoon with her new husband at The Mills House Hotel.

Getting Married at The Mills House Hotel

Southern weddings are still elegant affairs full of tradition and gracious hospitality at The Mills House Hotel. There are two areas for outdoor ceremonies: the **Courtyard**, framed by the hotel's brownstone facade and featuring a 19th-century fountain and graceful palms; and the second-story **Pool Terrace**, overlooking the hotel swimming pool and historic Charleston.

Steeped in history, each reception salon features understated elegance amid century-old surroundings. **The Planter's Suite**, named for the main plantation crops of 19th-century South Carolina, is ideal for mid-size groups of 120; **The Signer's Ballroom** pays tribute to a trio of South Carolinians who signed the Declaration of Independence and is ideal for large groups of 250; **The Middleton Room**, named for the fourth signer of the Declaration of Independence, is ideal for intimate groups of 40. Once the field headquarters for the legendary General Lee prior to the Civil War, **The Robert E. Lee Room** offers an historic setting for small gatherings of 14. The hotel also manages the adjacent historic **Hibernian Hotel**, once home to Charleston's St. Cecilia Ball, which features a two-story rotunda for groups of 250-500.

Rehearsal dinners offer the same southern charm at The Mills House Hotel. An arched entryway leads guests to the **Barbadoes Room**, named for the extensive trading done with the West Indies in the 1700s. The Barbadoes Room, with its gently moving paddle fans, offers a cozy setting for leisurely breakfasts, a bridesmaid luncheon, or pre-nuptial dinners. In the evening, diners can gather in the adjacent **First Shot Lounge**, which overlooks the fountain courtyard, or mingle in **The Best Friend Bar**, featuring live entertainment.

Honeymooning at The Mills House Hotel

Steeped in tradition and history, The Mills House Hotel is one of the last remaining symbols of the Old South. There are 214 guest rooms, including 19 suites, which harken visitors back to antebellum grandeur. Each room is draped in custom fabrics and wall coverings and feature demi-canopy beds, furnishings indicative of the era, and views of either historic Charleston or the hotel's pool and sun deck.

The **Patio Room**, named for its location, features French doors that lead to private terraces overlooking the hotel swimming pool. The **Petite Suites** and two-bedroom **Suites** are even more spacious with sitting areas and wet bars.

Mills House – Made For TV!

The Mills House Hotel was featured in the epic mini-series "North and South, Parts 1 and 2," a made-for-television movie depicting the rise and fall of the Confederacy. The mini-series, starring Patrick Swayze and Kirstie Alley, featured several scenes with the hotel's interior and exterior.

20. Tennessee

THE HERMITAGE SUITE HOTEL
231 Sixth Avenue North
Nashville, TN 37219
800/251-1908
615/244-3121

Accommodations
$145-$279

Celebrity Guest Register

- *Jennifer O'Neill*
- Bette Davis
- President and Mrs. Franklin D. Roosevelt
- Al Jolson
- President John F. Kennedy
- Al Capone
- Greta Garbo
- President Richard Nixon
- President Lyndon Johnson
- Gene Autry

A History

The Hermitage Suite Hotel was Nashville's first million-dollar hotel, and was considered by many to be the crown jewel of Tennessee.

Ground breaking for the hotel began in 1908, and only the finest materials were used: Italian sienna marble coated the main entrance, Russian walnut panels adorned the walls, a cut stain-glass ceiling covered the vaulted lobby, and overstuffed furniture sat atop plush Persian rugs. Each room featured a private bath, an amenity practically unheard of for its time. No expense was spared as each detail was carefully planned and executed.

Two years later, Nashvillians turned out in droves to attend the grand opening of Hotel Hermitage, as it was originally named. The Beaux Arts structure would soon become the focal point and social center for the visiting famous and infamous, from dignitaries to gangsters. American women would not easily forget the Hotel Hermitage. The hotel served as the 1920 headquarters for the suffragette movement, with Tennessee casting the deciding ballot giving women the right to vote.

Today, The Hermitage Suite Hotel is a landmark linking Nashville's past with its present. As the cornerstone for social buzz and activity, the words "meet me at the Hermitage" are spoken all over town.

Celebrated Honeymoons

Model and actress **Jennifer O'Neill**, best known for her portrayal of a young widow turned seductress in the 1971 coming of age film, *Summer of '42,* spent her honeymoon at The Hermitage Suite Hotel in September 1996.

Getting Married at The Hermitage Suite Hotel

The Hermitage Suite Hotel is a place where time stands still. Brides and grooms return to an elegant era for their celebration, as each ballroom and banquet suite transports its patrons back to the turn-of-the-century.

The historic **Grand Ballroom** has been the backdrop for many social occasions during the past 85 years. Featuring warm wood paneling, walls graced with portraits of former Presidents, floor-to-ceiling windows, and an intricate hand-carved ceiling, the Grand Ballroom creates a regal setting for ceremonies and receptions of 300. There are three reception suites, named for United States Presidents, ideally suited for small weddings and receptions: the **Johnson Suite** for groups up to 45, the **Jackson Suite** for parties of 50, and the **Polk Suite** accommodating groups of 65. Each banquet suite is elegantly appointed with creme hues and arched floor-to-ceiling windows.

The **Capitol Grille**, a popular gathering spot in the '20s, '30s and '40s, is an elegant setting for rehearsal dinners. The grille also features two private dining rooms for receptions, and can accommodate up to 45 guests. Behind a pair of antique French doors lies **The Verandah**, a favorite spot for post-rehearsal cocktails and light hors d'oeuvres. Atop the entrance of the hotel and overlooking downtown Nashville, The Verandah is a wonderful example of the Beaux Arts style with a graciously arched ceiling, paned floor-to-ceiling windows, and a tiled floor. Both the **Lobby Bar** and the **Oak Bar** offer a vintage-like setting for relaxing with family and friends.

Honeymooning at The Hermitage Suite Hotel

A honeymoon at The Hermitage Suite Hotel is ideal for those who enjoy an urban getaway coupled with southern hospitality.

Each room is a suite complete with a spacious living area, separate bedroom, and ample dressing area. Of the 120 suites, eight are luxurious two bedroom suites offering the ultimate in roomy surroundings. All suites are tastefully decorated in soothing tones of creme with floral accents, and feature a wet bar and large wardrobe for hanging wedding gowns and other related accessories.

Each morning, complimentary fresh brewed coffee is served in the lobby.

Dinah's Debut At The Hermitage
In 1946, a young Dinah Shore made her singing debut in the hotel's Oak Bar.

LOEWS VANDERBILT PLAZA HOTEL
2100 West End Avenue
Nashville, TN 37203
800/235-6397
615/320-1700

Accommodations
$119-$700

Celebrity Guest Register
- *Lorrie Morgan & Jon Randall*
- Stevie Wonder
- Johnny Bench
- Billy Joel
- Travis Tritt
- Bob Hope

A History
The Loews Vanderbilt Plaza Hotel opened with little fanfare in 1984 but has since enjoyed hosting some of the most celebrated artists in country music.

Immersed in Nashville's educational, medical, and business district, the hotel is adjacent to renowned Vanderbilt University. Within its confines, a subtle elegance prevails and modern appointments eclipse the stereotypical image of old-fashioned southern living. Charm gives way to state-of-the-art with towering colonnades, high ceilings, slick marble floors, and nouveau tapestries.

Within a short distance are some of Nashville's most prized possessions, including the famous Parthenon, Music Row, and Opryland USA.

Celebrated Honeymoons

Country music sensation **Lorrie Morgan** and guitarist **Jon Randall** met on the road when he toured with her entourage as an opening act. The two later recorded a duet together, *By My Side*, and were forever inseparable. In November 1996, Lorrie Morgan became Mrs. Jon Randall during a private ceremony at the bride's estate in Hendersonville, Tennessee. The bride wore a strappy white floor-length gown and ornate headband while the groom looked dapper in a dark suit and vest.

After the wedding and reception, the newlyweds made their getaway in a stretch limo and headed straight for the Loews Vanderbilt Plaza Hotel, where they spent their wedding night before enjoying a big city honeymoon in New York City.

Getting Married at Loews Vanderbilt Plaza Hotel

There are three levels of banquet space in which to host a wedding and reception at Loews Vanderbilt Plaza Hotel. The **Skylight Foyer**, named for its architectural features, is located on the Mezzanine Level and is an elegant setting for ceremonies of 200. The long, rectangular-shaped room features high ceilings and plenty of sunlight for afternoon weddings. The lobby level **Centennial Ballroom** is a favorite for receptions and can host up to 1,000 guests. or be tri-divided into smaller ballrooms for groups of up to 375. The ballroom boasts 18-foot ceilings, a collection of prism chandeliers, and rich gold brocade wall coverings. Fronting the ballroom is a magnificent pre-reception area with a wall of windows overlooking the campus of Vanderbilt University.

There are two restaurants for hosting pre-nuptial dinners and gatherings. The more casual **Plaza Grill** features a private dining area for up to 40 guests, and offers light, simple fare for those who are saving their appetite for the following day's wedding reception. **Sfuzzi**, part of a chain of Italian trattorias, offers a trendy atmosphere and good Italian cuisine or, for more traditional fare and ambiance, **Ruth's Chris Steak House** (another chain) serves hearty portions of beef. Those who wish to enjoy a nightcap will find the **Garden Bar** a lively place to gather with nightly entertainment.

Honeymooning at Loews Vanderbilt Plaza Hotel

Many honeymooners flock to Nashville for their love of country music, but by no means is this a cow-poke town. Instead, the city offers some of the best entertainment, dining, and cultural resources for those on the go, as well as a selection of superb accommodations including Loews Vanderbilt Plaza Hotel.

The hotel features 340 guest rooms comfortably appointed with conversation areas, writing desks, and floral embellishments. Honeymooners may wish to splurge for a room on the **Concierge Floors**, offering even greater luxury with plush his and her bathrobes in each room and a private lounge serving complimentary breakfast each morning and hors d'oeuvres and spirits in the evening. For the ultimate in pampering, each of the hotel's 13 suites offers a private balcony, working fireplace, second-floor bedroom, and wet bar.

Each room, standard or suite, offers sweeping views of Nashville, with the meandering Cumberland River and the wooded Tennessee hills beyond. All guests have access to the hotel fitness center.

UNION STATION HOTEL
1001 Broadway
Nashville, TN 37203
800/331-2123
615/726-1001

Accommodations
$129-$295

Celebrity Guest Register
- *Lari White*
- Mary Chapin Carpenter
- Tim Allen
- Danny Glover
- Reba McIntire
- Charles Kuralt
- (Former House Speaker) Tip O'Neill
- Olivia Newton-John
- Garth Brooks
- President Franklin D. Roosevelt
- Al Capone
- Waylon Jennings
- Mae West

A History
Built at the turn-of-the-century, the original Union Station was the hub of activity as passengers arrived to and from Nashville via train.

At times of war, it became a focal point for soldiers departing and returning from foreign soil. During World War I, thousands of civilians gathered outside the station to welcome home the 13th Division of the United States Army; throughout the Second World War, nearly three million servicemen passed through the station. The American Red Cross even constructed a make-shift canteen to feed the hungry soldiers during their brief Nashville stopovers.

When air travel came into fashion during the 1960s, train stations across America became virtual ghost towns. Nashville's Union Station was no exception. The buzz of locomotives lessened and the shuffle of weary travelers dwindled. In 1976, Union Station closed its doors and lay empty and dormant for nearly a decade.

In December 1986, Union Station got a new lease on life – not as a train depot, but as a grand hotel. Since that time, it has become once again the hub of Nashville activity.

Famous Nuptials

Nashville and country music are synonymous with one another. So when country singer **Lari White** (*That's My Baby* and *Now I Know)* married songwriter **Chuck Cannon**, it seemed fitting that the two would choose a Nashville location to celebrate. After exchanging vows in April 1994, the two hosted an elegant reception at the Union Station Hotel.

Getting Married at the Union Station Hotel

The Romanesque-Revival style facade of the Union Station Hotel leaves newlyweds and their guests with the feeling that they're not in Kansas anymore, or in this case Tennessee. With a 222-foot clock tower overlooking downtown, it's as if the hotel has come to life from the pages of a gothic novel set somewhere in Europe.

There are a trio of areas in which to be married and celebrate. A tiered, crystal chandelier is the focal point of the **Louisville and Nashville Ballroom**, which can accommodate groups of up to 300. The **Majors**, ideal for groups of 150, is reminiscent of 18th-century cathedrals with large windows and high ceilings, elegant woodwork, limestone walls, columns and chandeliers. The **Lobby**, an elegant venue for groups of up to 500, features a 65-foot-long barrel-vaulted ceiling, 127 original stained-glass panels, marble floors, a fireplace, hand-carved cherubs and gilded accents.

There are three restaurants well-suited for hosting pre-nuptial events. Fresh roses, antique lamps, an expansive ceiling, and stained-glass windows adorn the hotel's signature establishment, **Arthur's**. **The Broadway Bistro** offers casual all-day dining and cocktails, and resembles a New York cafe with neon lighting. Overlooking one of Nashville's main streets, Broadway, is **McKinley's**, an airy setting for breakfast featuring a decorative tile floor and limestone archways.

Couples marrying at the Union Station Hotel are assigned a personal wedding coordinator to ensure no detail goes unnoticed. A list of wedding-related services is available and includes photographers, florists, clergy and more.

Honeymooning at the Union Station Hotel

The first impression honeymooners see upon arriving at the Union Station Hotel is the elegant lobby. Serving as the hotel's centerpiece, the atrium boasts a 65-foot-long barrel-vaulted ceiling with 127 original stained-glass panels, marble floors, oak-accented doors and walls, a black marble fountain plus more than a dozen bas-relief angel figurines holding symbols of Tennessee commerce.

The 111 guest rooms and 13 suites are just as impressive. Each room features a 22-foot ceiling, expansive windows, and cozy sitting areas. Rooms overlook either the Nashville skyline or the hotel's exquisite atrium, with sliding doors opening onto an indoor balcony.

Too Wild For Nashville?

Wild boy Jerry Lee Lewis startled hotel guests late one evening by banging his favorite tunes on the lobby's black grand piano. The impromptu performance not only resulted in a large crowd, but caused quite a stir as well.

21. Texas

THE MANSION ON TURTLE CREEK
2821 Turtle Creek Boulevard
Dallas, TX 75219
800/527-5432
800/442-3408 (within Texas)
214/559-2100

Accommodations
$270-$1,640

Celebrity Guest Register

- *Victoria Principal*
- Reba McIntire
- Bill Cosby
- Johnny Mathis
- Dennis Hopper
- Jane Fonda
- Muhammed Ali
- M.C. Hammer
- Jonathan Frankes
- Jean Claude Van Damme
- Kevin Costner
- Heather Locklear
- Charlton Heston
- Kathy Bates
- Julia Child
- Anita Baker
- Naomi Judd
- Gregory Peck
- Kate Mulgrew
- Ernie Banks

A History

Long before the fictional J.R. Ewing of *Dallas* fame was hosting shindigs at Southfork, The Mansion on Turtle Creek was a gathering spot for lavish parties.

The Mansion was built in 1925 by Sheppard W. King, the wealthy son of a Confederate War veteran who acquired his riches through the cotton and oil industries. With the vision of recreating a 16th-century Italian Renaissance-style villa on the outskirts of Dallas, King and his wife Bertha traveled extensively throughout Europe with their architect in tow. The final results were magnificent with three levels sharing an ample 10,000 square feet of space that included eight rooms and five bedrooms downstairs, plus four baths and four maids' quarters upstairs. A nine-foot deep basement contained a silver vault, and the rusty pink stucco facade covered solid brick walls which varied from 15 to 36 inches in thickness. King spared no expense where the interiors were concerned, and European-style embellishments included imported marble, a cantilevered stairway, and Spanish cathedral hand-carved doors, just to name a few.

The Kings spent a decade at their mansion before losing their fortune in 1935. The home was then sold to oil tycoon Freeman Burford and his wife Carolyn, who sold the mansion again in the late 1940s to Toddie Lee Wynne, another oil tycoon. Wynne converted the mansion into offices for his American Liberty Oil Company, and during the '60s and '70s the former mansion accommodated various corporate owners.

In 1979, the property was purchased by a Dallas-based hotel group who spent the next two years, and $21 million, to restore the mansion to its original splendor. The refurbishment reflects the style of the original King Mansion without imitating it. As a result, The Mansion on Turtle Creek has recaptured the era of Sheppard King, creating a regal retreat for newlyweds and romantics.

Famous Nuptials

Victoria Principal, best-known for her role as Pamela Ewing on the hit television drama *Dallas,* married Los Angeles-based psychiatrist **Harry Glassman** at The Mansion in June 1985. The wedding took place in the Garden Room (since renamed The Promenade), which the bride bedecked with orchids, gardenias, lilies, and camellias. Dressed in a traditional white gown and veil, the bride made her grand entrance from the second floor private dining area, descending down a spiral staircase before reaching the altar.

After the "I Do's," the newlyweds hosted a small reception in the Sheppard King Room attended by family and friends, including members from the cast of *Dallas.*

Celebrated Honeymoons

After their Texas-style wedding, **Victoria Principal** and her bridegroom spent their first night as Mr. & Mrs. Glassman at The Mansion on Turtle Creek. Because of *Dallas'* popularity, the media desperately wanted a photo opportunity. The next day, after waiting several hours in the hot Texas sun, the newlyweds agreed to pose in the doorway of The Mansion to accommodate the press. Afterwards, they retreated to their elegant suite to enjoy some private time.

Getting Married at The Mansion on Turtle Creek

With six elegantly designed salons located in the original King Mansion, The Mansion on Turtle Creek offers opulent surroundings for weddings and receptions.

Wedding ceremonies are often performed in the **Sheppard King Suite**, which features a canopied terrace that overlooks Turtle Creek and can accommodate up to 75 guests. For intimate gatherings of up to 35, **The Hunt Suite** resembles an estate parlor with classic Empire-style chairs and a fireplace. **The Pavilion**, an exquisite ballroom housing up to 200 guests, can be coupled with **The Promenade** (formerly The Garden Room), an airy setting with Palladian windows and aromatic floral arrangements, to accommodate groups of 350. There are two very intimate salons perfect for small weddings and receptions: **The Wine Cellar**, once used as a silver vault for the mansion's original owner, offers a distinctive setting for groups of 12 or fewer; and **The Trezevant Room**, featuring French doors overlooking a landscaped courtyard and fountain, can accommodate up to 16 people.

A striking black and white marble rotunda leads to the award-winning **Mansion on Turtle Creek Restaurant**, which is well suited for rehearsal dinners. Carved doors frame the restaurant's entrance, which open to reveal an enclosed verandah, dual fireplaces, an impressive collection of art and antiques, original wood paneling, an intricate carved ceiling and leaded-glass windows throughout. The adjacent bar is an ideal spot for gathering with potential in-laws and friends. Unwinding before the "Big Day" is easily accomplished at the **Pool Terrace**, which features a cluster of cozy tables located poolside.

The staff at The Mansion on Turtle Creek can assist brides with even the most minor of details. For an elegant touch, chauffeur-driven cars for hire are available to pick up wedding guests at the airport and ferry them back in style in a stretch limousine. For last minute appointments and errands, complimentary sedan service is available to hotel guests within a five-mile radius.

Honeymooning at The Mansion on Turtle Creek

The Mansion on Turtle Creek spans more than four acres. While the dining and banquet facilities are located in the King Mansion, the guest rooms and suites are found in an adjacent nine-story tower, created to complement the architectural style of the original mansion.

The Mansion "experience" begins upon entering the dramatic floral-filled lobby with its 32-foot-high marble rotunda, which leads to a cozy conversational area complete with overstuffed chairs and fireplace. There are 126 guest rooms offering Texas-size accommodations, including a 450 square foot floor plan featuring a living area, bath, and vanity with elegant

French doors opening onto a small terrace. The 15 ample-sized suites offer one or two bedrooms, a living and dining area, a guest and master bath, fireplaces, wet bar, pantry and balcony.

Guests are treated to his and her plush terry cloth robes, cookies and lemonade upon arrival, and a hand written weather forecast with nightly turndown service. With Texas-style hospitality, a honeymoon at The Mansion on Turtle Creek is more like accepting a weekend invitation to someone's estate rather than staying at a hotel.

It's A Hit With Martha!

The Mansion on Turtle Creek is famous for its culinary masterpieces. Even the most simple of dishes get rave reviews. For instance, Martha Stewart, the queen of cuisine, has been known to order The Mansion's trademark Tortilla Soup when visiting.

22. Utah

RADISSON SUITE HOTEL
2510 Washington Blvd.
Ogden, UT 84401
800/333-3333
801/627-1900

Accommodations
$119-$219

Celebrity Guest Register
- *Rodney Dangerfield*
- Christian Slater
- Sigourney Weaver
- Sam Elliott
- Cyndi Lauper
- Nicolas Cage
- John Malkovich
- John Cusack
- Dennis Weaver
- Mike Farrell

A History
Nestled in the foothills of the magnificent Wasatch Mountains, the Radisson Suite Hotel made its 1927 debut as the Bigelow-Ben Lomond.

The Renaissance-Revival hotel towered 15 stories and was the result of a community effort to further the city's industrial and commercial growth. If the residents of Ogden had never been outside the city's limits, they were now able to travel the globe by merely stepping inside the hotel's gracious doors. Its interiors were hailed as exuberant and undeniably eclectic and featured a coffee shop with Middle Eastern influences, a ballroom emulating a Florentine palace, a Spanish motif dominating the businessmen's club, and an oak-paneled lounge that mirrored that of a chamber found in an English castle.

The hotel was ahead of its time, and people traveling through northern Utah often made a point of spending a few days in Ogden under the roof of the Bigelow-Ben Lomond. In 1977, the grandeur of the hotel came to a halt when Weber County acquired the property and transformed it into a building housing administrative services.

In 1986, the hotel was completely restored to its 1920s splendor and reopened as an all-suite hotel. Today, the Radisson Suite Hotel remains a showpiece for the community of Ogden, and a destination for those passing through Utah.

Famous Nuptials

Who says **Rodney Dangerfield** gets no respect? In late 1993, the comedian married his wife, Joan, at the Radisson Suite Hotel. The bride, a native of Utah, felt it fitting that the nuptials take place in her home state. It was a low-key event by Hollywood standards – only close friends and family were invited, and no photographers were invited other than the one the couple hired to capture the event.

Getting Married at the Radisson Suite Hotel

Weddings at the Radisson Suite Hotel seem to evoke thoughts of another era when the whole town used to toast the newlywed couple. While the entire community may not be aware of every wedding taking place on any given day, there is still that small-town feel on the streets of Ogden.

The hotel offers two splendid ballrooms in which to marry and celebrate. The ornate **Crystal Ballroom** is the perfect setting for grand affairs of up to 300 and retains the charm of years past, with original 1927 embellishments including chandeliers, an intricately carved ceiling, and cathedral-style windows. The rectangular-shaped **Grandview Room**, ideal for groups of up to 150, resembles a house of worship with a series of cathedral-style windows, candelabra-esque lighting, expansive ceilings, and a stone ascending fireplace.

For rehearsal dinners or pre-wedding gatherings, there are two restaurants available. The casual **Yesteryear's Restaurant** is located on the main level of the hotel and is ideal for enjoying breakfast with out-of-town guests; the more upscale **Skyline Restaurant** is located atop the hotel on the 11th floor and offers panoramic views of the city lights and burnished mountain ranges.

Each stay also includes a complimentary full breakfast in the hotel restaurant and use of the cardio-vascular fitness room.

Honeymooning at the Radisson Suite Hotel

Utah is often proclaimed as one of the most beautiful states in the country. Mother Nature seems to smile down upon its desert terrains and red clay mountains, where the grass seems greener and the sky bluer.

Honeymooners who enjoy skiing, golfing, and hunting for antiques can do it all from the Radisson Suite Hotel. Located just minutes from an array of ski resorts, golf courses, and the 25th Street Historic District, the hotel offers 122 chambers in which to slumber. Each room is actually a suite, with a living room, separate sleeping chamber, and wet bar, with views of downtown Ogden and the nearby Wasatch Mountains. Each suite also features armoires, wing-back chairs, comfortable sofas, and other period-style furnishings.

23. Vermont

THE EQUINOX
Historic Route 7A
Manchester Village, VT 05254
800/362-4747
802/362-4700

Accommodations
$169-$589

Celebrity Guest Register
• *Michael J. Fox & Tracy Pollan*   • Meg Ryan & Dennis Quaid
• President Theodore Roosevelt   • Mary Todd Lincoln

A History
Just 10 years after Manchester, Vermont, was established, the towns-people welcomed the opening of Marsh Tavern in 1769. As one of the state's first lodging establishments, it become the focal point for many historic gatherings and important guests, including memorable figures who played instrumental roles during the American Revolution. However, when owner and British loyalist William Marsh sided with the enemy, his tavern was the first seized in America to support the independence effort.

In 1780, Thaddeus Munson purchased the tavern from the local government. The property expanded in 1801, when Munson built a new inn next door, the first of 17 major architectural changes to occur. Each time the inn changed hands, more additions were made to the structure. Owner A.J. Gray changed the name from Marsh Tavern to the Taconic in the mid-1800s.

The name Equinox first appeared in 1849, when Franklin Orvis opened the Equinox House in his father's home, which stood beside the Taconic. Even in those days, a prominent name on the guest register could boost hotel sales. When Mary Todd Lincoln and her two sons vacationed at the inn in 1864, it quickly earned a reputation for being a premier summer resort. Mrs. Lincoln enjoyed her stay so much she planned to return the following summer with her husband, President Abraham Lincoln. A special suite was constructed in anticipation of the first couple's visit, but sadly, Lincoln was assassinated in the spring of 1865.

Orvis purchased the Taconic Inn in 1883 and connected it to his hotel, adding a third and fourth floor. Expansions and improvements continued after Orvis' death when his wife Louise was at the helm of the operation. In 1925, she commissioned the design and installation of an 18-hole golf course by Walter Travis; however, the additions of an airport and skeet field overextended the family during the Depression. In 1937, they were forced to surrender the hotel, and The Equinox enjoyed a series of owners. Today, The Equinox retains its 18th-century splendor, and has rightfully earned a space on the National Register of Historic Places.

Celebrated Honeymoons

Following their wedding and reception at West Mountain Inn in nearby Arlington *(see page 194)*, **Michael J. Fox** and actress **Tracy Pollan**, who met while starring opposite each other in the 1980s sitcom *Family Ties*, spent their wedding night at The Equinox before departing on an extended honeymoon.

Getting Married at The Equinox

With 1,100 acres to choose from, the spring and summer seasons are popular for outdoor weddings. Couples can marry beneath century-old trees located in the manicured gardens as guests bask beneath the sunshine to witness the nuptials.

There are a number of quaint rooms for receptions and indoor weddings, each boasting New England charm. **The Manchester** offers versatility and can be as elegant as you wish or toned down for a Western-style barbecue, accommodating up to 120 guests; overlooking a beautiful 14-acre mountain pond is the newly-constructed **Pond House**, featuring an enormous stone fireplace and unencumbered views, an ideal setting for parties of 100; and **The Garden Lounge**, for groups of 100, boasts views of Mt. Equinox, a covered terrace, a fireplace, and lush greenery.

An elegant and spacious setting can be found inside **The Colonnade**, featuring a hand-stenciled, vaulted ceiling, striking emerald chandeliers, French doors, a sleek hardwood dance floor and a cozy conversation area. The Colonnade can accommodate up to 200 guests. Smaller venues for 30-40 include **The Green Mountain Suite**, **The Arlington**, and **The Dorset**.

The Equinox features two restaurants for rehearsal dinners, pre-wedding gatherings, and private receptions. **Marsh Tavern**, the original structure seized during the American Revolution, is the hotel's showpiece and is ideal for casual meals. The seasonal **Dormy Grill**, a clubhouse setting located at the Gleneagles Golf Course, is ideal for afternoon bites.

Should you wish to marry at **Hildene**, the Robert Todd Lincoln Estate located a half-mile down the road, The Equinox can cater the event.

Honeymooning at The Equinox

The Equinox, with its white column buildings and green shutter accents, resembles a grand New England manor. There are 180 guest rooms located in 17 buildings offering oversized accommodations with either views of the garden, village, or nearby mountains. The upscale Charles Orvis Inn, a favorite for honeymooners, features nine suites containing either one or two bedrooms plus separate sitting areas.

While The Equinox began as a humble tavern more than two centuries ago, it has emerged a first-class resort. Within its confines guests can golf on an 18-hole course designed by Walter Travis in 1927, enjoy massage therapy and herbal wraps at the fitness spa, play tennis, swim laps at both an indoor and outdoor swimming pool, enjoy cross country skiing or simply relax underneath a shaded tree!

Lincoln's Choice

Robert Todd Lincoln, son of President Lincoln, so enjoyed summering with his mother at The Equinox that he returned years later to build his summer home in Manchester. The home, christened Hildene, is open to the public for tours and is also the backdrop for such cultural performances as the Vermont Symphony Orchestra. You can also arrange to get married at Hildene.

THE OLD TAVERN AT GRAFTON
Main Street
(Where Routes 35 & 121 Meet)
Grafton, VT 05146
800/843-1801
802/843-2231

Accommodations
$105-$575

Celebrity Guest Register

- *Rudyard Kipling*
- Joanne Woodward
- President Ulysses S. Grant
- Ralph Waldo Emerson
- Henry David Thoreau
- Daniel Webster

- Tom Cruise
- Treat Williams
- Paul Newman
- President Theodore Roosevelt
- President Woodrow Wilson
- Nathaniel Hawthorne

A History

The Old Tavern is the fifth oldest inn in Vermont and the centerpiece for the quaint town of Grafton. Located on the Boston-Montreal stagecoach line, the inn opened in 1801, the same year Thomas Jefferson was elected president of the United States. For nearly 65 years it was a convenient and well-regarded overnight stop for weary travelers and Yankee peddlers. In 1865, the inn really came into its own when brothers Harlan and Francis Phelps bought the tavern with California gold-rush money, renaming the tavern Phelps Hotel.

For more than three decades, Phelps Hotel was a boisterous place that attracted artists and Boston's literati, including the likes of Emerson and Thoreau. A hotel flier claimed that Grafton was a place void of mosquitoes and hay fever and was a cure-all for tired city nerves. Those on the campaign trail also found Phelps Hotel a convenient stop, and President Ulysses S. Grant spent nearly a week at the hotel in 1867 while campaigning for his first term. Presidents Woodrow Wilson and Theodore Roosevelt followed Grant's example during their own presidential campaigns.

While Grant may not recognize the world in which we live, he would surely feel right at home inside The Old Tavern. Echoes of the illustrious 19th-century gently mesh with today's standards of living, leaving guests wanting for practically nothing!

Celebrated Honeymoons

Rudyard Kipling, the renowned English-born author of the late 19th and early 20th centuries, gained fame for his children's books, including *The Jungle Book* and *Just So Stories*. Some well-known lines from his works include "East is east, and west is west, and never the twain shall meet" and "The female of the species is more deadly than the male." Many of his works have been adapted into motion pictures.

Kipling enjoyed his visits to Grafton so much that in 1892 he carried his bride over the threshold of The Old Tavern for a New England-style honeymoon.

Getting Married at The Old Tavern at Grafton

The Old Tavern at Grafton is the perfect setting for a country wedding.

Wedding ceremonies often take place in a nearby New England church dating back to the 1800s. Newlyweds emerge from the white-steeple structure to the sounds of bells ringing from the church spire, announcing to the residents of Grafton the beginning of a new life together. Other nearby wedding sites include wildflower-filled country fields and the public room at the inn.

When the wedding is held in town, the bride and groom may choose to be chauffeured by a horse-drawn buggy, passing white-clapboard homes and a covered bridge before finally reaching the reception site at The Old Tavern.

Each reception parlor reeks of New England charm. Located on The Old Tavern's property are two English-style homes: the **Whitegates House** and the **Barrett House**, both ideal for celebrations of up to 35. For those who desire a completely country wedding, **The Phelps Barn** is a rustic location for groups of up to 100.

Rehearsal dinners and pre-nuptial gatherings are enjoyed in The Old Tavern's **Dining Room**, which pays homage to the 19th century with a priceless collection of Chippendale and Hepplewhite antiques. Serving breakfast, lunch, and dinner, the Dining Room offers traditional New England fare and offers an extensive wine and ale list.

The Perfect Country Wedding

The entire inn may be rented to create the ultimate country wedding. An on-site wedding coordinator can assist with every need, including reserving the town's 1858 church, arranging for a horse-drawn carriage arrival, and reserving the Honeymoon Cottage stocked with your favorite edibles.

Honeymooning at The Old Tavern at Grafton

The Old Tavern offers a timeless example of colonial living with its hand-hewn beams, wide pine flooring, pewter and brass accents, and graceful decor. The inn boasts expansive grounds to include acres of forests, babbling brooks, and limitless meadows. Of the 66 authentic colonial-style rooms, 14 are found in the original main Tavern; and several elegantly preserved guest houses, dating from 1836 to 1971, shelter the remaining rooms. Each chamber features a private bath and period-style antiques. Guests are treated to a breakfast buffet each morning and a traditional afternoon tea.

The **Honeymoon Cottage** sits perched atop a rolling meadow just minutes from the main inn, and offers the most captivating views of the village below – not to mention total seclusion! Newlyweds share a queen-size bed, full bath and separate living room, plus a picture window big enough for two! The cottage rents for $235 a night.

The Old Tavern – Designed To Inspire!

While in residence at The Old Tavern at Grafton, acclaimed author Rudyard Kipling penned the classic tale "The Jungle Book;" and the Grant Room, so named for its most famous occupant, President Ulysses S. Grant, has been preserved to capture his 1867 visit with an array of eclectic Grant-esque memorabilia.

WEST MOUNTAIN INN
Route 313 & River Road
Arlington, VT 05250
802/375-6516

Accommodations
$105-$229

Celebrity Guest Register
- *Michael J. Fox & Tracy Pollan*
- Robert Redford
- Justine Bateman
- Christopher Reeve
- Meg Ryan & Dennis Quaid
- Leif Garrett

A History
Nestled on a picturesque hillside, this former farmhouse has emerged as a quaint bed and breakfast after years of architectural evolution.

The once humble home was built for Vermont farmers in 1849 and included 150 acres of fertile land. For decades the unobtrusive clapboard frame had little appeal other than to shelter its owners from the harsh New England winters. In 1924, new owners by the name of Rochester oversaw a series of drastic changes that would transform this former farmhouse into their magnificent dream house. They began by enlarging the home and adding the distinctive seven gables, giving the structure its unmistakable silhouette. Next, they had barns and small cottages built along the mountainside and covered the hillside with stone walls and fences. Once finished, the Rochesters had created an elegant summer estate.

After the Rochesters vacated the home, it remained a private residence until 1978, when the present owners fell in love with the stately
mansion and transformed it into a quaint yet elegant bed and breakfast.
Today, there is hardly a trace of the humble 1849 farmhouse, but the
Rochesters' hard work and vision for a refined estate remain very much
a part of West Mountain Inn.

Famous Nuptials

Michael J. Fox, star of the *Family Ties* TV series and the *Back To The
Future* trilogy, and actress **Tracy Pollan** met on the set of the 1980s sitcom
Family Ties. Fox played Alex P. Keaton and Pollan played his earthy
girlfriend Ellen. While no sparks ignited during their tenure on the show,
after Pollan departed the series the two began a lasting relationship.

In 1988, they managed to throw the papparazi for a loop when instead
of marrying at the groom's nearby Vermont home, they married at the
West Mountain Inn. The inn was chosen after Pollan fell in love with it on
a prior visit and decided this would be the place for her wedding. The
bride wore a simple off-white satin dress and veil, and the two exchanged
vows under a canopy in the backyard. Famous friends made the trek from
Los Angeles to witness the event, including *Family Ties* co-star Justine
Bateman, Woody Harrelson, Dennis Quaid, and Meg Ryan.

The new Mr. and Mrs. Michael J. Fox spent their wedding night at the
nearby Equinox hotel in Manchester *(see page 189)*.

Getting Married at West Mountain Inn

There is something romantic about being married at an historic New
England bed and breakfast such as West Mountain Inn. Wedding parties
take over the entire estate for the weekend as anxious bridesmaids pose
for pictures, a nervous groom paces the lobby, and a blushing bride gets
ready to make her once-in-a-lifetime entrance. The celebration begins
with a relaxed, pre-nuptial barbecue on Friday evening, creating an
informal setting as guests arrive for the weekend. Saturday, of course, is
the big day as the wedding festivities get underway, and on Sunday
everyone bids farewell after enjoying a gourmet breakfast buffet in the
inn's dining room.

The inn can host weddings from 24 to 120 people, making it a cozy
setting for exchanging vows. There are five unique settings for weddings
and receptions, including the **Side Yard**, where vows are exchanged
under a canopy with views overlooking the Green and Taconic Mountains; the 150-year-old **Barn**, where faint sounds of laughter and dancing
echo throughout the hillside; the **Gardens**, situated near the front of the
inn, features a pond and sweeping views of the mountains; the **Conference Center**, which complements the original architecture, offers cathe-

dral ceilings and ornate chandeliers; and the elegant **Dining Room**, outfitted in period-style antiques, is located in the main house.

Each wedding banquet is created by the resident chef especially for the newlywed couple.

Honeymooning at West Mountain Inn

After traveling along the country roads of New England, honeymooners are greeted by grazing llamas upon their arrival to West Mountain Inn. The inn can best be described as country chic, with each room offering its own unique style, such as pine paneled walls, lace-canopied beds, screened sun porches, fireplaces and bird feeding stations. The **Historic Millhouse Suites**, an annex located in the nearby woods, features three suites, each with a living room, kitchen, and two bedrooms.

Upon arrival, guests are presented with an African violet grown in the inn's flower garden. Each stay includes evening hors d'oeuvres, an elegant candlelight dinner in front of an open hearth, and a full country breakfast served in the inn's dining room.

Nearby activities include cross-country skiing, flyfishing, bird watching, hiking and, what most honeymooners yearn for, relaxing!

24. Virginia

THE INN AT LITTLE WASHINGTON
Middle and Main Streets
Washington, VA 22747
540/675-3800

Accommodations
$260-$595

Celebrity Guest Register
· *Alan Greenspan & Andrea Mitchell*
· Barbra Streisand
· Lynda Carter
· General Colin Powell
· David Brinkley
· Oscar de la Renta
· Paul Newman
· Katharine Graham
· Henry Kissinger
· Barbara Walters
· President Ronald Reagan

A History
While The Inn at Little Washington may be the most romantic find on the face of the earth, its history leaves little room for pounding hearts. Located one hour and 20 minutes from the political arena of Washington, D.C., the town of Washington, Virginia, dates back to the 1700s, when George Washington originally surveyed the area prior to the American Revolution.

The building that now houses the inn has undergone a series of transformations, from dance hall to garage to country store. Its final transformation to elegant inn began in the late 1970s when founders and culinary genius' Patrick O'Connell and Reinhardt Lynch were in search of the perfect spot in which to open a restaurant; the actual inn would materialize later. The duo scoured the countryside visiting existing inns in order to cultivate and refine their own concept. Eventually their journeys brought them to the historic town of Washington, Virginia, where they stumbled upon a vacant storefront for sale. With O'Connell and Lynch now holding a deed, the building would receive a new lease on life.

The two transformed the structure into a first-class restaurant and opened without any fanfare in January 1978. During their first weekend of operation, they served an impressive 75 dinners. From the onset, those motoring up from the nation's capital bended the the owners' ears with complaints of the lack of lodging in the area. The owners took their customers' concerns seriously, and soon plans were underway to add a second and third story above the restaurant. The rest, as they say, is history!

Since its opening, The Inn at Little Washington has catered (literally!) to Washington, D.C.'s urban dwellers as well as an endless list of celebrities and socialites, searching for nothing more than great food and a peaceful night's sleep.

Famous Nuptials

After a 12-year courtship, Federal Reserve Chairman **Alan Greenspan** and NBC news correspondent **Andrea Mitchell** married on April 6, 1997, at The Inn at Little Washington. The two looked radiant, she in a simple Oscar de la Renta dress carrying a small bouquet of roses, and he in a dark suit and tie. Washington's politicos were on hand to congratulate the two, and among those present were Virginia Senator John Warner escorting Barbara Walters, Henry Kissinger, David Brinkley, and Colin Powell.

Getting Married at The Inn at Little Washington

Couples pursuing a small, stylish setting for their wedding will applaud the surroundings at The Inn at Little Washington.

There is really only one area in which to be married and that is the enchanting **Courtyard**. Accommodating 50 or so guests, the Courtyard's ambiance is unprecedented with French doors creating an entry with an array of colorful flora and foliage dotted throughout. Receptions may also be held al fresco in the Courtyard or just inside the inn's elaborate **Dining Room**, which is a wondrous cocoon of luxury featuring a floral motif throughout. Another stylish area is the **Terrace Room**, which boasts yards and yards of draped fabrics and offers views of the inn's garden. Both rooms can accommodate up to 50 guests, and are ideal choices for hosting pre-nuptial gatherings.

Each stay includes complimentary afternoon tea and a sumptuous continental breakfast served in the sunny Garden Room.

Honeymooning at The Inn At Little Washington

Located in the lap of Virginia's Blue Ridge Mountains, The Inn at Little Washington sits in the shadow of the picturesque Shenandoah

Valley. Passersby barely notice the inn, not because it isn't worth a second glance, but merely due to the absence of signage.

The white-columned building is festooned with flags; and visitors are greeted by two gregarious Dalmatians. The mood at the inn is that of nesting at a friend's country house from another era, without sacrificing all the comforts and services of a first-class hotel! There are only 12 bedrooms and suites including a guest house annex. The interiors, created by a London stage and set designer, feature whimsical touches, yet no two are alike; each room offers its own period antiques and furnishings, fresh-cut flowers, and private baths.

Paul Newman's Pick

With all the money and prestige to travel anywhere in the world, Paul Newman chose the quaint surroundings of The Inn at Little Washington to celebrate his 64th birthday!

NORFOLK WATERSIDE MARRIOTT HOTEL

235 East Main Street
Norfolk, VA 23510
800/228-9290
757/627-4200

Accommodations
$165-$600

Celebrity Guest Register

• *Martin Lawrence*	• Will Smith
• Samuel L. Jackson	• Garth Brooks
• Tony Bennett	• Tisha Campbell
• Roberta Flack	• Herbie Hancock
• Gladys Knight	• Patti LaBelle

A History

While steeped in history and charm, Norfolk has often been over-shadowed by its more sophisticated sister cities, Richmond and Alexandria. But with the addition of Nauticus, The National Maritime Museum, and the Waterside Festival Marketplace (a harborside shopping and dining complex), Norfolk is fast becoming a destination for travelers.

Amid all this excitement lies the Norfolk Waterside Marriott Hotel, which opened its doors with precise timing in October 1991. Located in the bustling downtown waterfront district, the hotel's interiors are reminiscent of the Old South with dramatic stairways, ornate chandeliers, and rich woodwork.

While the hotel is only a few years old, its location is ideal for those who want to take advantage of such neighboring sites as Colonial Williamsburg, Busch Gardens, and the nearby Virginia beaches.

Famous Nuptials

On January 23, 1995, fans of comedian **Martin Lawrence** wanted to know *Wuz Up! Wuz Up!* It seemed the star of television's *Martin* traveled south to Norfolk, Virginia, to marry his girlfriend of two years, **Patricia Southall**, a native of Chesapeake and a former Miss Virginia. The wedding and reception were held at the Norfolk Waterside Marriott Hotel, as 18 groomsmen escorted a bevy of bridesmaids down the aisle while 600 guests looked on. Among those present were actors Will Smith and Eddie Murphy as well as Lawrence's co-star, Tisha Campbell.

Getting Married at the Norfolk Waterside Marriott Hotel

Modern brides with old fashioned tastes will be pleased with the selection of wedding and reception sites offered by the Norfolk Waterside Marriott Hotel. There are a trio of ballrooms, which span three levels, in which to marry and celebrate.

The elegant **Norfolk Ballroom** can be sub-divided into six separate salons with the flexibility to accommodate gatherings of 100 to 1,400. Located on the first floor near the lobby, the ballroom features opulent chandeliers, large framed mirrors, and a pre-reception area for cocktails and hors d'oeuvres. Crystal sconces grace the walls of the **Hampton Roads Ballroom**, which can accommodate large celebrations of 1,190 or, when sub-divided into eight salons, can easily adapt its size for smaller groups of 100. Perhaps the most elegant of all the salons is the **Marriott Ballroom**, located on the fourth level of the hotel. With a double-entrance staircase descending to a magnificent foyer, all eyes are focused on the bride as she makes her entrance. Beyond the foyer, double doors open up to reveal a ballroom bedecked with crystal chandeliers, hues of green and gold with specks of black and an array of sconces. Situated on the fourth floor, the Marriott Ballroom can also be divided into seven separate salons to accommodate intimate gatherings of 100 or gala celebrations of 720.

With two restaurants to select from, pre-nuptial celebrations can either be casual or upscale. **The Dining Room**, which overlooks the bustling harbor, is ideal for dressy gatherings, while **Stormy's Pub** is better suited for those who wish to host a more informal evening the night before the wedding. Afterward, everyone can unwind at **The Piano Lounge**, featuring live entertainment, fine spirits, and waterfront vistas.

Honeymooning at the Norfolk Waterside Marriott Hotel

With a state motto like *Viriginia Is For Lovers*, how could couples go wrong with a Virginian honeymoon?!

Couples wanting to enjoy day trips to Washington, D.C., Virginia Beach, Colonial Williamsburg, or Richmond, the state's capitol, the Norfolk Waterside Marriott Hotel is an ideal place to unpack your suitcase and begin exploring. The hotel features more than 400 guest rooms and eight suites, offering comfortable surroundings with king-sized beds, cozy sitting areas, separate dressing areas, and views of either the city or harbor.

25. Washington

THE WOODMARK HOTEL
1200 Carillon Point
Kirkland, WA 98033
800/822-3700
425/822-3700

Accommadations
$180-$1,250

Celebrity Guest Register
- *Cynthia Geary*
- Harry Connick, Jr.
- Sugar Ray Leonard
- Lisa Rinna
- Nastassja Kinski
- Harry Hamlin
- Richard Marx
- Tony Bennett
- Marcus Allen
- Paul McCartney
- Rob Morrow
- Quincy Jones
- Arnold Palmer
- Anthony Quinn

A History
The Woodmark Hotel has the distinction of being the only hotel located on Lake Washington in the upscale district of Carillon Point. Although the property has only been open since August 1989, the area on which it stands has a colorful history.

One of the pioneers in the area was Frank Curtiss, a native Seattleite who built one of the area's first homes in 1870. The house was later replaced by The Atlantic Park Dance Hall, a tourist attraction for passengers cruising Lake Washington. In 1901, the site was transformed into a shipyard where wooden ferries and tug boats were produced; eventually the yard made the transition from using wood to the more modern material of steel.

With the onset of World War II, employment at the shipyard increased from 300 to an overwhelming 9,000 employees. No longer were ferries and tug boats a priority, instead such naval ships as anti-submarine net tenders, flotation tanks, artillery lighters, and sea plane tenders were rolling off the assembly line. During those uncertain years, the shipyard built 28 ships and repaired nearly 500 vessels! In the years following the war the area was used as a freshwater winter tie-up for passenger liners and freighters of the Alaska Steamship Company.

In 1972, Seattle businessman David Skinner purchased the shipyard and launched a plan to bring the NFL to the then quiet town of Seattle. He developed the area into the headquarters and practice field of the Seattle Seahawks.

Today Carillon Point, located in Kirkland, just a few short miles from downtown Seattle, is an upscale waterfront community with The Woodmark Hotel serving as the area's centerpiece.

Famous Nuptials

When **Cynthia Geary**, best known for her role as Shelly on the television series *Northern Exposure*, married longtime beau **Robert Coron**, she opted for a more sophisticated setting than that of Cicily, Alaska, the fictional town in which her character lived and worked. Instead, the bride and her groom married and celebrated at The Woodmark Hotel on October 1, 1994, under a canopy overlooking beautiful Lake Washington.

Getting Married at The Woodmark Hotel

With Lake Washington gracefully stretched out in front of The Woodmark Hotel, it's easy to understand why every bride getting married at the hotel wants to do so outdoors.

Because of Seattle's notorious weather of overcast skies and constant drizzle, couples never have to fret since vows are often exchanged under a canopy. The canopies, aesthetically appealing, are equipped with transparent sides and heaters. In the distance, sailboats glide by as the gentle sound of water can be heard against the dock. After the "I Do's," the celebration can continue in the outdoor canopy or in one of two ballrooms. **The Marina Room**, which can accommodate up to 150 guests, is an elegant venue with a terrace that opens onto the Carillon Point Marina. Located on the hotel's lower level is the beautifully appointed **Lake Washington Ballroom**, perfect for groups of up to 120 or, when divided into three mini-ballrooms, is ideal for smaller gatherings. The adjacent outdoor terrace features a panoramic view of Lake Washington and the Olympic Mountains.

For rehearsal dinners, **Waters** restaurant eschews a stuffy, uptight atmosphere to embrace a more comfortable lakeside ambiance. Open for breakfast, lunch, and dinner, the restaurant features both indoor and outdoor seating. Named for its parlor-like setting, the **Library Bar** serves afternoon tea and espresso by day and offers cocktails and evening entertainment by night.

Honeymooning at The Woodmark Hotel

Located just seven miles north of metropolitan Seattle, The Woodmark Hotel affords honeymooners the benefits of the big city and that of a peaceful lakeside community. There are 100 contemporary-style guest rooms, including 21 suites featuring fireplaces, sitting areas, baths with marble accents, terraces and plush robes for lounging. Half of the rooms boast unobstructed views of Lake Washington and the Olympic Mountains, creating a romantic lakeside chateau setting.

Raid The Pantry In Style!

Added guest amenities include a courtesy van, use of the nearby fitness facility, evening turn-down service, and "Raid the Pantry" privileges for a selection of late-night snacks and beverages!

---

26. Washington, DC

ANA HOTEL
2401 M Street, NW
Washington, D.C. 20037
800/262-4683
202/459-2400

Accommodations
$270-$1,630

Celebrity Guest Register

- *Chris O'Donnell*
- Martin Scorsese
- Donald Sutherland
- Jean Claude Van Damme
- Susan Sarandon
- Nick Nolte
- Shaquille O'Neal
- Robin Givens
- Val Kilmer
- Chuck Norris
- Danny Glover
- Lisa Marie Presley
- Muhammad Ali
- Eddie Murphy
- Tom Arnold
- Gene Hackman
- Christopher Reeve
- Connie Chung
- Demi Moore
- Vanessa Williams
- Jack Nicholson
- Arnold Schwarzenegger

A History

Our nation's capital is home to some of the most renowned hotels in the country, having hosted many influential people over time – from presidents to princes. Since its opening in 1985, countless dignitaries, authors and movie stars have crossed the ANA Hotel's threshold...only to return again and again.

Located in the District of Columbia's fashionable West End, sandwiched between historic Georgetown and the downtown business district, the ANA Hotel is a commanding structure. Erected from granite, limestone, and glazed brick, the architecture emulates traditional dwellings found within the area. Its striking copper roof has become a showpiece and topic of conversation for residents and visitors alike.

While the exterior is quite appealing, the real beauty of the hotel is not always obvious to passersby. In order to truly appreciate the ANA Hotel, a spin through the revolving door is required. Visitors are deposited into the stunning atrium, where an array of immaculately arranged sofas and chairs create cozy conversational nooks. Just beyond, French doors lead to a beautiful interior courtyard with brick pathways meandering through a manicured grove of trees, shrubs, and bushes.

Located within walking distance of the White House, Georgetown, the Capitol, and Kennedy Center, the ANA Hotel is a magnet for savvy travelers who are determined to be at the pulse of the action.

Celebrated Gatherings

When papers across the United States reported **Chris O'Donnell** had married his longtime steady **Caroline Fentress**, the actor's female fans exlaimed "Holy Toledo, Batman, say it isn't true!" But true it was, as the 26-year-old groom and the star of such films as *Circle of Friends, Scent of a Women* and, of course, *Batman and Robin*, was married to the local kindergarten teacher on Saturday, April 19, 1997, at St. Patrick's Church in downtown Washington, D.C. The couple and their families began celebrating two days before with a rehearsal dinner at the posh Metropolitan Club, followed by cocktails and a mariachi fiesta at the ANA Hotel on the eve of the wedding.

The reception itself was held at the National Museum of Women in the Arts. Famous guests at the various events included actress Sandra Bullock, who co-starred with the groom in *In Love and War*; *Batman and Robin* director Joel Schumacher; and Senator Ted Kennedy, a friend of the bride's family.

Getting Married at the ANA Hotel

Outdoor weddings are few and far between in a metropolis such as Washington, D.C. Aside from public parks and private estates, many find it a challenge to be married outdoors. Surprisingly, the ANA Hotel has one of the most breathtaking settings for al fresco nuptials. The **Colonnade Garden Courtyard**, located in the center of the U-shaped hotel, features a three-tiered Italian fountain centerpiece, trees, and colorful flora, which are elegantly illuminated with twinkle lights for evening affairs. The courtyard can accommodate up to 150 guests for weddings and receptions.

Other venues include the spectacular **Grand Ballroom**, with a fleet of candelabra-style chandeliers, muted hues of gold, and double doors that lead to an opulent pre-reception foyer. The Grand Ballroom can be divided into a duo of separate salons for smaller celebrations and can accommodate up to 700 guests. With floor-to-ceiling pane-glass windows, the **Colonnade** resembles more of a solarium than an indoor banquet salon. Each table, regardless of its position, provides unobstructed views of the garden courtyard and can easily accommodate up to 300 guests. There are a number of small **Banquet Suites** for groups of 50 to 80 guests; although more streamlined in design than the ornate ballrooms, each offers tasteful decor for intimate gatherings.

Pre-nuptial celebrations offer a tranquil respite on the eve of a hectic day. **The Bistro**, with its antique mahogany bar, offers casual elegance for family introductions and also features a private dining area for up to 15 guests. The **Lobby Lounge**, located in the hotel's atrium, is an ideal location for reviewing last minute details while savoring an espresso and pastry. Each Sunday, **The Colonnade** doubles as a dining area for Sunday brunch and is a perfect place to say farewell to out-of-town guests.

Honeymooning at the ANA Hotel

Bordered by Rock Creek Park, foreign embassies, and Pennsylvania Avenue, a honeymoon at the ANA Hotel is a combination of history and culture.

There are 415 rooms located on 10 floors, each offering views of either the hotel's courtyard or the city below. Each room is tastefully appointed with writing desks, sitting areas, and large bathrooms. Those rooms gazing over the courtyard feature French glass doors which open onto balconies. For those who want to splurge, the 2,353 square foot **Presidential Suite** is one of three specialty suites designed for maximum comfort. Once inside, it's hard not to let your mind wander, thinking about who may have slept here on a prior visit. Occupants of the suite arrive on the ninth floor, which is privately accessed by a room key that also unlocks the door leading to the magnificent two-bedroom enclave. Lined from top to bottom with French glass doors that open onto a progression of balconies, the Presidential Suite features a marble foyer, living room, formal dining room, kitchenette and wet bar, master bedroom, guest bedroom and two full baths. Of course, luxury comes with a hefty price tag... $1,630 per night!

While accommodations throughout Washington D.C. may not seem like a bargain, keep in mind that honeymooners and visitors can tour and visit many city attractions for little or no money at all, including the various monuments, federal buildings, Smithsonian museums, and galleries.

> ## The Terminator's Capital Hotel
> *Guests and locals always know when Arnold Schwarzenegger is resting or lunching at the ANA Hotel when they spot his signature red Humvee parked right outside the hotel's main entrance!*

THE WILLARD HOTEL
1401 Pennsylvania Avenue, N.W.
Washington, D.C. 20004
800/843-2231
202/628-9100

Accommodations
$305-$3,300

Celebrity Guest Register
- *Ruth Gordon & Garson Kanin*
- President Abraham Lincoln
- Sarah Ferguson, Duchess of York
- President Ronald Reagan
- President Gerald Ford
- Martin Luther King, Jr.
- Melanie Griffith
- John Goodman
- Charles Dickens
- President Bill Clinton
- Don Johnson

A History
The Willard is not just a hotel, it is a 150-year-old institution.

Henry Willard, a born host and entrepreneur, purchased a hostelry on Pennsylvania Avenue in 1850. Henry, along with his brothers, introduced the grand hotel concept to the nation's capital and merged what were then four row houses into a four-story, 100-room hotel. To attract guests, Willard created an extravagant daily dinner menu that consisted of such indulgences as oysters, meat or poultry, and foie gras. As the 1850s progressed, the hotel expanded and Willard's dreams for a palatial hotel were becoming very much a reality. One amenity the hotel boasted was bathing rooms for both ladies and gentlemen; eventually the Willard would become one of the first hotels in America to install bathrooms on each floor, something unheard of for its time.

As the threat of a civil war grew, the Willard brothers tried to remain neutral by hosting members from both political parties. A man's loyalty was known by where he exited the hotel: Confederates departed The Willard via the F Street doors, and the Yankees used the Pennsylvania

Avenue exit. Throughout the Civil War, The Willard served as the focal point for Union generals, lobbyists, and politicians who sought refuge in the midst of chaos. It was during this time that Julia Ward Howe, a Bostonian of intellect and social pedigree, penned the words to the *Battle Hymn of the Republic* – a song that inspired a nation – while staying at The Willard.

Following the war, The Willard prospered as a never-ending stream of job seekers and carpet-baggers poured into Washington. Rooms cost in the neighborhood of $4 a day, and the luxurious hotel offered private baths in each room, mechanical elevators, and a newfangled refreshment called an ice cream soda. The turn-of-the-century ushered in the city's first skyscraper – the new Willard Hotel. The 12-story building was completed in 1904, and was designed by Henry Janeway Hardenbergh, who also designed New York City's Plaza Hotel as well as the original Waldorf-Astoria.

Following World War II, the Willard family sold the hotel for an estimated $5 million. As the nation experienced turbulent times during the 1960s, so would the legendary Willard Hotel. From 1968 to 1986, The Willard Hotel sat empty, its future uncertain.

In 1986, The Willard Hotel reopened once again to reclaim its title as Washington's grandest hotel and has once again become the hub for politicos of both parties.

Famous Nuptials

Accomplished writer and actress **Ruth Gordon**, best known for her roles in *Rosemary's Baby* and *Every Which Way But Loose*, wed **Garson Kanin**, director of such classics as *My Favorite Wife*, at the Willard Hotel on December 3, 1942. The bride rushed over to the hotel after her performance in *The Three Sisters*, which was playing nearby at the National Theater. The groom was one of many from the Hollywood community who enlisted during the war and was assigned to the Office of Strategic Services in Washington, D.C. After the nuptials, the two celebrated with a handful of friends at The Willard and postponed their honeymoon for a later, less hectic, date.

Getting Married at The Willard Hotel

With one of the toniest addresses in the District of Columbia, The Willard Hotel is a favorite gathering spot for celebrations. Wedding ceremonies, receptions, and rehearsal dinners are conducted in regal style in any of the 15 salons located throughout the hotel. Named for historic figures and politicos, each boasts its own unique decor, including mahogany paneling, brass or crystal chandeliers, and ample dance floors, and can accommodate from 20 to 200 guests.

The most popular salon for wedding celebrations is the historic **Crystal Room**, located on the lower level of the hotel. A narrow staircase off the lobby leads to its entrance. Once inside, it's easy to imagine newlyweds from another era waltzing beneath crystal chandeliers while gazing at their own reflections in the mirrored panels that still grace the walls today. The Crystal Room can easily accommodate up to 300 guests and doubles nicely as a ceremony site.

For elegant rehearsal dinners, the two-story oak paneled **Willard Room** offers unprecedented surroundings and impeccable service. Lively after-dinner conversation and politician gazing is enjoyed in the historic **Round Robin Bar**, named so for its circular configuration. The European ambiance of **Cafe Espresso** is ideal for spending some quiet time alone and offers flavored coffee drinks and light fare.

There are a number of professional florists, photographers, transportation companies and other wedding-related services located in Washington, D.C., and the hotel will be happy to make recommendations.

Honeymooning at The Willard Hotel

Located just one block from the White House, the regal structure of The Willard Hotel is an unmistakable icon to passersby. A revolving door leads honeymooners to the magnificent main lobby which boasts a towering ceiling artfully displaying each state's seal; great columns seem to effortlessly support the floors above; and crystal chandeliers hang suspended in mid-air.

Peacock Alley, an elegant breezeway that connects the Main Lobby to the F Street Lobby, is where a fleet of elevators ferry newlyweds to their honeymoon accommodations. Eleven floors share 341 first-class guest rooms and suites, each designed to combine historic elegance with modern amenities. Each chamber features marble-top mini bars, oversized bathrooms, and urban vistas of such monumental places as the Capitol, the Jefferson and Lincoln Memorials, and the Washington Monument.

Filming At The Willard

The Willard served as the backdrop for the 1993 movie Born Yesterday, starring Melanie Griffith, Don Johnson, and John Goodman. The film was a remake of the 1950 classic by the same name, which co-starred Judy Holliday and William Holden and, coincidentally, was written by Garson Kanin (who married Ruth Gordon here).

27. West Virginia

THE GREENBRIER
300 West Main Street
White Sulphur Springs, WV 24986
800/624-6070
304/536-1110

Accommodations
$308-$738

Celebrity Guest Register
- *Debbie Reynolds & Eddie Fisher*
- *Wallis Simpson*
- Bing Crosby
- President John F. Kennedy
- Jack Nicklaus
- Princess Grace Kelly
- Johnny Carson
- Phil Silvers
- Judy Garland
- *Joe & Rose Kennedy*
- *President Woodrow Wilson*
- Bob Hope
- President Bill Clinton
- Arnold Palmer
- Claudette Colbert
- Joan Crawford
- Steve Allen

A History
When Mrs. Amanda Anderson couldn't bear the pain of her rheumatism any longer, she was slung on a litter between two horses and taken to the edge of a spring in 1778. Her body was submerged in the sulfur water, and legend has it that the ailing Amanda Anderson leaped up from the water and exclaimed, "I'm cured, I'm cured!"

News of her magical recovery quickly spread, and soon a community of tents were pitched around the "magic spring." The first permanent buildings of what would become The Greenbrier resort appeared in the early 1800s, and are still in use today. Soon others flocked to the area to build their own mini-resorts. Stephen Henderson, a wealthy New Orleans plantation owner, is credited with building the first private cottages as well as the dome-roof Springhouse, where southern families made a daily ritual out of drinking from the nearby spring. John H.B. Latrobe, a Baltimore lawyer, created the Baltimore Row bungalows, which dotted the landscape.

The Grand Central Hotel, fondly called the "Old White," opened in 1858. Appropriately named, the hotel was 400 feet long and sheltered one of the largest ballrooms in America. The hotel, coupled with the cottages, was capable of hosting 1,500 guests at a time. During the Civil War, the magnificent Grand Central Hotel was transformed into an infirmary for injured soldiers for both Union and Confederate troops!

In 1910, the Chesapeake and Ohio Railroad purchased the resort and commissioned renowned architect Frederick Junius Sterner to design a modern, fireproof building adjacent to the Old White. Sterner sculpted a masterpiece consisting of a tall columned 250-room Georgian-style structure of monumental proportions. The building was christened The Greenbrier, and throughout the years additional wings were added, complementing and enhancing the existing structure.

It's been more than 200 years since Mrs. Anderson discovered the benefits of The Greenbrier's spring, an event that may have spawned the first American health spa!

Celebrated Honeymoons

Would they or wouldn't they? That was the bridal buzz surrounding America's sweethearts, actress **Debbie Reynolds**, who recently played Albert Brooks' mom in the critically acclaimed movie *Mother*, and crooner **Eddie Fisher**, in 1955. The two met while entertaining at the Army's Walter Reed Hospital in Washington, D.C., and had posed for a photo under the Washington Monument. Their first date was at a dinner party hosted by Dinah Shore, and from then on they were an item. They secretly married on September 26, 1955, at Grossinger's Resort in New York's Catskill Mountains, where the groom got his big break six years earlier. The ceremony lasted a total of three minutes, and the 23-year-old bride borrowed the wedding dress she wore in the movie *The Tender Trap!* After saying farewell to a handful of friends and relatives, the two divided their honeymoon between The Greenbrier and other locations in Florida, Virginia, and Pennsylvania.

Other famous honeymooners include **Joe** and **Rose Kennedy** in 1914 (who stayed in room #145), **President Woodrow Wilson** and his second wife in 1915, and **Wallis Simpson**, the future Duchess of Windsor, who spent her honeymoon at The Greenbrier with her first husband in 1916.

Getting Married at The Greenbrier

Set against the burnished Allegheny Mountains deep in the heart of West Virginia, a Greenbrier wedding comes alive from the pages of a bridal magazine. With more than 6,500 acres to choose from, sites for outdoor weddings are plentiful. Some of the more popular settings include the **Formal Gardens**, bursting with bouquets of aromatic flora, and the **Fountain and Gardens**, featuring a courtyard setting.

The Greenbrier features more than 30 ballrooms and salons throughout the main hotel. Among those favored by brides and grooms are the **Colonial Hall**, which features expansive ceilings, crystal chandeliers, a pre-reception area, and an outdoor terrace for celebrations of 500. The **Chesapeake Room** is ideally suited for groups of 250 or less and also features an outdoor terrace, gleaming chandeliers, and views of the surrounding mountains. Aside from the ballrooms, there are four elegant estate houses that create an unprecedented setting: the **Valley View**, **Top Notch**, **Colonnade**, and **Presidents**. Each is uniquely appointed with spacious living rooms, formal dining rooms, expansive terraces, glass-enclosed porches and separate sleeping chambers. These estate houses can accommodate parties of 150 to 200 guests.

With seven restaurants and lounges, pre-nuptial gatherings run the gamut from ultra-elegant to resort chic. The **Main Dining Room**, with its expansive ceiling, column supports, and arched windows, is without a doubt The Greenbrier's most elegant dining venue and is ideal for family introductions. A cozy, relaxed atmosphere is found in **The Tavern Room**, featuring an open kitchen, brass lanterns, and equestrian prints. Bistro-style tables overlook the green at **Sam Snead's**, named for the famed golfer who began his career at The Greenbrier, where rehearsal dinners take on a casual, carefree tone.

The informal **Ryder Cup Grille Room** is ideal for a quick lunch and is frequented by golfers in their sporting attire. Located off the shopping arcade is **Draper's Cafe**, named for renowned designer Dorothy Draper, which takes on a brasserie feel with checkered floors, tables for two, and a pink and white-striped motif. Draper's Cafe serves both breakfast and lunch and an enjoyable afternoon tea.

On the eve of the wedding, gather with friends at the **Old White Club**, a sophisticated lounge oozing with southern charm and elegant decor. The **Rhododendron Pool Lounge**, located adjacent to the indoor pool, offers a colonial garden-style setting for enjoying spirits and other thirst-quenching concoctions.

Honeymooning at The Greenbrier

Secluded. Grand. Romantic. These trio of qualities, peppered with countless others, are reflective of the majestic Greenbrier.

With 672 rooms and cottages, even the most discriminating travelers will be pleased with the selection. Built on an astonishing 6,500 acres in the Allegheny Mountains, your first impression of The Greenbrier is the great Georgian lobby, with a floor coated in black and white marble, 16-foot windows that drench the room in sunlight, and elaborately draped French doors that open onto the gardens. Guests often linger here to read or enjoy a cup of tea in the afternoon.

While the rooms in the main hotel are elegantly appointed and conveniently located, it is the 200-year-old cottages that harken honeymooners back to another era. Fondly referred to as **The Rows**, the clusters include **Spring Row**, **Paradise Row**, **Tansas Row**, **Baltimore Row** and **South Carolina Row**. Steeped in century-old traditions, the cottages were once the pied-á-terres for wealthy southern families. Although each "row" is unique, all share common characteristics such as fireplaces, covered porches, wicker furniture, and unencumbered vistas of the sprawling resort.

Each stay, whether in the main hotel or one of the many guest cottages, includes both breakfast and dinner, and guests may choose to dine at their own expense in any number of the resort's restaurants for lunch.

Harried honeymooners in need of pampering should make an appointment at **The Greenbrier Spa**, which features an indoor pool with heated wet-deck and tanning beds, state-of-the-art exercise equipment, and a full-service salon.

Resort activities include eight bowling alleys, three golf courses, 20 tennis courts, a trout stream, movie theater, endless trails for mountain biking and hiking, horseback and carriage rides, a trap and skeet range, an indoor swimming pool and a shopping esplanade.

Anyone booking a wedding, reception, or social function is required to also book at least 50 sleeping rooms as well. The sleeping rooms require a two-night minimum stay when associated with such an event.

Bob Hope's Favorite Golf Course

Rumor has it that entertainer and avid golfer, Bob Hope, shot his best round of golf at The Greenbrier!

28. Wisconsin

THE AMERICAN CLUB
Highland Drive
Kohler, WI 53044
800/344-2838
414/457-8000

Accommadations
$155-$715

Celebrity Guest Register
- *Brett Favre*
- Tim Allen
- Paul Newman
- Pearl Buck
- Clare Boothe Luce
- Wynton Marsalis
- Hedda Hopper
- Marcel Marceau
- Greg Norman
- Nelson Eddy
- Joe E. Brown
- Mario Andretti

A History
The American Club began as an immense rooming house in 1918 for the Kohler Company, makers of quality bathroom accessories, and its immigrant workers who were helping to shape the planned community of Kohler Village. Walter J. Kohler, Sr., president of the company from 1905 to 1940 as well as Wisconsin's 27th Governor, wanted to create a quality standard of living for his many employees.

The Tudor-style building featured three stories accented with a steeped green and purple slate roof, red brick exterior, and white trim. It contained 100 single bedrooms and 15 doubles, each equipped with enameled cast iron beds, a chair, plus a combination wardrobe and dresser. Several washrooms were located throughout the building boasting hot running water at any time of day, and home-cooked meals were served in a public dining room. During their off hours, workers passed the time by playing cards in the public lounge or in one of two reading rooms; there was even a bowling alley! In 1918, a resident of The American Club paid just $27.50 a month for a single room and board.

Throughout its history, The American Club would undergo several structural changes. In 1924, a three-story wing was added on the north end creating 88 additional sleeping rooms, a Tap Room, and a barber shop. With this expansion, The American Club was no longer just a boarding house for men with modest means; women were now welcome, too. In 1941-42, large portions of the interior were removed eliminating several rooms, yet creating larger chambers with such modern amenities as private baths and walk-in closets. It was during this time that the resort's function changed from a worker's dormitory to a public inn.

The resort's final transformation began in 1978, the same year it was listed on the National Register of Historic Places, and was inspired by Walter J. Kohler, Sr.'s nephew, Herbert. He wanted to convert the aging tenant home into a hotel of national renown. Local craftsmen were commissioned to artfully recreate details of wood moldings; original chandeliers were authentically replicated; and antiques from the era were collected to create the feel of the early 1900s. In recent years, two wings have been added to provide additional guest rooms, both maintaining the architectural integrity of the original structure.

Today, more than 75 years since its opening, The American Club has nurtured its humble roots to become a first-class resort.

Celebrated Honeymoons

Two-time league MVP **Brett Favre**, the quarterback who led the Green Bay Packers to Super Bowl victory in 1997, married his high school sweetheart, Deanna Tynes, on July 14, 1996, at Green Bay's St. Agnes Catholic Church. With football season just around the corner, the two barely had time for a honeymoon. That didn't stop the groom from going the whole nine yards! He booked a romantic suite at The American Club for his new bride, and both enjoyed some pre-season relaxing.

Getting Married at The American Club

The American Club, with its historic charm and country setting, is truly a find for brides and grooms. The **Gazebo Courtyard**, which can seat up to 200 guests, lends itself well to warm Wisconsin days and evenings as couples exchange vows under a flower-surrounded pergola. For indoor ceremonies, the intimate **Bay de Noc** salon features a draped, center portal where all eyes are focused on the bride as she makes her entrance.

Reception salons are found throughout the property, and each are varied in decor and appointments. The **Great Bay Room** features rich wood paneling, bold motif carpeting, and ornate chandeliers strategically placed throughout to enhance the natural lighting; the room can host up to 286 guests or be divided into a trio of smaller salons for parties ranging from 70-142. The spacious **Great Lakes Room** offers seating for 600 and features wood-beam 11 foot ceilings, a fleet of chandeliers, 11-foot ceilings, and intrepid hues of teal and gold. This salon can also be divided into five smaller salons ranging from 40-150 guests.

There are four restaurants suitable for formal pre-nuptial gatherings or casual bites. **The Immigrant Restaurant and Winery** offers a distinctive style reflecting the area's early European heritage and is an elegant setting for rehearsal dinners. A nostalgic setting awaits those in **The Wisconsin Room**, the resort's original dining hall, providing a relaxed atmosphere for breakfast, dinner, or Sunday brunch. The casual **Horse & Plow** features an array of cozy booths in a pub-like setting and, with a selection of 100 beers and ales, it's an ideal place to get reacquainted with out-of-town guests. A charming solarium, imported from Lancashire County in the north of England, is now home to **The Greenhouse**, a seasonal cafe specializing in afternoon and evening refreshments.

Honeymooning at The American Club

Newlyweds arriving at the all-inclusive American Club will feel as if they've embarked on a European sojourn. The resort's Tudor-style exterior evokes the image of a grand manor house in the English countryside. The main hotel features three parallel wings divided by four colorful courtyards. There are 184 guest rooms located in the main hotel, each named for a notable American. Rooms vary in size and amenities, yet each offers a trademark Kohler whirlpool bath. Other features may include courtyard views, wet bars, or sitting areas. The remaining 52 guest rooms are located in the historic **Carriage House**, featuring four-poster brass beds and one of the country's largest collections of original horse and carriage artwork. Spacious suites offer one bedroom, some with fireplaces and sitting areas, or second-floor stories.

Other amenities include pampering at **The Sports Core Salon and Day Spa**, tennis courts, golfing at the world-famous Blackwolf Run courses designed by Pete Dye, a private wilderness preserve and hunt club, as well as complimentary afternoon tea, guided historic hotel tours, and seasonal garden tours.

Hooray For The Red, White, & Kohler!
During the 1920s, patriotic musician John Philip Sousa once conducted the Kohler band in a noontime concert for employees on the front lawn of The American Club.

29. Canada

BANFF SPRINGS HOTEL
Box 960
Banff, Alberta
Canada TOL OCO
800/441-1414
403/762-5755

Accommodations
$155-$1,500

Celebrity Guest Register
- *Karen Percy & Kevin Lowe*
- Marilyn Monroe
- Clint Eastwood
- Jane Fonda
- Jane Seymour
- Ginger Rogers
- Robert Mitchum

- Rod Stewart
- Tina Turner
- Janet Jackson
- Arnold Schwarzenegger
- Wayne Gretzsky
- Bob Hope

A History
William Cornelius Van Horne was the general manager of the Canadian Pacific Railway during the late 1800s. He was instrumental in developing the nation's railway system and, at the same time, providing passengers with the most comfortable and luxurious surroundings.

Recognizing the potential of the hot springs that neighbored the Banff station, he set out to build a hotel that would cater to traveler's needs. He hired New York architect Bruce Price, father of etiquette expert Emily Post, and selected the nexus of the Bow and Spray Rivers in which to build the hotel.

The four-story structure with its dormered roof opened in 1888 as a seasonal resort. The railway company imported artists and photographers to create an extensive publicity campaign with the intent to lure wealthy tourists to the area.

During the next several years, new wings were added to accommodate the growing number of tourists flocking to the Banff Springs Hotel. By 1911, thousands of potential guests were being turned away because the hotel had reached its full capacity. The need for a new, much larger hotel was evident and construction began immediately. The Canadian Pacific Railway relied on the skills of Italian stonecutters and Scottish masons to create the baronial-style hotel. The hotel, as it appears today, was completed in phases, with the final phase finished in 1928.

Today, the Banff Springs Hotel is a first-class resort located an hour's drive from Calgary in the charming town of Banff.

Famous Nuptials

Banff native **Karen Percy**, a former member of the Canadian National Ski team, married Edmonton Oiler hockey player **Kevin Lowe** in the spring of 1990 at nearby St. Mary's Church. After being pronouned husband and wife, the new Mr. and Mrs. Lowe were transported by horse and carriage to the Banff Springs Hotel to celebrate. More than 400 guests, including "The Great One," Wayne Gretzky, filled the hotel's Riverview Lounge to celebrate the occasion.

Getting Married at the Banff Springs Hotel

Whether you are planning a ceremony for just the two of you or a gala reception for 1,200, the Banff Springs Hotel offers an overabundance of areas in which to say "I Do." Surrounded by a spray of fresh flowers, the **Garden Terrace** offers a picturesque area for exchanging vows. For indoor ceremonies, couples have a choice of six different rooms that can accommodate intimate groups of 10 or larger gatherings of 200 and include the **Oak Room, Manor Lobby, Strathcona Room, Mt. Stephen Hall, Ivor Petrak** and the **Conservatory**. For receptions, the choices are endless with more than 25 salons to choose from! The most opulant is the **Cascade Ballroom**, with its high ceilings, draped chandeliers, and views of the nearby mountains. The **Riverview Lounge** is another favorite of brides with waterfront vistas and an open, airy floor plan.

In addition, there are 17 casual-to-elegant restaurants housed under one roof, providing couples with their first major dilemma – which one to choose for the rehearsal dinner?

Honeymooning at The Banff Springs Hotel

Referred to as the *Castle in the Rockies,* the Banff Springs Hotel is steeped in history and tradition. Located in the heart of Canada's ski country, the Banff Springs Hotel is ideal for winter honeymoons.

Operated as a year-round resort since 1969, the hotel features 770 individual guest rooms and suites with views of either the valley or those of the majestic mountains, which loom in the background.

Besides skiing, the hotel offers an 18-hole golf course, bowling, an array of specialty shops and **Solace**, a world-class spa and retreat. The **Honeymoon Tower** houses a number of hidden suites featuring whirl-pool tubs and spiral staircases leading to the bedroom!

Wheeling Marilyn Around The Banff Springs Hotel

During the filming of Otto Preminger's 1954 movie "River of No Return," Marilyn Monroe and fellow cast members resided at the Banff Springs Hotel. While filming, Monroe injured her ankle and was at times confined to a wheelchair. Bellboys at the hotel nearly came to blows over who would have the honor of pushing the sex symbol's wheelchair!

LE WESTIN MONT-ROYAL
1050 Sherbrooke Street West
Montreal, Quebec
Canada H3A 2R6
800/228-3000
514/284-1110

Accommodations
$165-$247

Celebrity Guest Register
- *Celine Dion*
- Pierce Brosnan
- Eric Clapton
- Bob Dylan
- Ben Kingsley
- Yo Yo Ma
- Bette Midler
- Sinead O'Connor
- Donald Sutherland
- Melissa Etheridge
- Tori Amos
- Peter Gabriel
- Aretha Franklin
- Annie Lennox
- Madonna
- Liam Neeson
- Seal
- Tina Turner

A History
Le Westin Mont-Royal opened in 1976. Its purpose was to house wealthy visitors and athletes attending the Montreal Olympic Games. It

immediately earned a reputation around town for being *l'hôtel des stars* because of its impressive list of visiting celebrities.

The hotel's entry, framed in bronze, features a glass-revolving door which transports guests from the sidewalk into an elegant lobby, and was designed by the same team who created the Caroussel Food Complex at the Louvre in Paris. While modern in design, the hotel, as with the rest of the city, aligns itself with the culture and traditions of France.

Located in the heart of one of North America's most cosmopolitan cities, Le Westin Mont-Royal is within walking distance to some of Montreal's renowned museums, art galleries, and exclusive boutiques.

Famous Nuptials

When singer **Celine Dion** married her manager **Réne Angélil**, it was as if a fairytale had come to life, from her hand-pearled Cinderella-style gown and diamond-encrusted tiara to the gothic setting inside Montreal's Notre Dame Basilica. The event – *and it was an event* – took place on December 17, 1994, with eight bridesmaids and groomsmen plus more than 500 attendees. After the ceremony, guests made their way to the nearby Le Westin Mont-Royal for the reception, which included an elegant sit-down dinner. The wedding cake consisted of a mammoth tower of profiteroles, which the bride and groom fed to one another. Needing nothing more than each other, the newlyweds requested that donations be made to the Cystic Fibrosis Foundation in lieu of wedding gifts.

The couple had such a good time at their own reception that they stayed until 4 a.m. before retiring to their suite. The next morning they hosted a post-nuptial brunch at the hotel for 150 guests.

Getting Married at Le Westin Mont-Royal

Couples planning a wedding or reception at Le Westin Mont-Royal will discover an array of options in which to hold their celebration. Each of the eight salons, with their French pronunciations, are located on the first and second floors of the hotel.

Ceremonies are usually held in **L'Atrium** featuring a glass wall and ceiling, which provides a light, airy ambiance for daytime weddings or a dramatic backdrop for evening ceremonies. L'Atruim can comfortably house 180 guests. The expansive **Salon des Saisons**, the largest of the salons accommodating up to 550 guests, features a collection of crystal chandeliers encased in an intricate floral ceiling. The **Pierre de Coubertin**, ideal for groups of up to 350, is regal in its decor with crystal chandeliers suspended from the ceiling, floor-to-ceiling windows and bold hues of burgundy with gold accents. Understated elegance best describes **Salon**

le Printemps, ideal for celebrations of 250, with its crystal chandelier centerpiece, expansive windows draped in rich fabrics, and views of downtown Montreal; **Salon l'Ete**, similar in size and decor, can accommodate slightly larger groups of 280. For more intimate celebrations, from 16 to 80, **Salons l'Automne**, **l'Hiver**, and **Sherbrooke** each provide elegant accommodations on a smaller scale. **Le Cercle** offers a rotunda setting, iron balustrade, and intimate atrium, which can be adapted to various styles of entertaining for gatherings of up to 200.

For pre-nuptial gatherings, **Opus II** offers contemporary sophistication in a relaxed setting. The exotic **Zen** features Asian specialties and minimalist decor, providing an inviting contrast to the traditional rehearsal dinner.

Honeymooning at Le Westin Mont-Royal

There are 300 spacious guest rooms and suites housed on 31 floors at the Le Westin Mont-Royal. Rooms are adorned with rich mahogany furnishings, cozy sitting areas, subtle wallpaper prints, marble baths and views overlooking the city or the cascading Mount Royal.

Suites come with separate bedrooms, roomy floor plans, and elegant appointments. The split-level suites are larger than most apartments and include a living room, formal dining area, second-level bedroom, two baths and everything imaginable to create a home away from home.

Other guest amenities include **Gymtech**, with state-of-the-art exercise equipment, and an outdoor, year-round heated swimming pool located in the center of the hotel.

Le Westin Mont-Royal offers a splendid Honeymoon Package which includes an overnight stay in the plush Honeymoon Suite, featuring a tub for two overlooking Mount Royal, a bottle of sparkling wine, a full Canadian breakfast served either in the hotel restaurant or in the privacy of your suite, a bowl of fresh strawberries to nibble plus a fresh fruit basket upon arrival! The cost is just $288 per night.

Security For The Singer

Security measures at Celine Dion's reception could rival those taken to protect the First Family! Her party occupied 175 hotel rooms, not to mention every ballroom and restaurant. In order for the remaining hotel guests, who were not part of the celebration, to obtain access to their own rooms, each was required to check-in with security and obtain an identification pass!

RITZ-CARLTON KEMPINSKI MONTREAL
1228 *Sherbrooke Street West*
Montreal, Quebec
Canada H3G 1H6
800/363-0366
514/842-4212

Accommodations
$124-$405

Celebrity Guest Register

• *Elizabeth Taylor & Richard Burton*	• Harry Belafonte
• Nick Nolte	• Robert De Niro
• Isabella Rossellini	• Kathleen Turner
• Mick Jagger	• Pierre Cardin
• Liberace	• Sophia Loren
• Gene Kelly	• Margot Kidder
• Jack Palance	• Charles De Gaulle

A History

When the Ritz-Carlton Kempinski Montreal opened in 1912, Canadians of wealth and prominence discovered a new level of luxury within its confines.

Originally it was to be named the Carlton, paying homage to a famous London hotel. However, one of the project's investors approached Cesar Ritz, whose name was synonymous with the finest hotels, and he agreed to have his namesake appear on the marquis with the understanding that his high standards were to be met. Ritz's laundry list of musts included, among other things, a bathroom in every chamber and a kitchen on every floor so room service meals could be served course-by-course. When the last carpet was laid and the furniture in place, the total cost to complete the hotel was $3 million, a staggering sum for its time.

During the Great Depression, when millionaires were instantly transformed into paupers, the hotel saw a decline in occupancy. Rather than compromise its standards, the Ritz-Carlton chose to keep a portion of its suites cloaked in dust covers and, like millions elsewhere, patiently waited for an economic recovery.

Today, the gilded era that was once a way of life during the beginning of this century remains intact at the Ritz-Carlton Kempinski Montreal. Sadly, the Ritz-Carlton is the only Montreal hotel from its period still in existence today.

Famous Nuptials

When **Elizabeth Taylor** met British-born actor **Richard Burton** during the filming of *Cleopatra* in 1961, the two were very much married – to other people; she to crooner Eddie Fisher and he to his longtime wife and companion, Sybil. Nevertheless, the two fell madly in love and decided they couldn't live without one another. In 1964, they tied the knot at the Ritz-Carlton Montreal. For her fifth trip down the aisle, and her first wedding to Burton (they were married twice), the 32-year-old bride chose a low-cut, bright yellow chiffon gown accented with a $150,000 emerald-cut brooch given to her by the groom.

Getting Married at the Ritz-Carlton Kempinski Montreal

Brides and grooms who dream of marrying in old world Europe but wish to remain in North America will find the best of both at this Ritz-Carlton. Located in the heart of the 350-year-old Canadian city, where both English and French are the spoken languages, the Ritz-Carlton could easily have been the setting for a Victor Hugo novel.

The Ritz-Carlton offers eight magnificent salons for both weddings and receptions. Named for its unique configuration, the **Oval Room**, which can accommodate up to 600, is the hotel's pièce de résistance boasting classic French decor, crystal chandeliers, and floor-to-ceiling windows. The adjacent **Palm Court** provides added elegance for pre-reception cocktails. The **Ritz-Carlton Room**, with its marble fireplace and collection of antique paintings, offers superb surroundings for groups of 90. Oriental embellishments are hallmarks of the **Blue Room**, suitable for celebrations of up to 175, and is ideal for couples with a taste for the exotic. The **Gold** and **Grey Rooms**, named for their prominent hues, are ideal for small groups of 70 or larger groups of 400. Additional salons, which offer breathtaking backdrops, include the **Vice-Royal** for celebrations of 130 and the **Canadien** for smaller gatherings up to 75.

The Ritz-Carlton surpasses all expectations when it comes to pre-nuptial gatherings. The hotel offers two restaurants, including **Le Cafe de Paris**, serving classic French cuisine in a refined setting, and the seasonal **Le Jardin du Ritz**, featuring outdoor dining amid the hotel's magnificent gardens. For after-hour socializing, **Le Ritz Bar** features a cozy piano lounge, light meals, and refreshing cocktails.

Each wedding package includes, among other things, a complimentary overnight stay for the bride and groom plus continental breakfast and a personalized picture frame to remember the moment.

Honeymooning at the Ritz-Carlton Kempinski Montreal

Embracing the grandeur of a lost era, the Ritz-Carlton Kempinski Montreal is known as Le Grande Dame of Sherbrooke Street. Newlyweds are pampered with a special **Honeymoon Package**, which includes a bottle of champagne, a box of home-made chocolates, complimentary parking, and breakfast for two in the privacy of your room. The cost is $179 (U.S. currency) per night for a deluxe room, or $245 (U.S. currency) per night for a suite.

Each of the 230 guest rooms and suites offers high ceilings, expansive windows with views of either the city or the St. Lawrence River, large bathrooms and, in some cases, sitting areas and fireplaces. Other amenities include plush terry robes and the use of a fitness facility.

Mr. Jagger, Can I Get You A Clip-On Tie?
When the Rolling Stones stayed at the hotel during the 1970s, they entered the Cafe de Paris without jackets...a major faux pas for the time. They were politely asked to return to their rooms to retrieve them. These bad boys of rock were true English gents and returned moments later looking dapper in their evening attire!

THE VICTORIA REGENT HOTEL
1234 Wharf Street
Victoria, British Columbia
Canada V8W 3H9
800/663-7472
250386-2211

Accommodations
$159-$699

Celebrity Guest Register
- *Teri Hatcher & Jon Tenney*
- Goldie Hawn & Kurt Russell
- Margot Kidder
- Tony Geary
- Mel Gibson
- Gregory Hines
- Emma Samms
- James Garner

A History
Located on the inner harbor in the quaint island city of Victoria on Vancouver Island, the contemporary Victoria Regent Hotel is a stunning contrast to its nostalgic surroundings of flower-draped lamposts, vintage double-decker buses, and cobblestone sidewalks.

The hotel was born a condominium complex in 1980, but shortly after its opening the concept was altered to create a luxury hotel. The 10-

story structure, which balances delicately on pylons, boasts a futuristic look of mirrored glass and is literally built right on the water.

When in town, celebrities seem to favor The Victoria Regent Hotel because of its "home away from home" feel and its central location to Victoria's major attractions.

Celebrated Honeymoons

After their 1994 nuptials, **Teri Hatcher**, who plays sexy Lois Lane on television's *Lois & Clark: The New Adventures of Superman*, and actor **Jon Tenney**, co-star of the romantic comedy *Fools Rush In*, traveled to the charming island of Victoria to celebrate. They stayed at The Victoria Regent Hotel for three days and spent much of their time behind closed doors. Travelers at heart, the newlyweds also chartered a yacht and sailed away on a Fiji honeymoon.

Getting Married at The Victoria Regent Hotel

Because the hotel was originally built as a condominium complex, no spacious ballrooms were incorporated into the design. But that doesn't stop couples from hosting receptions at The Victoria Regent Hotel.

The two-story **Regency Suite** offers an elegant setting for groups of up to 60 guests and features a spacious living room, den, kitchen, two fireplaces and an open deck overlooking the the inner harbor and distant mountains. Rehearsal dinners are just an elevator ride away at the waterfront **Water's Edge Restaurant**, located on the lobby level.

There is no on-site catering available at the hotel, but the staff will be more than willing to recommend a reputable caterer along with other wedding-related services to make everything as stress-free as possible.

Honeymooning at The Victoria Regent Hotel

Honeymooning at The Victoria Regent Hotel offers ultra-luxurious surroundings, daily maid service, and spectacular harbor and city views.

There are 42 suites with one or two bedrooms, king-sized beds, living rooms, dining rooms, full-sized kitchens and balconies overlooking the inner harbor or city; **Executive Suites** include fireplaces and Jacuzzi bathtubs. Other amenities include complimentary continental breakfast, morning newspaper, a waterfront dock for boaters, and laundry facilities.

Bird On A Wire

During the filming of "Bird On A Wire," both Goldie Hawn and Mel Gibson, who co-starred together in the action-comedy film, brought their families with them on location and everyone resided at The Victoria Regent Hotel.

30. Mexico

LAS ALAMANDAS
Quémaro, Costalegrie
Jalisco, Mexico
888/882-9616
011/52-328-55027

Accommodations
$210-$730

Celebrity Guest Register
- *Richard Gere & Cindy Crawford*
- Patrick Stewart
- Francis Ford Coppola
- Ellen Degeneres
- *Rod Stewart & Rachel Hunter*
- Robert De Niro
- Elle MacPherson
- Carrie Fisher

A History
Owner Isabel Goldsmith has garnered as much press attention as has her secluded hideaway of Las Alamandas. The Parisian-born daughter of British financier Sir James Goldsmith and the granddaughter of "Bolivian Tin King" Don Antenor Patino, who built Las Hadas resort in neighboring Manzanillo, Goldsmith inherited a taste for luxurious surroundings.

Her grandfather had envisioned a large-scale resort for Las Alamandas, named for the fields of bright yellow flowers which blanket the Mexican countryside. Patino never lived to see his vision flourish, but Goldsmith kept the project in motion after she acquired the land in 1982.

Not one to remain idle, Goldsmith quickly put her creative forces in motion. Instead of a sprawling, cookie-cutter resort, she opted for a cozy, private retreat that would attract a clientele of discriminating tastes. The results were spectacular, with four pastel villas surrounded by a 1,500-acre private paradise consisting of exotic trees, palm fronds, bouquets of wild flowers, several species of birds, scattered lagoons and endless white sand beaches.

Since its opening in 1990, Las Alamandas has remained one of this decade's best kept secrets, which is exactly why Hollywood heavyweights return again and again.

Celebrated Honeymoons

When actor **Richard Gere** and supermodel **Cindy Crawford** decided on an impromptu Las Vegas wedding, they made sure not to take a gamble on their honeymoon. Instead, the two headed for Las Alamandas where they relaxed, worked out, and sailed to a nearby island to enjoy a private picnic.

Other famous honeymooners include rocker **Rod Stewart** and supermodel **Rachel Hunter**. Always the romantic, Stewart led his picture-perfect bride down a candlelit path where she discovered a bonfire dinner for two, all masterminded by the groom himself!

Getting Married at Las Alamandas

Wedding ceremonies at Las Alamandas are spontaneous affairs, as couples are swept away by its beauty. Because of its secluded location and ability to accommodate only a limited number of guests (a maximum of 22), the mini resort lends itself well to the most intimate of weddings and celebrations, and the entire place can be rented out for such gatherings.

Ceremonies most often take place on the beach with the bleached sand serving as a natural runner. Receptions are held in **La Palala**, where newlyweds and their guests are surrounded by swaying palm trees and colorful flowers. The oceanfront restaurant is illuminated in the evening with scores of candles with the moon bouncing off the Pacific Ocean. Specialty receptions include an elaborate dinner buffet complete with local mariachi music.

For the ultimate in casual dining, the **Oasis** is a shady retreat with an ideal beachfront location, reclining chaise lounges and swinging hammocks. Private parties can be arranged to include an authentic Mexican buffet and grill, frothy margaritas and a beach bonfire.

Drenched in nature's beauty, Las Alamandas is ideal for those who want a relaxed, no-frills wedding. The inn is devoid of sports jackets, ties, stiletto heels and other restrictive devices. The staff is ever-so-accommodating and assists in making sure each wedding celebration is unforgettable.

Honeymooning at Las Alamandas

The famed Mexican Riviera is the backdrop for a sun-drenched honeymoon at Las Alamandas. There are four villas named for their dominant interior color: **Casa del Sol** (yellow), **Casa del Domo** (shocking pink), **Casa Azul** (blue) and **Casa Rosa** (hot pink) and each are encased in pink stucco. Guests seem isolated from the rest of the world, as the inn can only accommodate a limited number of guests – a prime location for honeymooners!

Mosaic stones embedded in pale yellow paths lead to 11 spacious guest rooms. Each casita reflects the festive culture of Mexico with bright vibrant colors draped throughout; many hand-painted artifacts are artistically displayed. Each villa is cleverly hidden among a fragrant garden of gardenias, bougainvillea, night-blooming jasmine, and, of course, the resplendent alamanda flower for which the resort was named. Each room is unique, offering shaded terraces blanketed in white ceramic tile, oversized bathrooms, and fully-equipped kitchens; some rooms feature private dining areas, indoor gardens, and rooftop terraces.

Added amenities include a 60-foot fresh-water swimming pool, a tennis court, horseback riding, bicycling, hiking, a fully-equipped gym, boogie boarding, croquet, ping-pong and beach volleyball. In addition, the hotel can arrange for boat rentals and romantic balloon rides which carry lovers across the coast.

De Niro's Mexican Retreat

Frequent guest Robert De Niro often books the entire place from Christmas through New Year's, enjoying a Mexican-style holiday with those friends and family lucky enough to be invited!

ROSARITO BEACH HOTEL
#31 Benito Juarez Blvd.
Rosarito, Baja California Norte
Mexico
800/343-8582
011/52-661-2-0144

Accommodations
$69-$369

Celebrity Guest Register
- Burgess Meredith & Paulette Goddard
- Leonardo DiCaprio
- Clark Gable & Carole Lombard
- David Faustino
- Marilyn Monroe
- Al Capone
- Buster Keaton
- La Toya Jackson
- Edward G. Robinson
- Morgan Fairchild
- Spencer Tracy

- Humphrey Bogart
- Jack Palance
- Tiny Tim
- Vincent Price

A History

When the beachfront Shore Acres Country Club opened in 1926, Rosarito Beach was nothing more than a village with dusty, dirt roads leading to a handful of ranches. The club was tailored to the tastes of wealthy Americans who resided on the other side of the border. With only 12 private rooms and a number of tents for rent, it was promoted as a hunting and fishing club with a small restaurant and dance hall for evening socializing.

In 1928, Mexican entrepreneur Manuel Barbachano purchased the resort and built a magnificent mansion as a wedding gift to his bride Maria. Señor Barbachano continued to expand the facility, now referred to as The Rosarito Beach Hotel, and as the resort grew in size, so did the town of Rosarito. Throughout the '30s, '40s, and '50s, the resort attracted Hollywood's jet set who slumbered in private bungalows, dined on fine cuisine, and took a gamble in the casino. There was even a landing strip for small planes that arrived and departed with rich and famous passengers.

When Señor Barbachano died in 1954, his widow reluctantly leased the hotel property to a commercial operator. Two decades later, the Rosarito Beach Hotel was returned to the family circle with the managerial appointment of the Barbachano's nephew.

What started out as a 12-room enclave in 1926 has now grown to a 275-room premiere resort situated along the Mexican coast. Today, the Rosarito Beach Hotel not only appeals to a younger, hipper Hollywood, but to those who fondly remember the Rosarito Beach of yesteryear.

Celebrated Honeymoons

Stars from Hollywood's golden era found the Rosarito Beach Hotel the ideal honeymoon hideaway. **Burgess Meredith**, who found renewed fame with a younger generation of movie-goers when he played Sylvester Stallone's manager in the underdog film *Rocky* as well as three of its sequels, and the former Mrs. Charlie Chaplin, actress Paulette Goddard, who is remembered for her roles in *The Women* and *Modern Times,* just to name a few, honeymooned at the hotel following their wedding in the 1940s.

Comic genius **Buster Keaton**, star of *It's A Mad, Mad, Mad, Mad World, Sunset Boulevard,* and *Lil' Abner,* also spent his honeymoon at the Rosarito Beach Hotel.

Getting Married at the Rosarito Beach Hotel

With the Pacific Ocean glistening at sunset and an infinite stretch of sugar-like sand, weddings become extraordinary affairs at the **Beach Gardens**, where couples pledge to love, honor, and cherish. Situated along the ocean, the Beach Gardens offers the flexibility of accommodating from 30 to 1,000 guests, and provides a wonderful photo opportunities to capture the moment.

There are four salons for post-wedding celebrations, and for those who prefer to recite their vows indoors, each area also doubles as a ceremony site. For large groups of 500, **Salon Mexicano**, built in the 1930s, features decor indigenous to Mexico with bright, vivid colors, tile floors, and stucco walls. Atop the resort's newest eight-story structure is **Hugo's**, which gazes down upon the Pacific Ocean and Rosarito Village, and welcomes parties of up to 80. Hand-painted tiles encircling the room depict the story of Don Quijote de la Mancha inside **Salon Quijote**, which can accommodate up to 70 guests. **Salon Maya**, named for Señor Barbachano's heritage, features Mayan architecture and decor and can host up to 80 guests.

There are a few choice restaurants for hosting prenuptial gatherings that take on a somewhat casual air. Each restaurant offers its own unique setting with nuances of classic Spanish architecture. **Salon Azteca** is the hotel's main dining room and is a fun spot to gather for a hearty breakfast, leisurely lunch, or candlelit dinner. The elegant **Chabert's** pays homage to Señora Maria Barbachano's French heritage in both decor and cuisine. The glass-enclosed poolside **Cabana** serves casual fare and is a sought-after location the day after a big fiesta. The night before the wedding, guests may want to gather at one of two lounges: the more tamed **Beachcomber Bar** offers lovely views of the ocean for margarita-sipping lovers, while the **Salty Dog Bar**, which has earned a reputation as the hippest dance spot in Rosarito, is more for those who truly want to party.

Honeymooning at the Rosarito Beach Hotel

Although the Rosarito Beach Hotel has grown considerably from an eight-room casita to a sprawling 275-room beachfront hotel, its 1920s charm still remains.

The hotel is a showpiece of Mexican colonial design and art. A red-tiled arched portal entices guests through the white-washed complex, a design replicated throughout the hotel. The ornate lobby is adorned with large, romantic murals painted by the 1930s Mexican artist Matias Santoyo, while brightly colored tiles complement the carved and hand-painted woodwork found throughout. Arched passageways lead to many of the sleeping chambers, and nearly all the guest rooms and one-bedroom suites offer oceanfront views; those that don't overlook the hotel gardens. While the accommodations are plainly decorated, the vistas observed from each room's terrace are phenomenal!

In addition, the stately mansion that Señor Barbachano built for his bride has been transformed into **Casa Playa Spa**, offering massages, facials, herbal and seaweed wraps, sauna, steamroom hydro-baths and more. Aside from the beautiful beach, other recreational outlets include two swimming pools; courts for tennis, racquetball, basketball, and volleyball; a museum; and a shopping area.

Bibliography

Wendy Goldberg and Betty Goodwin, *Marry Me!*, Simon & Shuster, New York, 1994.

Robert S. Conte, *History of The Greenbrier*, Pictorial Histories Publishing Co., West Virginia, 1989.

Stan Cohen, *The Pink Palace*, Pictorial Histories Publishing Co., Montana, 1986.

Victoria Houseman, *Made In Heaven*, Bonus Books, Illinois, 1991.

Julie Nixon Eisenhower, *Pat Nixon, The Untold Story*, Simon & Shuster, New York, 1986.

Alexander Walker, Vivien, *The Life of Vivien Leigh*, Weidenfeld & Nicolson, New York, 1987.

In Style Magazine, February 1997, *Enchanted Evening*, by Bonnie Siegler, pages 114-118.

In Style Magazine, February 1997, *Perfect Match*, by Leslie Marshall, pages 121-122.

In Style Magazine, February 1997, *Elements of Style*, by Louise Lague, reported by Sean Elder, page 128.

In Style Magazine, May 1996, *The Ultimate Wedding Album*, by Melanie Acevedo, pages 104, 106, 108.

People Magazine, May 5, 1997, *The Agassi and the Ecstasy*, by Janice Min, Danelle Morton, Elizabeth Leonard, Paula Yoo, Tom Cunneff and Mary Huzinec Anthony Duignan-Cabrera, pages 48-52.

People Magazine, May 5, 1997, *Robin's Nesting Instinct*, by Anthony Duignan-Cabrera, page 55.

People Magazine, February 10, 1997, *Weddings of the Year*, pages 64, 67, 71, 72, 73, 132, 142.

234

Celebrity Index

Destination Index

HELP US UPDATE!

Our goal is to provide you with a guide book second to none. Please bear in mind, however, that things change: phone numbers, admission price, addresses, etc. Should you come across any new information, we'd appreciate hearing from you. No item is too small for us, so if you have a great recommendation, find an error, see that some place has gone out of business, or just plain disagree with our recommendations, write to:

Celebrity Weddings & Honeymoon Getaways
Open Road Publishing
P.O. Box 284
Cold Spring Harbor, New York 11724

NOTES

NOTES

NOTES

NOTES

NOTES

NOTES

NOTES

NOTES

NOTES

NOTES